Contextualising Tukadoji's Gramgeeta

Trajectories of Tradition and Reality

Ratnakar D. Bhelkar

ATLANTIC
PUBLISHERS & DISTRIBUTORS (P) LTD

ATLANTIC
PUBLISHERS & DISTRIBUTORS (P) LTD

7/22, Ansari Road, Darya Ganj, New Delhi
Tel.: +91-11-4077 5252, 2327 3880
E-mail: orders@atlanticbooks.com
Web: www.atlanticbooks.com

Published by Atlantic Publishers & Distributors (P) Ltd 2024

Printed & bound in India by Atlantic Print Services

Introduction

The explosion of information and knowledge, the increase in migration, and the process of globalisation have transformed the world into a global village with multi-variant realities. From the standpoints of appearance—virtual illusion, reality, and tradition—*Gramgeeta* offers the blueprint which is symptomatic as well as curative. In the global context where there is an increasing divide among material and spiritual, knowledge and wisdom, biological reality and psycho-social evolution, and sprawling cities and crawling villages, there arises a need for rural restructuring and agricultural reform to avert communal riots and violence by fundamentalist forces.

Born on 30th April, 1909 at Yawali (in the Central Province in the colonial India and, now, in Maharashtra), Manik was educated at Yawali and Warkhed, along with assisting his father's tailoring work. He learnt *khanjiri* and *ektari* to sing *bhajans*, initiated by Samarth Adkoji, his mentor, who addressed him as Tukadya while sharing the piece of morsel, and the title became popular to attribute his identity. He fulfilled the arduous task of pennance at Kapurbawadi, Narayan hill in the forest of Ramtek, Gondoda, and Tadoba forest. He was instrumental in organising Salbuldi *yagnya* (1935) to ban animal sacrifice which was protested earlier by Buddha and Mahavir to instill the spirit of unity for mass enlightement. For a month in 1936, he was at Bapukuti in Sevagram, on the invitation by Mahatma Gandhi, where he interacted with the Indian nationalists, such as Rajendra Prasad, Jawaharlal Nehru, Vallabhbhai Patel, Lal Bahadur Shashtri, and Maulana Abdul Kalam Azad. He composed and sang the patriotic songs with *khanjiri*, and with the accomplices of the activists of *Aarti Mandal*, ignited the masses to involve in Quit India Movement (1942) to topple down the colonial power. His *bhajan* with the militant tone:

> Trees, brooms will be weapons; devotee army
> stones will be bombs; the boat will be the shore.[1]

was banned by the Britishers, recalls Subramania Bharati's verses in Tamil, and he was imprisoned in the Central Jails of Nagpur and Raipur.

The publication of the monthly, *Sri Gurudeo* (1943) and the foundation of *Sri Gurudeo Seva Mandal* (1943), known as *Aarti Mandal* earlier, at Gurukunj Mozari, were the practical parameters to propagate and implement Tukadoji's conceptual perceptions. The women wing of the *Mandal* was steered by Vimala Thakar, activist and thinker, and with the cohort, Prabhatai Deshmukh, Radhadevi Goyenka, Venutai Wankhede, Narmadabai Sapkal, Renukadevi Birle, Sarojabai Malgujar, Hiratai Boke, and Rukhminibai Goswami, she embarked on enpowering women, making them conscious of rural reality and national upheavals. Tukadoji ventured to eradicate superstitions with Gadge Baba (1945), and to open access to untouchable at Pandharpur temple, with Sane Guruji (1947), and at other places practiced collective meal (1947), reminding *langar* in Sikh tradition, irrespective of caste, creed, and religion.

After the Indian independence (1947), in the post-colonial India, his insistence was on constructive governance with self-reliance of nation and secular approach, epitomising the constitutional values of the free nations, freedom, unity, equality, and justice. He awakened masses on the border of Nizam province to resist *Razakar's* drive against integration of Hyderabad state into domination of India. He addressed *Sarvodaya* meets at Sevagram, Banaras (North India), and Kanchivan (South India). Dr. Rajendra Prasad, the President of India, graced the first Gandhi Memorial Celebration (1949) at Gurukunj and bestowed upon Tukadoji the honour of 'Rashtrasant', envisioning his humanitarian vision of national welfare, the confluence of conceptual approach, and programmatic stance. Anticipating the call by Vinoba Bhave, he participated in the Land

Donation Movement (1953) and donated 11,410 acres of land to landless tribals at Aheri and Bastar zones. For rural reform, he coordinated Ideal Villages Convention on 20th, 24th, and 30th January, 1953, in which Lal Bahadur Shashtri and Guljarilal Nanda were present at Amagaon which included 100 villages.

The World Religion Conference for World Peace was organised from 23rd to 25th July, 1955 at Simizyu, Japan in which representatives from various nations, such as U.S.A., England, Greece, Indonesia, and Malaysia were invited. The conference was inaugurated by Rashtrasant Tukadoji with his *bhajan*,[2] "the mover of world, render me the consciousness of the world",[3] and his discourse stressed on co-ordination, love, freedom, peace, unity, and equality. Tukaramdada Gitacharya, Appex Officer of *Sri Gurudeo Seva Mandal,* accompanied him as bilinqual, besides Shivacharan Sinha Wirik, the representative from the Indian Embassy. Paying heed to his humanitarian spirit and co-ordinative endeavour for word peace, he was nominated for the Advisory Committee of World Religion Conference. Unifying energy, which conjectures diversities, is enthused in the *bhajan*, composed in Tokeyo, on 3rd August, 1955:

> You in every nation, You in every attire
> Your names many, You are one
> Filled this world, Your stage ||

In all sports, harmony and spirit are imminent in every attire. The world is a stage and though, you exist in transformative forms, but the beauty is in all being 'one'. Though waves on surface seem different, water beneath is same. Panchshil Resolution (Five parameters for word peace) was accepted in World Religion Conference in Tokyo, because of the leadership of Tukadoji, which was put earlier in Asian-African Conference in Bandung, Indonesia, in April 1955.

He made a discourse at All India Vedant Conference (1955) in Amritsar (Punjab) and addressed the valedictory session of All Religions Meet (1956) at Srikshetra, Nathdwara (Rajasthan). He motivated the natives in Goa Freedom struggle to break the shackles of Portuguese; resolved to utilise one crore donated time hours for "Mass Enlightenment" on the completion of 2500 years of Buddha's *nirvana*; opened a tribal school at Kamalapur; established an Ayurvedic College at Gurukunj; and organised Indian Farmers Rail Fare (1961) to visit dams, water storages, and projects to increase production. At the time of Indo-China War (1962) and the aggression by Pakistan (1965), he motivated soldiers with his spirited *bhajan* to combat with enemies and addressed the National Security Conference in 1966. During the disaster phases of Koyna earthquake and Bengal famine, he involved in rehabilitation of the affected people and consoled the sufferers with performance, compassion, and empathy.

Being multifaceted, like 12th–13th centuries bilingual saint poet Namdev, Tukadoji, a bilingual, who penned in Marathi and Hindi, was a poet, writer, singer, *khanjiri* player, and reformer. His literary oeurve comprises of the anthologies of *bhajan, abhang, powada,* letters, essays, travelogue, autobiography, and *Gramgeeta,* magnum opus. When we trace the location of his poetry in the ambit of Marathi poetry, it has nuances with saint's progressive thought in devotional poetry; the reformative fervours in the *abhanga*; *powada* of Jyotirao Phule who whipped on slavery, social stratification, and orthodox religion, and insisted on the investigation of truth; his closeness with the lyrics, *abhanga* of Keshavsut who resisted socio-economic unequality, oppression, and superstitions, and appealed for awakening to combat against the counter forces; had kinship with Kusumgraj's lyrics which dealt with peripheral, deprived, and exploited, and highlighted national spirit in Indian freedom struggle to revolt; and joy, wish, and fulfillment in independence of Bal Sitaram Mardhekar's poems, the derivative of tradition and modernity, imbue *abhang* as traditional form in saint's poetry with modern import to stress bloodshed in communal riots, derosion of values paving road to new, cleavages between rich and poor, inner impovershment, and spiritual orientation. Tukadoji's hindi poetry reveals the parallel with the tradition of *Nirguna* devotion of Ramanand and Kabir; spiritual urge of Tulsidas, Raidas, and Meerabai; the unity between Hindu and Muslim in Sufi poetry; and the patriotic vein in the poetries of Maithilisharan Gupt and Ramdhari Singh 'Dinkar'.

In the backdrops of Indian cultural renaissance in 19th and 20th centuries; the reformative measures by Jyotirao Phule, Gopal Ganesh Agarkar, Vivekananda, Raja Ram Mohan Roy, Dayananda Saraswati, Rajashri Shahu Maharaj, Vitthal Ramji Shinde, Lokmanya Tilak, Periyar Swami, Narayana Guru, Mahatma Gandhi, Babasaheb Ambedkar, Karmaveer Bhaurao Patil, Panjabrao Deshmukh; the crucial transformative events as the Second World War and its socio-economic-psychological-philosophical impacts; and the political freedom of India and decolonisation process in the world, *Gramgeeta* was published in 1955, the post-colonial zone, and then translated in English, Hindi, Sanskrit, Urdu, Gujarati, and Telugu.

We observe that during the national and global events on socio-economic fronts such as the two World Wars and the crisis and migration during Indo-Pak partition, Indian English poetry had a lull period. It is rare that the poets attempt to look beyond personal experiences in the context of larger Indian reality to hobnob with the spirit of soil and develop with it. But, we perceive that it has happened in the poetical creations of Sarojini Naidu, Aurobindo, Rabindranath Tagore, A.K. Ramanujan, Jayant Mahapatra, Dilip Chitre, and Arun Kolatkar. Tukadoji created the poetry, beginning from individual to collective consciousness, in terms of village, society, the world, and then to cosmic vision, rooted in indigenous culture and moving beyond its contours too.

In the post-colonial expanse, *Gramgeeta* has oriented Indian poetry from elitism to masses. It is conscious and assures: "... the *Mandal's* philosophy is aloof from the confinces of caste-cult-party-religion-region-language, and beyond it. The ideal of humanity and human religion are dear and near to it. I observe, with my eyes, the world is slowly slowly orienting towards this".[4]

Sevamandal's philosophy is relied on human essence and human religion, and in the phase of national and international turmoil and unrest, it is indispensable as it is oriented towards life and searching the values in life. Tukadoji discerned in his last performance at Pandharpur:

Say Tukdya, to bring tempest; to live though demised
Intend to revolt some; to ebb the wave of this energy.[5]

These lines reveal Tukadoji's vision of life to use potential energy to kinetise it to revolt and bring reformation and transformation. From Bombay Hospital, he appealed fervently to his readers, audiences, and activists "to be dutyful to propagate his literature to crores of tongues and ears". Hon'ble President of India, Pratibha Patil, on the Birth Centenary lecture on 6th January, 2010, reiterated the legacy of Tukadoji's poetic tradition and the indispensability of *Gramgeeta's* vision in the present time and its repercussion in future.[7] As, thus, it is of paramount significance to translate such literary text and treasure of literatures in indigenous languages to render wider canvas of receptors in India and abroad, envisaging in linguistic and cultural diversities.

The critique, contextualising *Gramgeeta* and mapping out the trajectories of tradition and reality, articulates the exploration of Indus culture, Vedic time and post-Vedic culture, Indian devotional poetry, sufi poetry and post-colonial reality (Chapter I); approaches to religion, science and religion, the perception of religion in the text and its cosmic dimension (Chapter II); utopia as the fantasy mode and its practicability (Chapter III); and mass culture and society, mass psyche and mass communication, and indigenous culture (Chapter IV), exploring post-colonial discourse in historical and cultural contexts with new comparative critical assertions. The comparative cultural analysis and interpretation purport to answer the problems: How does the text, here, deconstruct the authoritative text? How does cultural hegemony operate? How does the post-colonial discourse deconstruct the text? The corollary questions are: Does the text offer paradigms to fill void and fissures in multi-variant realities, which post-modernism celebrate? Do we listen the subaltern voice?

I express my gratitude to Tukaramdada Gitacharya and Laxmandada Narkhede, Directors, *Voice of Saint Tukadoji*, Quarterly in English, who rendered me the opportunity to edit it since July 1997, which triggered my critical insight and enthusiasm to delve deep in Tukadoji's literature and translate the *Gramgeeta*, making its analysis and interpretation in comparative cultural contexts; to S.R. Raut for international distribution of the Quarterly, *Akhil Bhartiya Gurudeo Seva Mandal*, Gurukunj Mozari, *Atmanusandhan Kendra*, and Adyal Tekdi for their missionary services; to the University Grant Commission, New Delhi, for financial assistance; to B.B. Taywade, Principal, Dhanwate National College, for motivation and unstinting support; to Sharayu Taywade, Dean, Faculty of Arts, Rashtrasant Tukadoji Maharaj Nagpur University, Nagpur, for involvement in this endeavour; and to Head, Department of Marathi, Mumbai University, who provided cue to undertake the venture sincerely. I am also grateful to Sahitya Academy, New Delhi; British Council High Commission Library, New Delhi; Indian Council of Historical Research, New Delhi; Asiatic Society Library, Mumbai; Pune Nagar *Vachan Mandir* and Pune Marathi *Granthalaya*, Pune; Jaykar Library, Savitribai Phule Pune University, Pune; Osmania University Center for International Programmes, Osmania University Campus, Hyderabad; Banaras Hindu University, Banaras; Indian Institute of Advanced Study, Shimla; Center for Religious Studies, University of California, Riverside; Libraries, Ramkrishna Mission; and Dhanwate National College, Nagpur for conducive academic environment and enrichment. I am very thankful to Anand Patil, Comparative Culturalist, Translator, Professor, and Head, Department of English, Goa University, Goa; Usha Bande, Critic, Principal, and the Fellow of Indian Institute of Advanced Study, Shimala; Sachin Ketkar, Poet, Translator, and Professor of English, The Maharaja Sayajirao University of Baroda, Vadodara, Gujarat; and Sunil Sawant, Translator and Professor of English, Kisan Veer Mahavidyalaya, Wai, Maharashtra, for their deliberations and suggestions to furnish clues to explore and update the contexts.

My sincere thanks to P.K.U. Pillai, Chairman, Board of Studies of English; Pramod Sharma, Dean, Faculty of Arts; D.V. Naik, Principal, R.K. Mokhare College; and Urmila Dabir, Principal, Rajkumar Kewalramani Kanya Mahavidyalaya, Rashtrasant Tukadoji Maharaj Nagpur University, Nagpur.

At this juncture, I experience the blessings of Deorao Bhellar, my father, with aesthetic sensibility, Producer of drama troop, Adarsha Kala Niketan, and Radha, my mother, with transparancy of heart; both abided to black soil in farm and when my tree's leaves rustle, buds bloom, and flowers blossom permeate vicinity with fragrance.

I acknowledge the interest that Pralhad Ande (my brother-in-law), Usha Ande (my sister), and Prabhakar Bhelkar (my brother) have taken in the venture to boost up my investigative spirit. I am thankful to T.V. Warhekar of International *Gurudeo Seva Mandal*, Warud, for missionary zeal and anticipate the words with warmth of Waman Borade, Anant Zade, Keshav Dahikar, and Anil Zade, who encouraged me. Without endurance and patience of Sangita R. Bhelkar, Yugandhar R. Bhelkar, Vaibhavi Bhelkar-Zade, Abhijit Zade, and near and dear ones, the challenging task would have not seen the sunlit expanse.

Hope, through this endeavour of mine, the present readers as well as the generations to come would cultivate orientation to read the source text, *Gramgeeta,* translated by me in English, and its comparative cultural exploration would find the entire enterprise as enriching as we did.

Ratnakar D. Bhelkar

Notes

(a) *Khanjiri* is a circular shaped indigenous musical instrument in folk tradition; on the rim of which, the seasoned skin of monitor lizzard is stretched, with thin metallic disc structures in the peripheral zone. It is prevalent in Rajasthan, Gujrat, Madhya Pradesh, and Maharashtra. With the accomplices of *tabla, tal,* and harmonium, Tukadoji deployed *khanjiri* to sing *bhajans,* which cast magnetic spell on masses. In childhood, he learnt to play on *khanjiri* from Hanuwantibuwa. *Khanjiri* accompanied through out his hectic schedules and rendered the service for peace and revolt.

(b) *Ekatari* is a single stringed instrument used in the traditional music of South Asia. It is used in the devotional practice of singing to maintain tempo rather than providing base note. From Saint Kothalikar, Manik learnt to play *ekatari*. Surdas and Mirabai also played *ekatari*.

(c) *Bhajan* is a traditional Indian folk form of singing devotional songs and was practiced by Kabir, Guru Nanak, Narsinh Mehta, Raidas, Surdas, Mirabai, and Chaitanya Mahaprabhu. Tukadoji's identity was his *khanjiri bhajan*, means of mass communication, in which he infused contemporary themes relating to *bhakti*, society, nation, political scenario, slavery, war, freedom, and constructive citizenship. For more, see *Gramgeeta*, Canto VI, 'Impact of Good Company', Canto XII, 'Village Purification', Canto XXX, '*Bhajan* Influence', in *Gramgeeta,* (tra.), Ratnakar D. Bhelkar, Atlantic Publishers and Distributors (P) Ltd., New Delhi, 2023.

(d) *Yagnya* is the ritual to lit fire out of sacred wooden sticks, with chants, which in the course of time, was associated with animal sacrifice. Salbuldi *yagnya* was the deviation from the traditional sacrifices. He alerts:

'What makes food available to labourer; a work, the best than *yagnya*

Otherwise something else not to support by mentioning *Geeta*. ||21||

(Canto XVIII, 'Labour Wealth')

Gadge Baba and Tukadoji, both worked to eradicate orthodoxy and superstition.

(e) *Langar* is a form of community meal, started by Guru Nanak to uphold the principal of equality. It expresses the ethics of sharing, community, feeling, inclusiveness, and oneness of all humankind. In their prayers, the *sikhs* seek the favour, "Loh Langar topde rahin" (May the iron pots of langar be ever warm in service).

(f) *Powada* is a narrative genre of Marathi poetry, a kind of ballad writing. Its folk form was sung to narrate valours of heroes/heroines with *duf* and *tuntune* by *shahir* to motivate the listeners. In the modern garb, Tukadoji infused democratic spirit in *powada*. Refer Canto VIII, "Significance of Propagation".

(g) *Abhang* is a form of devotional poetry, composed of *ovis*, which is in couplet and has *cesuras* at four places and internal lines rhyme. *Abhanga* is a composite form of *ovis*, practicised by saints in Maharashtra and deployed in Marathi poetry to imbibe social stratification, discrimination, post-war reality, industrial impact, spiritual desolation, and experimentation by Jyotiba Phule, Keshavasuta, Bal Sitaram Mardhekar, Vinda Karandikar, Madhukar Keche, Tulsiram Kaje, and Sudhakar Gaidhani. Also, see Canto XXX, '*Bhajan* Influence', Canto XXVI, 'An Idol Worship'.

References

1. Tukadoji, (2016), *Rashtriya Bhajanavali, Gurukunj Ashrama: Sri Gurudeo* Publication, p. 26.
2. Tukadoji, (2016), *Meri Japan Yatra, Gurukunj Ashrama: Sri Gurudeo* Publication, p. 148.
3. *Ibid,* p. 145.
4. *Sri Gurudeo*, August 1968, p. 5.
5. The last *bhajan* sung at Pandharpur on 6th July, 1968.
6. *Sri Gurudeo*, Sept., 1968, p. 2.
7. *Sakal*, 7th January, 2010.

Contents

Chapter 1

Indus Culture, Vedic Age and Post-Colonial Reality

The Indian tradition of poetry, from *Upanishad* onwards, has tended to be highly mystical and charged. *Bhakti* (Devotional) poetry had its inception in the eighth-century Tamil Nadu and moved upward through the tenth-century Karnataka and thirteenth-century Maharashtra, and spread to the entire North, West, and East of India. By the sixteenth-century *bhakti* poetry had reached to almost every corner of India. It was like national movement enriching and inspiring people, and cementing differences. In the twentieth century, in Maharashtra, Tukadoji had penned *Gramgeeta*. The purport of this research endeavour is to analyse the content and interpret the data in its diverse manifestations in the contexts of tradition and reality in *Gramgeeta*. Analysis and interpretation cut across the disciplines of Sociology, History, Political Science, Economics, Philosophy, and Science, and as thus, the explorative approach is multi-disciplinary. The research method applied in the present study is critical, analytical, and interpretative. The endevour is directed to evaluate *Gramgeeta* in the context of dynamics in post-colonial world, the projected reality, and tradition which imbibes historical sense in the ensuing chapters, 'Indus Culture, Vedic Age and Post-Colonial Reality', 'Towards Cosmic Vision' 'Utopia and its Practicability', and 'Mass Culture and Society'.

This chapter points at Indus culture, vedic age, post-vedic Indian devotional poetry, Indian English poetry, and the location of *Gramgeeta* in literary, historical, and cultural contexts; and *Gramgeeta* as post-colonial text.

Indus Culture and Pre-Vedic Society

After the measurements of Hubble telescope over the past few decades, the most recent and best measurements have directed to the estimated age for the universe within the range of 10 to 15 billion years. As the universe expanded, matter transformed into clouds that began to condense and rotate, forming the forerunners of galaxies. Some stars, inclusive of our Sun, were formed in the middle of a flattened spinning disc of material. The gas and dust within this disc collided and aggregated into small grains and then formed into planetesimals (small planets). In successive stages, these planetesimals culminated into the nine planets and their satellites. The rocky planets, including the Earth, were near the Sun, and the gaseous planets were in the distant orbits.[1] The evidence reveals that bacteria like microorganisms lived on the Earth about 3.5 billion years ago and they might have existed before, when the first solid crust formed almost 4 billion years ago. These early microorganisms must have been simpler than the microorganisms today. There must have prime structures, building blocks of life, that one would not call 'alive' but that are now the components of living beings. Unicellular animal later on evolved by natural selection and adaptation, Darwinian principles, in non-chordates, and then into chordates, inclusive of primates, monkey, gorilla, chimpanzee, and humans. The evolutionary span of man's primitive ancestors Australopithecus, biped, apparently evolved in Eastern Africa around 4 million years ago, as per paleontological and archaeological sources, and Homo-erectus, upright man, advanced from the earlier, 1.8 million years ago, on the basis of fossil evidence, and then Homo-sapiens, thinking man, is the odyssey of struggle, persistent efforts, and wanderings. DNA plays crucial role in transmission of beings' traits, coded in genes, to next generation.

Pre-Aryan Indian Sindhu culture (3300 B.C.-1300 B.C.) was the representative of bronze era. Its devastation during 1500-1400 B.C. relates to the discovery of iron. Indus valley culture, which was in existence before the invasion of Aryans, has resemblances with Mesopotamia's Sumerian culture (5000

B.C.-3500 B.C.) and Elam, the pre-Iranian culture (2700 B.C.-539 B.C.), in the parlance of well built houses with amenities, king or petty chief, seal with picture, progress in language, pictorial scripts, signs, and faiths. In Sindhu culture, there may be some places for worship, but there was no presence of any form of image worship. In writing, sign system and cannoting words were operable. In contemporary context, the writing system in China kept parallel to it. Certainly, it was not Sanskrit language, but it is sceptical whether it was Dravidian language.

Aryans were in the phase of herdsmen, when they entered in India. Aryans, comprised of many tribes, were frequently combating among themselves and with the various tribes of non-Aryans, such as Dasas, Dasysu, and Pani. They treated themselves as Aryan, means "noble of birth and race", in opposition to black natives Dasysu or Dasas. Purus, Turvasas, Yadus, and Sudas were the chiefs of Aryans, and Sambara was the militant leader of Dasas.[2]

After strenuous struggle, when they got settled, they paved the way to new economic system, co-ordinating herdsmenship and farming. New economic system had triggered of the division of labourers for fulfillment of needs. King or petty chief, *rajpurohit* or family priest, and skilled and unskilled labourer were the important facets in the human society in the pre-vedic period.

Ancient literatures around the world, such as Sumerian literature, Akkadian literature, Egyptian literature, and Greek literature concern with myriad hues of struggles. The dialectics and binaries, victorious and defeated, Aryan and non-Aryan, king and slave, priest and others are the crucial components of Ancient literatures; *Ilid, Ramayana, Mahabharata,* and Vedic literature are not distant from it. *Rigveda* is the assemblance of the poetic chaants and hymns to pray for the nature deities for happiness on the earth. *Upanishad* is a philosophical poetry, analytical of existence of being and interpretating it, unfolding nature of human life, its purpose, and *sreyas.*

Ancient Indian poetry has a rich tradition of philosophical poetry. In *Veda* and *Upanishad,* we find the seeds of philosophical poetry. As compare to philosophic poetry of *Upanishad*, *Vedic* poetry is a composition of philosophical poetry and situalistic poetry. The mother of Indian philosophical poetry, upanishadic poetry is manifestation of mysticism. *Ishavasya Upanishad* is an example of ancient mystical poetry as well as of ancient philosophical poetry.

The root of *Bhagwatgeeta's* core principles, the crux of Indian spiritualism, is in *Upanishad.* The statement, "This entire world is infused with God and there is no place in the world without Him" in *Upanishad* is the root of *Bhaktiyoga* in the *Geeta*. The statement, "Though you will live for hundred years you continue your life with work. There is no alternative to it" is the base of *Karmayoga.* The statement, "In God, all elements are merged and in all elements God is infused" is the base of *Jnanayoga.* These tri-formulae in ancient Indian philosophical poetry operate in epics like *Ramayana*, *Mahabharata,* and *Bhagwatgeeta* and Indian saint poetry, in diverse manifestations.

Ancient Indian philosophical poetry has attained spiritual height as well as poetic height because of search for self-principle and realisation. In *Ishavasya Upanishad,* the approach to self-principle is as follows:

- Self-principle is movable and immovable.
- Self-principle is far away and nearer.
- Self-principle is within and without.

The mystical language in *Upanishad* is manifested in the *Geeta* and Indian saint poetry in various forms. It continues in the tradition of philosophical poetry in *Veda* and *Upanishad,* and in the tradition of epics, such as *Ramayana, Mahabharata,* and *Bhagwatgeeta.*

Indian literature has a history that dates back to almost four thousand years. While a chronological listing would suffice to show its antiquality, range, and development over the centuries, what is of greater interest is its evolution, and the themes and concern with which it began, some of which continue even today. It is a common place to refer to Indian literature as one, though written in many languages, but until the roots of this literature are explored, the visible branches and the offshoots around cannot be understood in their historical and literary contexts.

The earliest writings in India were in Sanskrit, Pali, Prakrit, Tamil, and Kannada. The writers of each language worked within a distinct socio-historical context and yet shared a common frame of reference as far as recurring patterns of thought are concerned. The relationship of man with the world around him and with the creator of this world were the subject matters of the earliest known texts.

The Vedic Age and After

The earliest period of Indian literature in Sanskrit was the *Vedic* age, which scholars tentatively believe, lasted untill around 1200 B.C. It saw the emergence of the oral tradition of the *Sruti* texts, including the *Vedas*, that were meant to be recited and heard. The word '*Veda*' is derived from the word 'vid' that means 'to know' and it is believed that the *Vedas* were the creations of God and the human narrator was only the medium to convey the message. The *Rigveda* is the earliest known work of this type and contains hymns and prayers addressed to various gods. In this and later *Vedas—Yajurveda, Samaveda, and Atharvaveda*—is visible man's earliest attempts to understand his position in the world and create the possibility of a dialogue with the unknown, through supplication, philosophical enquiry, and speculation. These *Vedas* are *samhitas* (collections; literally joined together), written years together by multiple hands and contain hymns, prayers, benedictions, sacrificial formulae, and litanies.

The central motif in the *Vedas* is that of the sacrifice or *yajna* and the injunctions for its performance in honour of various gods, to request their benevolence. The primary impulse of these prayers is man's desire for the good life—a long and healthy life of cattle, offspring, and the like. The supplicant hoped that these wishes would be fulfilled by the propitiation of a benign deity. The deities were those who governed natural phenomena like fire, water, wind, and the earth.

The eleven *Brahmanas* are a large corpus of prose texts that comment on the *Vedic* mantras and prescribe their application in different sacrifices. The speculations are not only theological, but also philosophical, grammatical, etymological, and metrical. The three *Aranyakas*, on the other hand, were meant for study in the seclusion of the forest. These texts were ritual explorations and allegorical speculations that represented a transitional phase of enquiry into the knowledge, contained in the *Vedas*. After the *Aranyakas,* the *Upanishads* came. The word *Upanishad* means sitting down with devotion near the teacher to receive instruction. There are thirteen principal *Upanishads* which are primarily metaphysical in content and reflect man's yearning to find answers to the eternal questions of life, death, immortality, happiness, truth, God, and the origins of life.

The *Sruti* texts contain whatever is heard and revealed, and are made up of all that are remembered, recorded from memory, and later consolidated into a literary tradition. The *Smriti* texts are break from the earlier *Vedic* tradition as they are attributed to human creation and also deal with a variety of subjects as diverse as phonetics *(siksa)*, metrics *(chanda),* grammar *(vyaakaran),* etymology *(nirukta),* astronomy *(jyotisha),* and rituals and ceremonies *(kalpa).* The body of *Smriti* literature consists of the six *Vedangas*, which are adjuncts to the *Vedas*, the epics—the *Ramayana* and the *Mahabharata,* and the *Puranas,* most popular of which is the *Bhagavata-purana* that tells the story of the life of Krishna. The *Sruti* texts are written in the *sutra* (thread) form and lead to the realisation of *dharma*—which sustains, is firm and durable, and governs all human life. These writings are not only didactic in intent but also display a development in form and structure as they use a variety of narrative techniques and introduce an element of drama as the destiny of mankind unfolds and the listener/reader is entertained and instructed through the story. Sanskrit poetry in the post-*Vedic* age ranges from the amatory to the moral and the renunciatory. The poems were composed in courts under royal patronage and diverged from their predecessors as they became more secular in tone and temper.

In the development of Sanskrit drama, the foremost is the name of Bharata, whose *Natyashastra* (of the first century B.C. to the first century A.D.) is a theoretical text on the performing arts and sets the ground and the parameters for Sanskrit aesthetic theory. Most of the plays written at the time were structured around romantic love or heroic valour and had a noble and godly hero, and began and ended with a benediction for universal peace and prosperity. The story chosen for dramatic treatment would illustrate the hero's achievement of one of the four socially accepted goals of *dharma* (righteousness), *artha* (wealth), *kama* (pleasure), and *moksha* (liberation). Destiny played an important role as did the natural environment of birds, flowers, animals, clouds, and so on. The sources were mainly the *Vedas*, *Puranas*, and history; and the characters were drawn from a cross-section of the society. Besides romantic and heroic plays written by dramatists like Bhasa and Kalidasa, some dramatists like Shudraka also wrote social comedies, while others like Visakhadatta wrote about political intrigues and life in the courts.

The other forms of literary composition of that age are *Mahakavyas*—long poems that conform to the prescribed rules of poetry; *Laghukavyas*—lyric poetry; inscriptions that stylistically illustrate the use of ornate prose and verse with striking imagery and introduce the genre or the *prasasti*—the eulogy of the ruling king; *Gadyakavya*—literary romantic prose; *Akhyayika*—invented stories of historical characters; scientific prose on medicine, astrology, grammar, prosody, astronomy, erotics, politics, performing arts, and law; champu-mixed prose and verse; and fables, the most popular among which remain Visnu Sarma's *Panchatantra* and Somadeva's *Kathasaritsagara*. Taxonomy can be seen as the hallmark of Sanskrit thinkers with their penchant for classification and analysis of language, natural phenomena, and even emotions. The world view is one of a hierarchical social order and the regulation of human life by *dharma*, and is not open to debate or opposition. By the sixth century B.C., knowledge had been codified and there were strict rules for literary composition and even appreciation. This had changed with the growing influence of Buddhism and Jainism in the subcontinent.

Literature in Prakrit and Apabhransi

If Sanskrit was the principal refined language of literary speech and rituals and required training, Prakrit, meaning 'natural' or 'common', was the language of everyday conversation and commerce among many. The relationship between these two languages that developed side by side was one of complex negotiation and exchange. In many Sanskrit plays, some of the characters, especially the women and servants, spoke in Prakrit; and Prakrit texts used Sanskrit themes and rewrote them in the context of folk traditions. The major evidence of Prakrit being used in literary compositions can be seen in the inscriptions of Ashoka which represent the earliest dated Indian literary records. By the fifth-century A.D., Prakrit was also being used in songs, Buddhist *gathas,* Jaina writings and doctrinal treatises, and a large mass of secular literature like the *Sattasai* (anthologies) to which women also contributed. Grammars, lexicons, works of poetics, metrics, and astronomical and medical texts were also written in Prakrit.

Another language used at the time was *Apabhramsa.* By the seventh-century A.D., it had become a literary language. This language was originally used in Jaina writings and, therefore, had an overtly religious tone, but later on it also began to be used for the composition of *samdhi-bandhas*—stories from the *Puranas,* biographies, and religious narratives; and the *rasa-bandhas*—lyrical compositions which employed a fixed metre for the main body of the text and a range of other metres for variation.

Sangam and *Bhakti* Literature in Tamil

The ancient period of Tamil literature is popularly known as *Cankam (Sangam)* and the earliest known work is the *Tolkappiyam,* usually ascribed to anywhere between 300 B.C. and the first-century A.D., which is the first complete, classified, and comprehensive treatise on the Tamil grammatical system. The two major forms of literature as enunciated in the *Tolkappiyam* are the *'Akam'* and the *'Puram'.* The *Akam* is the interior landscape of the writer's imagination and deals with love in all its variations and moods. The poems are located in a specific space and time, and the characters are not named, but identified by their gender, occupation, region, and role in the love and relationship. The *Puram* is the outer world, marked by feats of heroism, war, court life, and the poet in search of a generous patron. The *Cankam* poetry of love and war, composed between 300 B.C. and 100 A.D., is conceived in a secular milieu, and the relationship between nature and man's emotions and experiences is explored in all its dimensions.

The next phase of ancient Tamil literature, between the second and third centuries A.D., is the didactic phase in which the influences of Jainism and Buddhism are prominent. The most famous work of this period is the *Tirukkural,* which developed the earlier two-fold division of literary composition into a three-fold one of love, virtue, and matters relating to policy and society. In this period, many major epics were also composed, like the *Cilappatikaram* and the *Manimekhalai.* They represent a departure from the Sanskrit epics and reflect a prominent world view of Buddhism and Jainism. At the centre of the narratives are strong women who are empowered and invested with moral authority that reinforced with religious sanction, and who anticipate the rebellious women of the *Bhakti* period.

Bhakti, which in Tamil means 'partaking of God', found expression in the Tamil speaking region around the sixth/seventh-century A.D. The literature of this period is made up of a large body of devotional hymns sung by *Shaiva* saints called the *Nayanmars* and *Vaishnava* saints called the *Alvars*. The songs were composed in a spirit of protest against conventional rituals and scripture, and the intercession of priests between man and God. Each *bhakti* poet worships a personal God and the poems are emotional, ecstatic, and erotic, and explore the relationship of the self with his/her god.

Early Kannada Literature

Any introduction to the literature of ancient India would be incomplete without a reference to literature in Kannada. Based on linguistic evidences available from rock edicts and inscriptions, it is believed that the Kannada language must have existed as early as the third-century B.C. It was influenced by Sanskrit, Prakrit, Vedic, and Jaina legends, and also by the stories from the *Ramayana* and the *Mahabharata*. The earliest known literary work in Kannada is *Kavirajamarga* (ca. 850 A.D.) and like the first book in Tamil, it is a treatise on rhetoric, grammar, language, and prosody, and also contains observations on contemporary society, religion, and culture. Influenced by the epics, the *Ramayana* and the *Mahabharata*, grand narratives were also composed in Kannada at that time and they took well known episodes from these sources and reinterpreted them in a local context.

In the tenth-century A.D., which is often referred to as the Golden Age of old Kannada literature, the most important writers were Pampa, Ponna, and Ranna. Their works are a reflection of the social, cultural, and political milieu of the time. Most of the writings in Kannada at that time attempted to create a distinct identity through language, landscape, myth, literature, and culture. Jainism, its beliefs and social practices, had gained a wide acceptance which is also evident in most of the writings of the time. In fact, the dilemma of a man caught between his desire to live a full life and the contrary tendency of renunciation—the dual vision of affirmation and denial—informs the whole corpus of Jaina-inspired writings. Thus, one of the threads that binds the literature in all the languages mentioned above is the juxtaposition of two parallel archetypes—movement towards life in all its variety and passion and the wish for the fulfillment of erotic and material desires and a tradition of renunciation, a moving away from life. It is only with the *Bhakti* movement that the duality of 'here' and 'hereafter', 'physical' and 'metaphysical', 'material' and 'transcendential', and 'visible' and 'invisible' could be reconciled; and it is during the *Veerashaiva* movement that the *Vachanakaras,* the makers of divine poetry in Kannada, composed songs that blended all disparate emotions to achieve an integral vision.

Medieval Indian Literature (1000 A.D. to 1800 A.D.)

Moving into the eleventh-century A.D., the map of the Indian subcontinent began to look different, as various political and social changes ushered in an era of dialogue between cultures, religions, and languages. The most fascinating dimension of this age of Indian literature was the development of modern Indian languages. In the next seven centuries, all the Indian languages as we know them today would have developed a distinct literature of their own. This era was marked by foreign invasions, cultural contacts, large-scale migration, religious conversions, military conquest, and changing patterns of socio-economic relations.

The Past and the Present—Identity and Difference

The first distinct feature of medieval Indian literature was the translation, adaptation, and transcreation of stories of the *Ramayana,* the *Mahabharata*, the *Puranas*, myths, and legends into a large number of languages. These texts in their new forms reflected the local ethos of the region into which they were translated, and also became the classics of the host languages. For example, Kamban's *Ramayanam* in Tamil and Nannaya's *Mahabharata* in Telugu are considered landmarks in the development of these literatures.

Each of the languages also retained folk elements in their literature, leading to the development of distinct identities, as seen in languages like Maithali, Manipuri, and Nepali. Drama and performance continued to flourish which was most evident in the folk theatre and local style of performances that developed, like the *Bhavai* in Gujarat. Literary texts were written to accompany performances, like the *Attakathas* in Malayalam which complements the *Kathakali* performances. In fact, a lot of the literature at that time retained its orality as what was written, was incomplete without the music and gestures that accompanied it.

The *Bhakti* Movement

The *Bhakti* movement was the phenomenal attempt of the marginalise segment (i.e., regional languages and literature, the lower castes and classes) at decentralising the hierarchy imposed by the *brahmin* fraternity. From its inception, the *Bhakti* ideology was guided by a humanising cosmopolitanism, an emotional fervor, and a thirst for the divine essence and experience. The socio-political factors propelled the *Bhakti* movement from its inception in the eight-century Tamil Nadu with the *Shaiva* and *Vaishanya Bhakti* Cults, to the elevanth and twelfth centuries Lingayats of Karnataka; the *Mahanubhav panth* (sect) and the *Warkari panth* of Maharashtra in twelveth and thirteenth centuries, respectively; Ramananda's school which initiated *Nirguna bhakti* in the fourteenth-century North-India; *padam* tradition in the fifteenth and sixteenth centuries in Andhra Pradesh; and the Chaitanya School of *Saguna Vaishnava bhakti* in Bengal and Orissa, which had a parallel following in the *Saguna* poets of Gujarat. Composed during the quarter of the sixteenth-century, *The Bhakti-ras mrta-sindhu* of Rupa Goswami is the critical document on *Bhakti* to bring it in the ambit of the *rasa* theory. Goswami cities the examples of *Bhakti* from the *Purana* literature, and in his he except on *Bhaktirasa,* he views:

> Exceptionally wonderful supernatural powers, long-enduring worldly and heavenly pleasures, long and lasting experiences of *Mukti* as *Brahmasukha* (felicity derived from knowledge and realisation of impersonal *Brahman*), and eternal and ever-progressive and supreme flow of transcental felicity (from realisation of the Supreme Lord) are attainable by *Bhakti* in Lord Govinda (Krishna), who is the Lord of all senses...[3]

He further compares in *Bhava-Bhakti,*

> In the *Puranas* and Dramaturgy both *Rati* and *Bhava* have been used in the same sense; here *Bhakti* literature is also... they are conceived as equivalent to each other..."[4]

The *Bhakti*, which is emphasised here is visible in the poetries of Surdas, Meerabai, Chaitanya, and the Vernsular languages in India. The translation of the original text by Tridandi Swami in 1965 was also used for spiritual upliftment of masses.

Ganesh Devi has disseminated that Rupa Goswami was not trying to explain *Bhakti* poetry in terms of the *rasa* theory of *Bhakti* poetry as engrained in the poetic practice in Sanskrit in the owntime.[5] *Bhakti* is presented as the highest *rasa,* and beside it, for him, *Bhakt* in real life itself is a *rasa*, which is indistinct from the *rasa* in poetry. While evaluating Keshavadasa (1555-1617), he has observed that *bhakti* was not an additional *rasa*, a new sentiment not known to Bharata, but that *bhakti* is an aspect of all sentiments[6] described by Bharata and Abhinavagupta.

The *Bhakti* movement was the creation of an extensive literature in the vernacular languages. Envisaging the *Bhakti* movement as the link with the development of regional vernacular languages and with that of the marginalised social segments, A.K. Ramanujan writes:

> Like a lit fuse, the passion of *Bhakti* seems to spread from region to region, from century to century, quickening the religious impulse. Arising in particular regions, speaking the local languages, it is yet interregional—both parochial and universal. Even modern urban *Bhakti* groups include in their hymnals, songs of several languages and ages.[7]

As the consequence, from the *Upanishads* onwards, a large number of smilies and analogies are applied in the *bhakti* poetry and the tradition of mystic verse writing continues.

While all languages saw the growth of devotional and philosophical literature, a distinct feature of this age was the resurgence of *Vaishnavism* and *Shaivism,* and the rise of the *Bhakti* movement. The dialogue between man and God infused a new spirit in the whole body of songs in many languages across the length and breadth of the country. These harbingers of a new faith also wrote commentaries on the *Bhagavadgeeta* and the *Puranas* as seen in the works of Jnaneshwar in Marathi, and the *Padmapuranas* in Assamese. This age also saw the emergence of writing by women saint poets, the most prominent among them are Lalleshwari known as Lal Ded, and Habba Khatoon in Kashmiri, Meerabai in Hindi, Mahadamba, Janabai, Muktabai, Bahinabai in Marathi, Avvaiyar in Tamil, Muddupalani in Telugu, and Akka Mahadevi in Kannada. An interesting relationship was set up between literature and ideology as the saint-poets spoke of faith in a new idiom. Their vibrant message of love and humanism transcended barriers of region, language, and class. Buddhism and Jainism continued to exercise an important influence, and were joined by the stories from Islam and Christianity with the coming of the Muslims and the Portuguese. This was supplemented by the impact of Guru Nanak Dev's *Adi Granth* which speaks of a religion as a way of life that combines elements from all the belief systems and also incorporates the humanistic ideals of the *Bhakti* and *Sufi* poets. This trend was also seen in Sindhi writings of the time, which was profoundly influenced by *Sufi* ideas and world view. While the literary works in some languages like Dogri, Manipuri, and Kashmiri make reference to local deities and the objects of worship and veneration, which are pan-Indian.

The conversion to Jainism and Buddhism in the eighth-century, the conversion to Islam to escape the burden of jizya tax in the fourteenth and fifteenth centuries, and the conversion to Christianity to elevate status, were largely from the down strata of society. The *Bhakti* movement was the revolt within the Hindu structure which paved the passage for the marginalised and triggered of the humanisation of social structures. Sisir Kumar Ghosh views:

> The mystic belongs to the family of man and more than man, he has his comrades and is at home everywhere and nowhere. He alone has conquered alienation and looked into the heart of the human situation... I (Mystics)...do not consider organised religion as enough, (but) an vitally concerned with collective salvation, a divine milieu.[8]

The *bhakti* poetry has the traits of mystical poetry but it points at reformation of society and improvement of spiritual fabric.

From ancient time, the system which was developed, was dominated by the privileged class. The non-privileged class was deprived of ancient discipline, Oriental study, and from this standpoint, Shambuka is an illustrative example. Buddha had rejected these notions and in these prohibited area, downtrodden masses (grass root people and women) were accepted and for the discussion on knowledge, the mass language was in operation. The clash of the currents of ancient discipline oriented and mass oriented is prevalent from centuries together. In many centuries in India, the influence of Buddhism was visible but the dominance of the currents of *Sruti-Smruti* was not feeble.

Saint poets had given new direction to religion and society. They extracted out devotion, knowledge, penance, ancient disciple-study, spiritual reflection, and philosophical debates from the limited range to the masses of society, who were marginalised. They enlightened self-realisation by the medium of devotion in the masses and put a question mark on the verdicts which were discriminatory. They developed the devotional currents parallel to *Sruti-Smruti,* and oriented and joined all classes and castes with them, who were totally fragmented in the society.

In Dravidian area, i.e., South India, this tone of devotional poetry was emerged in ninth and tenth centuries. It had travelled from Maharashtra and Gujrat to North India. It was more intensified in Punjab where Guru Nanak, founder of Sikhism and the first Shikh Guru, though not from downtrodden strata, had not anticipated *Sruti-Smruti* oriented life style based on inequality. He linked himself with the tradition of Namdev, Kabir, Dhanna, and Saina Wali. This tradition believes in the Supreme Power without form and rejects idol-worship and incarnation; and deviates from *Sruti-Smruti* proposed God-abode, pilgrimage, and orthodox rituals to accept self-experience. It not only accepts devotion and tiny currents in spiritualism and philosophy but also welcomes Sufi approach. It reinforces counter discourse against *Sruti-Smruti* oriented approach to heaven, modes of devotion, and insistence on rituals.

Adi Grantha by Guru Arjan, the sacred scripture of *Sikhism*, includes couplets of the Sikh Gurus and various early and medieval saints of different religions and castes—Jaydeo, Ramanand, Parmanand, and Surdas were *brahmins*; Pipa was *kshatriya*; Trilochan was *vaishya*; Shaikh Farid, Kabir, and Bhikha were *Muslims*; and Namdev, Ravidas, Sadhana, Saina, Dhanna, and Beni were from downtrodden castes. It contains 541 couplets of Kabir, 122 of Sheikh Farid, 60 of Namdev, and 40 of Ravidas. As per the parameters of *Sruti-Smruti*, these saints were discarded. Namdev is famous in Punjab where place to place centers on his name are opened. He is a link for cultural dialogue between Maharashtra and Punjab.

Medieval Indian Poetry (1000 A.D. to 1800 A.D.)

Saint poets emerged in different states in India. Medieval Indian poetries were written in regional languages, but they had the potential to cross the language barriers. But, ancient Indian poetry was in Sanskrit. Regional poetry had initiated the new era of medieval regional poetry. Regional language was mass language, akin to common man. Saint poets of medieval period were from the different castes and tribes, and they represented the masses. Saint poetry is devotional poetry and in true sense, it is religious and spiritual poetry. Keeping aside outer decorum and meaningless ritualistic practices, it gives the message of good conduct. This poetry had touched the heart of masses. Its ideals were great ancient sages who wrote philosophical poetries. Like poetries, lives of ancient poets and medieval saint poets had philosophical base. Medieval saint poetry was emphatically philosophical poetry. Medieval saint poets propounded truth, non-violence, and peace in their poetry, and rendered the message of equality and unity. Hammering on religious and social corruption prevalent in the society, they did religious and social awakening. In the medieval age, the *Bhakti* movement had proved to be the phase of social as well as self-consciousness awakening in India. The regional saint poetry had widened the orbit of Indian poetry. Experiencing the futility of blood-shed in the Kalinga war, Ashoka accepted Buddhism and propagated it. Royal patronage no longer remained the exclusive priviledge of Vedic tradition.

With rise of the mercantile community between 200 B.C. and 300 A.D., both Buddhism and Jainism saw their decline. Differences in the interpretation of the preceptor's teachings, formation of sub-sects, distancing from the common man, and isolation in monasteries were some of the pitfalls of Buddhism and Jainism. New cults of devotion to Vishnu and Shiva—the *Bhagvata* and the *Pashupata* cults—with an emphasis on personal worship rather than sacrificial ritual, had arrived upon the scene. Jainism and Buddhism had to gradually pave the way to this new form of religious worship.

Tamil society, at the threshold of the *Bhakti* era, was fragmented by caste hierarchy with the distinction between the Sanskrit literate class and the vernaculars. A process initiated during the Gupta period (320 to 540 A.D.), it had exerted considerable influence and secured the favour of southern royal. The politics of exclusion/expulsion created the non-priviledged and marginalised classes (*Vaishyas*, *Shudras*, and other non-castes) who were desirous of raising their status and hence, conducive to conversion. The democratic fervour of Buddhism and Jainism was the outlet for status promotion. Reformative measures were introduced within the Hindu fold to speed up the flow of conversion.

Both Gautama Buddha and Mahavira were *kshatriya*. They discouraged animal sacrifices, appealed to downtrodden, opposed caste system, and used the vernacular form of Prakrit for spreading their respective faiths. They were the first to protest the systems of ritual and caste, and counter cultural voices to resist the traditional dominance of orthodoxy in religion, rituals, and caste monocentricness. As a consequence, they were received by the *Vaishyas* who were economically powerful but deprived of social status and the *Shudras* who were oppressed. In 510 B.C., Mahavira (aged 30) renounced his family for asceticism and wandered for twelve years until he gained enlightenment in 498 B.C. Initially Jainism spread to the western part of the north and south of Mysore. Its trust on non-violence and strict limitation on property made it popular with the trading community. The Prince Siddhartha (born in 566 B.C.) had left his home and became an ascetic. After six years of wandering as an ascetic, he turned to meditation as the means for salvation. On the 49th day of meditation, he received enlightenment and gave the first sermon at Sarnath, four miles away from Banaras. He preached eight-fold path of *nirvana* (enlightenment) which enlisted eight principles of action—right views, right resolution, right speech, right conduct, right livelihood, right effort, right recollection, and right meditation, the combination of which is called as the middle way. Later Buddhism spread to many parts of Asia. The religion continued to grow in the centuries in vicinity and received royal patronage. Chandragupta Maurya towards the end of his life converted to Jainism and became an asectic.

Envisaging socio-religious tension between orthodox and non-orthodox sects, between 200 B.C. and 500 A.D., the period that followed between 600 A.D. and 800 A.D. saw the revival of Shiva and Vishnu, not with their orthodox accessories but through the *bhakti* cult. The *bhakti* cult recognised no middleman between devotee and God. It revolted against the tyranny of ritual and caste practices. R. Champakalakshmi comments on the *bhakti* cult as having brought back the *Puranic* religion:

> Marked by intense religious conflict, persecution and royal conversions in favour of the 'orthodox' religions, the first phase witnessed the establishment of *Puranic*

> religion through the *bhakti* cult, supported by new institutional forms. It also represented the culmination of the process of acculturation, i.e., the assimilation of folk cults into, and imposition of local cults over the *Brahmanical* religions systems of *Vaishnavism* and *Shavism*. The religious aspects of the change are seen in the spread of Puranic and epic stories, new iconographic concepts, both *Vaishnava* and *Shaiva*, introduction of Agamic worship and above all building of temples by the ruling families.[9]

Popularisation of *Puranic* religion and Agamic forms of worship was achieved through the ideology of *bhakti* or devotion expressed through the hymns of saints. The former was sponsored by elite groups for mutual benefits like social dominance and political influence. While the latter was seen in the resurgence within the masses through a personal communion between individuals and with God through devotion. As thus, the option of vernacular language was also open.

Tamil hymns made available for community singing (*kirtana*) added to the movement's popularity and opened the avenue for the lower caste and out-caste (subaltern). The sectarian religions of *Shaivism* and *Vaishnavism* evolved out of older beliefs of popular worship and cult practices.

The presence of popular and fast spreading religions like Jainism and Buddhism, had provided an opportune escape to the oppressed masses, whose exodus into the Jain or Buddhist fold sent alarm bells ringing among the *brahmin* community. The cult of *Vaishnava bhakti* was born at the time when Jain and Buddhist faiths were on the decline. The masses were encouraged to join the worship ritual which favoured emotional fervour and devotion to God. Its pioneer poets (the twelve *Alvars*) were from high caste *brahmins* who lent their verses for the purpose of devotional singing.

As poems, the Alvars' hymns were the forbearers of later *Vaishnava* poetic traditions, influencing nearer home, the *Varkari* movement of the twelfth-century Maharashtra and the *Padam* tradition of the fifteenth-century Andhra Pradesh.

Padams were composed throughout India. Early examples in Sanskrit are those occurring in Jaydev's famous devotional poem *Gitgovinda* (12th Century). *Padams* are short musical compositions of light classical nature. In the fifteenth and sixteenth centuries, they were sung and performed by devadasis and their counterparts, both in the temples and royal courts. Telugu *padams* being devotional in character were included in the wider corpus of South Indian *Bhakti* poetry. The following poem by Tallapaka Annamacharya is in the *padam* tradition:

These marks of black musk
on her lips
red as buds
what are they
but letters of love
sent by our lady to her lord?
Her eyes, the eyes of a *chakor* bird,
why are they red in the corners?
Think it over my friends:
what is it but the blood
still staining the long glances
that pierced her beloved
after she drew them from his body
back to her eyes?[6]

In the eleventh and the twelfth centuries Karnataka, the *Shaiva* movement known as the *Veerashaiva* or *Lingayat* movement, received momentum. It created space for the participation of lower classes. The *Lingayats* were iconoclastic, questioning prevalent conversions, deconstructing ritual practice, inducing social reform, and propagating a return to conscience and essence. The eminent *lingayat* poets were Basavanna, Dasimayya, Allama Prabhu, and Mahadeviyakka.

Shaivism is based on the dual principles of Shiva-Shakti. This provided a wider base due to incorporation of the worship of mother-goddess which absorbed all tribals and popular forms like the tree and pillar, and deities associated with funerary practices. *Murugan*, Tamil tribal deity, was absorbed in the

Shaivite pantheon. Shiva was the deity of those people belonging to agricultural classes and the craftsmen, professionally and socially differentiated from the higher agricultural and ruling families. *Veerashaivism* was largely the accepted faith of the ruling elite, i.e., the landed chieftains called *velif*. The concept of Vishnu as the protector of the earth, as the husband of *Sri* or Wealth or prosperity, and the inclusion of *Bhudevi* as his second consort, all such connections made *Vaishnavism* the religion of the upper-classes. By and large Vishnu remained alienated to Tamil society. Shiva, the destroyer of evil, became the pan-Indian God of large number of lower class people. The local deities and their symbols had been absorbed under the two heads of Shiva and Vishnu. The local cult centers or spots, like enclosed tree trunk or a pillar, were replaced by a temple or a shrine to the worship of Shiva or Vishnu. The priests of the converted local cult centers were also integrated into the new order of worship. *Vaishnavism* had its major centers in the northern and southern most parts of Tamil Nadu and a few in the Kaveri delta region. *Shaivism* was mainly concentrated in the Chola region, i.e., in the Kaveri valley and in and around the Pallava and Pandya capitals of Kanchipuram and Madurai.

Among the twelve *Vaishnava* saints (called Alvars), only two belonged to the low castes. Similarly, a majority of the *Shaiva* hymnists, known as Nayanmars, also hailed from the higher castes. They were mystic poets and scholars who spoke of equality of all humans at the feet of God.

Some desirable changes were to take place in the second major phase of societal transformation between the tenth and thirteenth centuries. This was also the period of Chola dynasty. The Cholas took active interest in the development of temple centers and used the temples to widen the sphere of their royal authority. However, it was *Shaiva* temples and the *Shaiva* faith at large that flourished under the Chola region. An impetus to speedy liberalization in temple worship was the desire to retain the popular sway which *Shaivist* faith had come to establish. Tirunavukkarasar, the seventh century poet and scholar, who on being reconverted to *Shaivism* from Jainism, had reconverted the Pallava King Mahendravarman to *Shaivism*. The Nayanmars,

Sambandar (seventh century) and Manikkavachakar (eighth century) of Madurai, contributed immensely towards the spread of *Shaivism* in the Pandya court. The songs of the Nayanmars were surcharged with devotional feelings.

Vaishnavism had initially been patronised largely by high-caste *brahmins* and the elites. Reformative attempts were made in the twelfth-century when Ramanuja (1017 to 1137 A.D.), born at Sriperumbudur, tried to provide *Vaishnavism* with the wider base of popularity. Ramanuja believed that liberation was possible only after death. It was person's *bhakti*, true love, and meditation that led to the goal of *mukti* (liberation). But, God's grace (*prasada*) plays the crucial role without which man's efforts cannot bear fruit. Both Kabir and Nanak laid emphasis upon 'divine grace' in their ethos of *bhakti*. Ramanuja attempted to synthesise the vedic philosophy with the element of *bhakti*. He strived to ensure the participation of devotees from different social strata by ascribing to them same aspects of ritual and management. The *Shaivas* viewed that *Vaishnva* attempted to reform as a threat to their religious networks. However, Ramanuja's attempts at liberalisation were not shared by his successors in the south, and by the fourteenth-century there arose among the *Vaishnavas* its schism into the northern (*vadakalai*), and southern (*tentalai*) schools, based on their differences regarding the participation of low-caste members in the rituals of worship.

Veerashaiva

Veerashaivism, the *Shaivist bhakti* cult of Karnataka, was more radical and reformist in its approach. *Veerashaivas* were a group of Kannada speaking Shiva *bhaktas* living in the tenth to twelfth centuries Karnataka. They challenged the caste system and attacked orthodox ritual, sacrifice, and superstition in worship. With ironical and satirical tones, Basavanna writes:

> The sacrificial lamb brought for the festival
> ate up the green leaf brought for the decorations.
>
> Not knowing a thing about to kill,
> it wants only to fill its belly:

born that day, to die that day.
But tell me:
did the killers survive,
O lord of the meeting rivers?

(*Speaking of Shiva*, p. 73)

Veerashaivas had their small rituals. They wore the *linga*—a small stone-emblem of Shiva—in a chain or string around their necks.

Mahadeviyakka chose to address her lord Shiva by the epithet "O Lord, White as Jasmine". Allama Prabhu writes,

Vishnu and Brahma
are my kingmen and sidekick.
You are the father-in-law
and I, the son-in-law
O Lord of Caves (161)

The *Vachanas*, the Kannada *Upanishads*, record the voices of protest and reform in Hindu society. *Veerashaivas* were men and women from a large cross-section of society. The *Vachanas* don't adhere to traditional metres, discipline of literary genre, division of prose and verse, and use the colloquial diction in Kannada. The *Vachana* tradition was enriched by Dasimayya, Basavanna, Allama Prabhu, and Mahadeviyakka. Basavanna (1106 A.D. to 1167 A.D.) was a political activist and a social reformer, and established the *Veerashaiva* movement in the tenth-century Karnataka.

The famous Kannad poet, Basaveshwar was the major force in establishing Anubhava Mantapa. He treats himself as '*chakor*'. *Chakor,* day and night, watches the moon and likewise real devotee concentrates on God. Basaveshwara views *chakor's* longs for stars, lotus for rising Sun, and honeybee for honey in flower, and craves for Lord. He was poet and singer. He was spiritual practitioner besides social reformer and vehemently attacked religious corruption and social injustice. In one of the *vachanas*, he writes that people who offer milk to stone-snake but kill real snake, reveals social irony.

A.K. Ramanujan in his *Speaking of Shiva* highlights the poets of the *Veerashaivas*:

> Basavanna helped to create a new community. Many great men like Allama Prabhu, saint of saints, were in Kalyana in that period. He helped to clear and shape the ideas of the *Veerashaivas*. Many others like Siddharama, Machideva, Bommayya (the lute-playing Bommayya), and the remarkable radical woman saint Mahadeviyakka were part of the company of saints. A religions centre called *Anubhava mantapa,* (the hall of experience), was established in which the great saints met for dialogue and communion shaping the growing community—a hundred and ninety thousand jangmas or mendicant devotees are counted as having lived in Kalyan under Basavanna's direction, helping spread the new religion. (64)

In Basavanna's new perception of religion, his legs are pillars, the body is shrine, and head a cupola. To him, whatever is stagnant, will crumble, and moving will stay for ever. He pens:

> The rich
> Will make temples for Shiva
> What shall I,
> A poor man
> Do?
> My legs are pillars,
> The body the shrine,
> The head a cupola
> Of gold
> Listen, O Lord of the meeting rivers,
> The things standing shall fall,
> But the moving ever shall stay.

(Basavanna, tr. A.K. Ramanujan 19)

Akka Mahadevi was the contemporary of Basveshwar. She emphasised upon the freedom of woman and elevated Indian poetry to spiritual height. She realised the presence of God in cosmos and, also, in micro-forms.

In the sixteenth-century, Purandara Dasa, singer and poet, was devotee of Vitthal and disciple of Madhavacharya. To him, a person becomes *brahmin* not only on the basis of caste but because of spiritual power. Kanaka Dasa was contemporary saint poet of Purandara Dasa. He was born in a shepherd family and never believed in discrimination on the basis of religions, caste, and cult, and criticised social inequality.

Many saint poets existed together in the same place at the same time and all shared the ideal of devotion. *Anubhava Mantapa* or assembly of saints at Kalyan, near Kalburgi in Gulbarga district, is the symbol of devotional movement. There devotee and saints used to come together for spiritual practices and religious discussion. Keeping aside orthodox practices, the propagation of religious principles to reach them to masses was the core work of the assembly. No discrimination was made on the grounds of *varna,* cult, caste, and gender. The assembly was with social commitment and progressive religious tradition. Collective spiritual practice and religious discussion were new experiments in medieval period. It recalls the galaxy of saint poets of *warakari* cult in the vicinity of Pandharpur in Maharashtra.

Alvars

Shaivism was more popular in the earlier stages of the *Bhakti* movement and *Vaishnavism* received momentum in the later stages in the West, North, and East of India. Alvars were saints who wrote the earliest devotional poems for Vishnu. 'Al' means "to immerse, to be lowered, to be deepen". Hence, Alvar means one who is immersed in God. It began with Ramanuja of the twelveth-century, who attempted to widen the frontier of *Vaishnava* to the non-priviledged. He ventured to synthesise the vedic tradition with the Tamil tradition of Alvars and fuse the metaphysical terrain of the *Vedanta* and the tradition of *bhakti.*

Alvars identified *Mayon* with the dark hued Vishnu or Krishna and it is reflected in Nammalvar's poem from *Hymns for the Drowning*:

> If I see you anywhere
> I'll gather you
> and eat you up,
> he beat me to it
> and devoured me entire,

my lord as dark as raincloud,
my lord self-seeking and unfair (69)

The twelve Alvars were Poykai, Putam, Pey, Tiruppan, Tirumalikai, Tontaratippoti, Kulashekaran, Bhutath, Periyalvar, Andal (a woman poet), Tirumankai, Nammalvar, and Maturakavi; of these, the first three were called the mudal Alvars who belonged to the seventh-century and attempted to merge Vishnu and Shiva, and practiced Hari-Hara sect. The remaining nine Alvars who lived in the nineth century revitalised Hinduism and checked the spread of Buddhism and Jainism, absorbing some of their features, such as the use of vernacular language, the defiance of vedic authority, crossing the barriers of castes, and creation of the religious texts. A.K. Ramanujan commented on the spread of *Vaishnavism* and *Shaivism* in Tamil Nadu in his *Hymns for the Drowning*:

> The saint-poets wandered all over the Tamil countryside, inspiring and converting kings, *brahmans,* and peasants, affirming in poetry the holiness of hundreds of Tamil places dedicated to Vishnu or Shiva. Their pilgrimages, their legends, and their hymns (which they sang by the thousands), literally mapped a sacred/geography of the Tamil regions and fashioned a communal self image that cut across class and caste. They composed the most important early *bhakti* (i.e., devotional) texts in any Indian language. The two rival movements despite differences in myth and ritual created and shared a special idioms, a stock of attitudes and themes, and a common heritage alive to this day.[7]

Vaishnava bhakti was charged with a spirit of reform and humanism. The Alvar lyrics encompass pure urge of human mind for divine, all immanent, and omnipotent. Of the twelve Alvars, only two belonged to the lower castes, the rest came from either from the *brahmin* castes or from higher *velala,* i.e., *shudra*, ruling classes. During the upward course of *Vaishnava bhakti,* it spread across the west, north, and east of India, within a century.

Nammalvar (880 A.D. to 930 A.D.) was the competent Alvar poet, born into a princely, *velala* family. He was prolific of the twelve Alvars and wrote one thousand two hundred and ninety six poems out the four thousand poems that make the Alvar literature. After his death, Nammalvar's images were installed in temples of South India, and revered as the very feet of God. Nathamuni, a priest at the Srirangam temple (the tenth-century), was the first to compile in an ordered manner his compilation, "The Four Thousand Divine Compositions" (Naalayira Divya Prabandham). The singers of the Tamil hymns led the temple processions and walked before the image of God.

The Alvar's hymns were the forerunners of later *Vaishnava* poetic tradition which influenced the *Warkari* movement of the twelfth-century Maharashtra, and the *Padam* tradition of the fifteenth-century Andhra Pradesh. Tallapaka Annamacharya (1424 A.D. to 1503 A.D.), Kshetrayya (1595 A.D. to 1680 A.D.), and Sarangapani (early eighteenth-century) were the major poets of the *Padam* tradition.

Purandaradasa (1480 A.D. to 1564 A.D.) of fifteenth and sixteenth centuries Karnataka and Tyagaraja (1767 A.D. to 1847 A.D.), a Telugu speaking poet of the eighteenth and the nineteenth centuries, contributed significantly to both the terrains of poetry and music. The *Bhakti* movement provided new energy not only to the tradition of Indian poetry but also to Indian music.

Warkari Movement

In the twelfth and the thirteenth centuries, Sri Chakradhar and his disciples, such as Nagdevacharya, Mhaibhat, Mahadaisa, Changdev, and others contributed to social and religious reforms, focusing on social equality, and said that all have rights for religion, salvation, and *bhakti*. *Mahanubhav* cult, which resisted *vedic* tradition, was crucial in socio-religious movement in Maharashtra. In its cultural history, Sri Chakradhar's philosophy of equality and acceptance of vernacular language, Marathi, had played reformative role in socio-religious and cultural matrix.

In the thirteenth-century, the *Bhakti* movement in Maharashtra, under the aegis of Jnanadev, took the form of the *Vithoba* cult (*Vithoba* is regarded as a form of Vishnu). *Vithoba*, the black-coloured deity of Pandharpur, was worshipped by the pilgrims of the *Warcari* cult, with whom it was regular practice to journey to Pandharpur and back at least twice every year. A *warkari* is one who made a *wari,* i.e., a round trip pilgrimage.

In the twelfth and the thirteenth centuries in Maharashtra, on social scenario, the dominance was of religious power, *varnashrama*, and traditional rituals. On the basis of religious scripts, important decisions were taken on religion and social counts. The seats of religion power were the pilgrim places at Paithan, Nashik, Wai, and Pandharpur. This period was of decline in religious domain. *Vedic* tradition was ineffectual. In religious institutions, strength was not left to motive society as per changing situation. Religious sector was synchronised to penance, *yagnya* sacrifice, and chanting. As more importance was being given to unreal and orthodox practices, human values were dwindling. Common man, deprived of general knowledge, became victim of social inequality. Traditional philosophy, rituals, and signs exploited common and downtrodden people of the society. Since, precise meaning of the religion was not known, many evil tendencies and orthodox practices were surging up. Human minds were contaminated by inequality in *Varna.* Roots of discrimination based on higher and lower castes were deep in the society. Turning away from life, men of flesh and blood, people were engrossed in idol worship. No road to self confidence was visible.

During Jnaneshwar period, *Jain*, *Lingayat,* and *Mahanubhav*, the three sects were hammering on Vedic religion. During this period, more importance was attributed to deities, penance, and sacred hymns, and the focus was on exterior of religion forgetting internal, stressing on non-violence and equality. *Jain, Lingayat, and Mahanubhav* were opposing *chaturvarna.*

In Maharashtra, the rule was of Ramdeorao in Yadava period and he was a militant person. He was all time engaged in the stories of Haridasa, the penance of Hemandri, and not paying attention to state and soldiers. It had negative repercussions in the visible form of the attack by Alauddin in 1216. The kings in Karnataka and Konkan surrendered to Alauddin. State, village, caste, and religious institutions were extracting more parts of the agricultural produce from the farmers. King was treated as a part of Vishnu. Due to orthodoxy of religion, farmers were starving. Political power was soverign and uncontrolled, and its contact with farmers was only with reference to taxes.

Religious innocence of people and intellectual slavery were the supports to *brahminism*. *Joshi* was an element of village institution. Kulkarni, Deshpande, Pandit, and Purohit were dependent on political power. They were shareholders in the income of government institutions and attempted to firm the grip on masses. Practices as directed by ancient scripts and birth based caste system had permitted no scope to personality development. To lower class people, psychic slavery was more imposed than economic slavery.

Saints were neglected sometime due to caste system and sometime due to the distorted conception of social dignity. The right to *Vedant* and devotion to God and their practices were not monopoly, and this roar was reverberated everywhere. In Canto 9 of *Srimad Bhagavadgita*, Krishna told the devotee confined to any caste to devote to achieve salvation and then to merge.

समोऽहं सर्वभूतेषु न मे द्धेष्योऽस्ति न प्रियः।
ये भजन्ति नु मां भक्त्या मयि तेतेवु चाष्यहम्।।29।।

अपि चेत्सुदुशचारो भजते मामनन्यभाक्।
साधुरेव स मन्तव्यः सम्यग्व्यवसितो हि सः।।30।।

क्षिप्रं भवति धर्मात्मा श श्वतच्छन्तिं निगच्छाति।
कोन्तेय प्रतिजानीहि न मे भक्तः प्रणश्यति।।31।।

मां हि पार्थ व्यपश्रित्य येऽपि स्युः पापयोनयः।
स्त्रियो वैश्यातथा शूद्रस्तेऽपि यान्ति परा गतिम्।।32।।[12]

I am equally present in all beings; there is none hateful or dear to Me. They, however, who devoutly worship Me abide in Me; and I too stand revealed in them. (29)

Even if the vilest sinner worships Me with exclusive devotion, he should be accounted a saint; for he has rightly resolved. (30)

> Speedily he becomes virtuous and attains abiding peace. Know it for certain Arjuna, that My devotee never suffers degradation. (31)
>
> Arjuna, women, *Vaisyas, Shudras* as well as those of impious birth, whoever they may be taking refuge in Me, they too attain the supreme goal. (32)

The base of Jnaneshwar's social magnanimity is this philosophical approach and the base of devotional road in Maharashtra is firmly relied on this sublime thought.

Because of material deterioration and psychic slavery common people were with inertia and inactive. The Saint movement emerged to free masses from that pathetic situation. The canvas of this movement to the most extent was religious and cultural. It was touched by the core questions of social life. Keeping intact the tempo of Vedic tradition, saints (Jnaneshwar and Eknath) moulded tendencies and, thus, saint literature became hybridised.

Maharashtra is the link between north and south India. Culturally, in Marathi saint poetry, north and south Indian cultures of poetry are merged. Pilgrimage of Jnaneshwar and Namdev to north is a crucial sign of communication between Hindi and Marathi saint poetries. Namdev wrote in Marathi and Hindi, and his poems are included in *Granth Sahib*. Eknath lived in Varanasi for a long period to study and was exposed to Hindi saint poetry. Tukaram referred to Kabir, Ravidas, and Meerabai in his poetry. In *Gramgeeta*, Tukadoji referred to Guru Govind Singh (Punjab), Sri Chakradhar Swami (Gujrat/Maharashtra), Guru Nanak Dev (Punjab), Kabir (Varanasi), Swami Dayananda Saraswati (Gujrat), Ramakrishna Paramahansa (Calcutta), Meerabai (Rajasthan), Chaitanya Mahaprabhu (Bengal), Raman Maharshi (Tamil Nadu), Tulsidas, Namdev, Surdas, (north), and Aurobindo (Pondicherry) from out of Maharashtra.

Marathi saint poetry's relation with Hindi saint poetry is as important as its link with Kannada poetry. The deity of Marathi saint, *Kanada Vitthal* had come from Karnataka to Maharashtra and brought rich tradition of Kannada culture. Kannad saint poet, Purandaradas was devotee of *Vitthal.*

Gulburga in Karnataka near the boarder of Maharashtra was the working place of Basaveshwara for socio-religious and political reformation.

Etymologically, the name of the city, Pandharpur goes back to Pandurang, a name of Shiva, the deity originally worshipped in that place. The overlapping of Pandharpur–*Pandurang*–*Vithoba* is the fusion of *Vaishanava* and *Shaiva bhakti* cults whose motive was to point at the same one God or divine truth, which exists beyond all superficial compartments. From the thirteenth-century onwards, Pandharpur emerged as the pilgrim centre of the *warkari bhakti* movement which had the galaxy of saints, such as Namdev (1270 A.D. to 1350 A.D.), the tailor; Jnanadev (1275 A.D. to 1296 A.D.), the outcaste *brahmin*; Eknath (1533 A.D. to 1599 A.D.), the householder, *brahmin*; and Tukaram (1608 A.D. to 1659 A.D.), the *shudra* saint poet.

Jnaneshwar, basically initiated from *nath* cult, was the torch-bearer of *warkari* cult and composed philosophical treatise *Amritanubhava*, *abhanga* (religious poems), and an extensive poetic commentary on the *Bhagavadgita* titled, *Jnanesvari*. His writing concerns with a genuine inner evolution in the consciousness of being. Fred Dallmayr in his book, *Jnandev and the* Warkari Movement, alleges:

> Appreciation and admiration are bound to deepen by a closer reading of these texts...despite a diversity of genres, Jnandev's writings are held together or animated by a common concern or theme. This theme.....is the centrality of love or *bhakti,* where *bhakti* does not mean an emotive sentimentalism but rather a genuine turning—about of the whole being (including mind, heart, and senses)...[13]

Namdev, who sought advise from his *guru*, Visoba Khechar, was the pillar of the *warkari* movement, and later continued to bring to its fold a number of mystic poets from all across Maharashtra. The poets were a potter, a gardner, a barber, a banker, a beggar, and a *mahar*. The *Warkari* movement was resurged with Tukaram and Eknath in the seventeenth-century. Jnandev has friendship with Namdev who was five-years older to him. At Pandharpur, he became a devotee of *Vithoba*. In Marathi poetry, his orientation was towards *Saguna bhakti*, and Jnaneshwar honoured him with Vitthal as 'treasure of love'. Coordinating knowledge and *nam*, he cited the principle of self-sacrifice. He was the founder of *kirtan cult* in *warkari* mode and vowed to "dance in the dye of kirtan; light the lamp of knowledge."

Soon after, the two saints went together on a prolonged pilgrimage, visiting most of the holy places in northern India including Banaras and Delhi. After return, Jnandev entered in *samadhi* at Alandi. Experiencing desolation, Namdev left for the north again and visited holy places in Gujrat and Rajasthan, and finally reached Punjab where he settled at a village called Ghuman in Gurudaspur district. He spent about twenty years of his life, spreading the cult of devotion and, thus, preparing the people of north India to face the wave of Islam which was fast engulfing Hinduism. At the end of the thirteenth-century, he initiated the *Bhakti* movement in the north and eventually inspired poets like Kabir and Nanak. The following lines have been taken from the Guru *Granth Sahib*:

> As the deer followeth the huntsman's bells,
> And giveth up its own life rather than cease its attention,
> In the same way I gaze on God...
> As the kingfisher gazeth on the fish,
> As the goldsmith meditateth stealing gold while
> Fashioning it,
> As the lustful man gazeth on the wife of another
> As the gamber meditateth cheating while playing cowries,
> So *Nama* ever meditateth on God's feet....
> Wherever I gaze there is God.[14]

Namdev was the first major poet of *nirguna bhakti* which manifests in his Hindi poetry. The poets of *nirguna bhakti* perceives God as formless, while the school of *saguna bhakti* attributes to God a physical form and believes in the theory of *avatarwad,* i.e., reincarnation. *Warkari* cult emphasises upon castelessness, non-hierarchy, and caring human fellowship. Under Namdev's ambience, the movement gathered in its fold the galaxy of saints and poets from the cross-section of Maharashtra, and included Parisa Bhagat, a *vaishanav brahmin;* Changdev, the *yogi* turned saint; Gora, the potter; Savata, the gardner; Sena, the barber; Jagamitra Naga, the banker turned begger; Janabai, the serving maid; and Chokhamela, the untouchable. Chokhoba asks to *Vitthala*:

> Down my caste, God, how can avail your service? ||
>
> Away, Away they say, in which way I meet you? ||[15]
>
> (Chokhoba, Tr. Myself)

Karmamela, the son of Chokhoba asks:

> Our caste made down, don't you understand Lord Sripati?
>
> Life spent eating waste food, don't you experience shame?
>
> (Karmamela, Tr. Myself)

Chokhoba tells about economical discrimination and poverty to Pandurang:

> Seat for one, raiment for one, some walk naked ||2||
>
> Stale food for one, sweet for others, no food to same ||3||
>
> Wealth for one, honour of state, other beg village to village ||4||
>
> Justice this in you home, Chokha says, Hari, work mine ||5||
>
> (Chokhoba, Tr. Myself)

Sawata Mali says, "Sawata says low caste, grace you *Sripati*". During Chokhoba's time, in society, one class was rich and luxurious, and other was starved, wearing torn clothes. The discrimination was also made on the ground of caste. The cleavage was deep between rich and poor. Though, others were robbers, corrupted were right, and in his life, baseness was due to caste. He says that in their company he experiences pain. Chokhoba hammers on social system and he is the saint who outright speaks in language with revolutionary spirit; but he, in the end, succumbs to destiny and prestorage of work in the past. Saint Sena writes, "I am in low caste, retain my respect".

Mahanubhav and *Warkari* cults have written in Marathi for masses. *Mahanubhav* cult opposed *Vedas* and religious scripts as *chaturvarna* proposed social system and caste system. When *Mahanubhav* cult was propagating, Hemadpant, the Prime Minister of Ramdeva Yadava, had written *Chaturvary Chintamni* in which there were two thousand penance practices. To eradicate inequality only utterance of equality was not sufficient but new self reliant social system was the call of time.

Basaveshwar and Chakradhar were all religious reformers and their stance was also for social revolution. Out of reform and revolution, two tendencies, reforms and change, were prevalent before pre-British period. *Jain* and *Mahanubhav*, two cults, are renunciation oriented. Tendency not to believe in caste discrimination, teaching to renounce family, and lesson for body punishment have an impact to some extent on the devotees of Vitthal, Kabir cult, and the disciples of Dadu.

Muslim Invasion

The full force of the *bhakti* upsurge was to decline after the departure of Namdev in 1350 AD. Muslim rule began to dominate public life. A century later, the Deccan governments had began to give precedence to the Maratha people and Marathi language over the Afgani residents and the ruthless Muslim officials. Despite the subjugation and harassment, the Maratha people led vigorous and enlightened lives. Shivaji (1630 A.D. to 1680 A.D.) appeared on the scene in the seventeenth-century and fought to free from the clutches of the mulsim rule; and remained in contact with Tukaram (1608 A.D. to 1659 A.D.) and Ramdas (1608 A.D. to 1681 A.D.). The saint literature had the strength to light up the spirit of masses and create the flare of spiritual faith and militant fervour. Tukaram was described by his contemporary Bahinabai as "the spire or crown of the temple at the *warkari* tradition of *Bhakti*".

An important social contribution of *warkari* cult adopted by Tukaram and Indian *bhakti* movement is that it abolished the class of oppressors who were performing the role of mediator between God and common man. Tukaram, the poet with spiritual mould, urging for perpetual cosmic spirit, attained salvation. Often animal's comprehension is in two dimensions but man evolving comprehended the world in three dimensions. Onward the fourth dimension develops in evolution, means, comprehension of reality above creation and destruction; and beyond present, past, future, perpetual, and eternal. Tukaram proved through his experiences that he had developed the consciousness of the fourth dimension.

Dilip Chitre views *Bhakti* poetry in the light of nativism in his introduction of *Says Tuka*:

> This poetry was sung and performed by audiences that joined poet-singers in a chorus. Musical-literary discourses or *keertans* that are a blend of oratory, theatre, solo, and chorus singing and music, were the new art form spawned by this movement. *Bhajan* was the new form of singing poetry together and emphasising its key elements by turning choosen lines into a refrain. These comprise a new kind of democratic literary transcation in which even illiterates were drawn to the care of literary text in the collective realisation of some poet's work. This open ended and down-to-earth nativism found its fullest expression in Tukaram; three centuries after Jnandev and Namdev had broken new ground by founding democratic Marathi poetry itself.[16]

This statement is valid for the entire *Bhakti* movement in India which surged upwards from the southern peninsula and spread to the west, east, and the north of the country. V. Raghavan writes in his essay on the saints of Medieval Hinduism:

> From the Tamil country this movement of saint-singers of philosophical and religious songs in regional languages spread to the Kannada-speaking area, whence the spark was ignited in Maharashtra; then the Hindi-speaking areas took it up and the whole of North India was a flame with this resurgent and fervent faith. This popular presentation of the teaching of the *Upanishads*, the philosophical schools and the Puranic love, coincided with the linguistic phenomenon of the growth of the neo-Indo Aryan Languages of the

> North and the flowering forth of the literatures of the Dravidian family of the languages in the south.[14]

A prominent feature of the 14th century, the period by which the *Bhakti* movement had covered the entire country, is the presence of Islam and Islamic culture. Its forced conversions and numerous raids enacted under the rule of the Mongol, Afghan, and Turkish invaders culminated into the Mughals (beginning with Babur in 1506 A.D.) establishing a stable Mughal empire by the earlier half of the sixteenth-century.

The pillaging of Buddhist monasteries and Hindu places of worship was the direct expression of Muslim antagonism towards any religion other than Islam. The inception of the *Bhakti* movement and the coming of Islam (and the *sufis*) to India were curiously simultaneous in the north and north-west of India. The *Bhakti* movement was stimulated by their influences. The *sufis* (who were in fact rebels against orthodox Islam) and the Hindu saints (who were placed against the *brahmin* orthodoxy) were become the meeting points for Islam and Hinduism.

In enlarging the orbit of Indian poetry, *sufi* poetry plays significant role. In medieval age, *sufi* poetry had infused the current of Persian poetry in Indian poetry. In the eleventh-century, originated in Persia, the poets like Attar, Hafij, Jami, and Omar Khayyam emerged. In the twelfth-century, *sufi* saints started coming to India and this cult expanded from Kashmir to Marathwada and Punjab to Bengal. To propagate *sufi* cult, *sufi* saints applied the means of poetry and wandered village to village, communicating sufi poetry to masses. *Sufi* poetry is philosophical as well as mystical. *Sufi* cult being influenced by Buddhism and Christianity was progressive.

In sufi poetry, some images of romantic poetry are seen on symbolic level. God-lover, devotee, and beloved are popular metaphors in *sufi* poetry. Consequently, sometime God is husband and devotee is wife. This style of *sufi* poetry had influenced medieval Indian saint poetry and European poetry. 'Trabudar', the cult, emerged in South France in twelfth-century, had influence on *sufi* poetry. Those 'Trabudar' poets were singers and they sang their poems on tune of the stringed instruments like fiddle. In such poetries, philosophical and romantic poetries are mixed together. The 'Trabudar' poetry was motivating force for imaginist poets like Ezra Pound. Indirectly *sufi* poetry, because of ramification, linked Indian and European poetries. In the history of Indian poetry, its place is unique as cultural and literary endeavour for Hindu-Muslim unity due to progressive strategy had been accepted by *sufi* poetry.

Because of native influence of ancient Indian poetry and foreign influence of *sufi* poetry, medieval Indian poetry had become more progressive, inclusive, and enriched. Medieval Indian poetry had provided a wide geographical canvas enlarging its empire from Punjab to Kerala and Rajasthan to Bengal. Medieval Indian poetry had infused diverse colours of languages and enriched regional culture. Though it was written in different regions and in various languages, it has internal relation. The base of ancient Indian philosophical poetry and relentless search for spiritual and mystical experience are the nuances of internal relation. It reveals that medieval saint poetry has unity in diversity, in spite of linguistic variations and regional and cultural diversities.

History had stood witness to the fact that an invading culture always appeals to the lowest section of the society. The *sufis*, who were rebel saint poets within the Islamic culture, were placed vis-à-vis the Islamic orthodoxy, its *Ulemas* and *Mullahs*. The saints and the *sufis* were representing marginalized classes, subaltern, and the periphery, while the *brahmin* orthodoxy and the Islamic fanatic were the priests—heads of the central ruling class.

Among the prominent *sufi* poets were Chishti, Qadiri, Suhrawardi, and Naqshbandi. Chishti Silsilah proved to be the most brilliant in terms of (a) the great *sufi* poets it produced, (b) the large areas it spread into, and (c) the large followers it carried. Chishti Silsilah is a harbinger of Hindu-Muslim unity like that of Kabir and Nanak.

Origin of *Sufism*

Sufism was born in the nineth-century Arabia and during its travel through Iran and India, it underwent perceptional shifts.

It stressed upon the emotional content of devotion, as against the dry-as-dust self-denial of the Arabs.

> The Arabs laid stress on asceticism and disciplining of the body, while the later *sufis* in Iran and India, under the influence of Greek philosophy, Platonic ideology, Christian faith, Vedantist thinking, Buddhist lore, etc. believed in leading an emotionally rich life. They drank and danced and advocated that physical love could sublimate itself into spiritual love. They had faith in God; they loved the Prophet but they maintained that the Murshid or Guru could also lead to realisation of the Divine Reality.[17]

Between the ends of the twelfth and the fourteenth centuries, three great orders had migrated from Iraq and Persia into northern India. They were the Chishti, the Suhrawardiyah, and the Firdausi. The *sufis* had followed the Muslim conquerors to India with a view to propagate in India. They established several centres at Lahore, Pakpattan, Kasur, Multan, and Uch in Punjab. Their approach to God was that of a beloved-wife who pines for a reunion with her lover-husband, suffers, repents, undergoes ascetism, and finally gains enlightenment and merges with God.

> *Sufi* is a lover of God, and as such he stands in a different relation to God from others who are merely 'abd' or slaves. The Indian *sufis* laid stress on repeating the name (*Japu*), concentration (*dhyan*), and meditation (*habs-i-dhyan*)...like the Iranian *Sufis* who sang the praises of Yusuf Zulaikha, Laila Majnun, and Shirin Farhad, the *Sufis* in the (17th, 18th century) Punjab idealised the romances of Heer Ranjah, Sohni Mahiwal, and Sassi Punnun.[18]

Khwaja Moinuddin Chishti of Ajmer, Baba Sheikh Farid of Ajodhan, and Hazrat Nizamuddin Auliya of Delhi were conspicuous *sufi* saints. Chishti established his Khangah at Ajmer during the period of the Gorian conquest of India in the closing years of the twelfth-century. Baba Sheikh Farid (1173 A.D. to 1265 A.D.), who came after him, was the most remarkable of the next generation of popular *sufis* of Chishti Silsilah and the disciple of Muhammad Bakhtiyar Kaki.

Many of Hindu saint poets and Muslim *sufis* strived to rise above the Hindu-Muslim differences. The two saint poets who had been mainly responsible for the spread of *bhakti* in the northern belt, were a tailor, Namdev from Pandharpur, and Ramananda, the *Vaishanava* of Banaras. They made masses conscious to shed the orthodoxy of rituals and superstitions.

Ramananda, Tulsidas, Kabir, Raidas, Nanak, and Dadu Dayal

Medieval saint poetry in North India reveals medieval saint culture. Ramananda's verses are included in the *Granth Sahib* and due to Ramananda, Guru Nanak is linked with this tradition of saint poetry. Ramananda writes, "कत जाइए रे, घर लाग्या रंगु." The meaning of this verse is that Ramananda's house is filled with myriad colours which are of Lord and there is no reason to search him out. Brahma is inside and this is self-principle. This realisation is an internal fabric which unites medieval Indian poetry.

Ramananda, originally educated under the more conservative school of *Vaishnava brahminism*, was the one who relaxed the rigidities of the system, introduced egalitarian reforms, and readily accepted disciples from lower castes and communities; thus, dismissing the sanctity of casteism. He occupies a unique place in the history of religion in medieval India. Among his twelve disciples were Asananda, Surasurananda, Sukhananda, Paramananda, Mahananda, Pipa (Rajput Ruling Chief), Kabir (a weaver), Bhavananda, Sena (a barber), Dhanna (a jat peasant), Ananda, and Ravidas (a cobbler). Ramananda borrowed ideas from the various religious schools that flourished before him and vitalised them with the devotion of his heart. He cleansed and refurnished the school of *Vaishnava bhakti* with his enlightened and humanistic approach. It was this path which Kabir and others followed later and decorated with their lives, their faiths, and their rich poetries. The most accepted dates of Kabir are 1440 A.D. to 1518 A.D. Kabir was contemporary of Sikandar Lodi who ruled from 1489 A.D. to 1517 A.D. Nanak met Kabir in 1496 A.D.

It is believed that Ramananda did for north India exactly what Nayanmars did for the south India. He shed the use of

Sanskrit in favour of the vernacular, which made the Hindu God accessible to the common man by bringing Him out of the *brahmin* dominated temple and installing Him in the heart of all humanity. He initiated the regular practice of *satsang* (i.e., community singing—a parallel example in Christianity would be the choir practice), *naam japna* (i.e., meditation), and common kitchen where all cook and sat for meals together.

> To the Lord's temple, I hurried for worship,
> But that temple, the Guru revealed,
> Was within[19]
>
> (Ramananda, *Adi Granth*, 112)

> Light a lamp inside you
> That does not need any oil.
>
> (*Adi Granth*, 204-205)

After Ramananda, the saints such as Namdev, Ravidas, Kabir, Dadu Dayal, Nanak, and the Sikh *gurus* opened a new chapter in *nirguna bhakti*.

Tulsidas was a philosopher and a narrative poet who constructed the base for medieval Hindi saint poetry. *Tulsi Ramayana* is a narrative poetry and its philosophical content is also significant. Tulsidas has oriented ancient Sanskrit epic *Ramayana* towards masses by writing it in Hindi in the context of medieval masses. He awakened society by pointing at dwindling moral values which appealed more to masses. To him Lord is inside and outside. He illustrates his verdict with the metaphor—as red colour is hidden in but it is not visible with scrubbing leaves. This red colour is of devotion. He doesn't differentiate 'in' and 'out' with reference to Lord as with attributes and without attributes. He writes, "सगुनहि अगुनाहि नहि कुछ भेदा." He operates the metaphor of water. Water is one though it manifests in the forms of vapour, ice, and cloud. He calls himself *chatak*. He reiterated the significance of relentless chanting of the name, Rama. Stressing the importance of the chanting of the name he alleges that 'name' is like a lamp on a tongue. It illuminates internal and outer.

Tracing the saga of Arab and Turk raids upon the Indian subcontinent, the first forays of Muslim soldiers into India were in the year 712 A.D. in the province of Sindh. The raids and loot campaigns of Muhammad of Ghazni upon the Indian subcontinent ended in 1030 A.D. With the death of Ghazni, his raids upon the north and north-west of India had paved the way for further attacks from aspiring Turks, Afghan, and Mongolian nobles, desirous of expanding their boundaries, or of setting up new empires.

The saga of Islamic advent and settlement in the Indian subcontinent began in the end of the twelfth-century. By 1192 A.D., Indus Valley and the rich regions of Punjab, Lahore, and Delhi were conquered. 1206 A.D. marked the beginning of the Delhi Sultanate or the rule of the Turkish and Afghan Sultans. The Slave Dynasty founded by Qutb-ub-Din Aibak ended in 1265 A.D. with the assassination of Queen Raziya Sultan (Aibak's brilliant niece).

Around 1290 A.D. another group of Turks, the Khaljis, came to power. By this time, the levying of the Jizya (the tax on non-Muslim) had become a reality and to escape from it many Hindus began converting to Islam. By 1320 A.D., the Khalji dynasty gave way to the Tughlaq who ruled ruthlessly for about a span of eighty years. This was the time when the influx of *sufis* was on the accent and saints like Namdev who spent twenty-years in Punjab and Ramananda of Benaras were working with a missionary zeal to enlighten masses.

On the north-west Indian border, the Mongols had been threatening to invade from time to time. They had been successfully kept at bay by the Tughlaq dynasty. In 1398 A.D., the Mongols under the leadership of Timur at last broke through north India. After sacking Delhi, Timur left for Central Asia and in his absence, his nominee seized the opportunity to capture Delhi and become the founding Sultan of the Sayyid Dynasty. The Sayyids ruled over north and central India until the earlier half of the fifteenth-century. It was the period that saw saint and *Sufi* movements in India. Such was the political backdrop of the time in which our revolutionary and reformist poets Kabir and Nanak lived. This was the time when both Islam and Brahminism in north India were challenged and ridiculed for their sentiments of fanaticism and rituals.

The period saw mass conversions of lower caste Hindus into casteless Muslims. The conversts were a section of the society who were Hindu in their bearing but Muslim in their identity, following the newly embraced festivals, dress code, and the new God, Allah, along with their age-old plethora of Hindu deities, customs, and food habits. The saints spoke of a religion of love and of God who resides in the temple of the heart.

Kabir (1440 A.D. to 1518 A.D.) was nourished in Hindu-Muslim culture and in his poetry we find the convergence of ancient Indian philosophical poetry in Hindu tradition and *sufi* poetry in Islamic tradition. *Tulsi Ramayana* is a narrative poetry and Kabir's poetry is at the core philosophical poetry. Kabir deems Lord as 'निरंजन', "देव निरंजन और न दुजा। परम पुरिख तहँ देव अनंता।" In *Upanishada*, Lord is described as "निरंजन: परमं साम्यमुपैति:।" It unfolds how Kabir's poetry is influenced by ancient Indian philosophical poetry. 'निरंजन' means pure Lord or *Brahma* without the layer of darkness. Lord is not visible because of darkness/illusion. 'अंजन आये अंजन जाये' but the form of 'निरंजन' remains pure. Kabir writes, "कहै कबीर भरम में मन भागा। एक निरंजन सो मन लागा।" Because of निरंजन darkness/illusion vanishes. Immersed in this illusion Mullaha calls for Allaha in high-pitched voice treating oneself deaf and inserting fingers in ears. Kabir satirises the illusion of Hindu's meaningless chanting. He honours the image of *Guru* as the image of Lord. He compares *Guru* with Swan who separates milk and water. *Guru* differentiates material life and life–beyond. He calls *Guru* 'Sikalgar', 'कुम्भकारा' divine truth. As a potter outerly and innerly shapes pots, *Guru* moulds disciple. He realises Lord's colour, rhythm, luminance, and *rasa* is in his poetry. "लाली मेरे लाल की जित देखौं तित लाल। लाली देखन मैं गई मैं भी हो गई लाल। is experience of colour. "रोम रोम सुर उठत है" is mystical experience of rhythm in body. "रोम रोम दीपक भया" is experience of luminance and "चुवत अभी रस भरत ताल जब शब्द उठै असमानी हो" is the collective experience of *rasa* of ambrosia and timeless rhythm in the sky. To Kabir this *rasa* sometime is *'Harirasa'* and sometime *'Ramrasa'*. The divine *rasa* in Kabir's poetry is wine. This intoxication of wine is divine realisation. Kabir compares intoxicated devotee with an elephant, and imported divine intoxication from *sufi* poetry. Language of love in Kabir's poetry is akin to the language in *sufi* poetry. In Kabir's poetry, there are love, waiting, and separation. His words, "मेरा मुझमें कुछ नहीं" are the flight of his realisation of cosmic spirit.

Saints emphasised upon religion of love and of God who resides in the temple of heart, and were mass oriented. Such an arrangement was very convenient and desirable during the times when political instability, forced conversion, and violence of all sorts were rampant. The emotional appeal, spiritual richness of the experience, the simplification of the divine, and the rhythm and joy of community-singing (*bhajan-kirtan*) provide a therapeutic release. As William Dwyer observers in *Bhakti in Kabir*:

> National consciousness, love of country, and pride of freedom were smothered under the weight of a mass of rituals and social connections, a petty-minded vanity and narrow selfishness as the Muslim power was consolidated the clash between expanding Islam with its official patronage and Hinduism, was to aggravate social and religious unrest in northern India.[20]

Dwyer holds such transitional circumstances responsible for the anti-Islamic stance that Kabir took despite being raised in Julaha (weaver) community which was that section of Hindus who had converted to Islam, but the process of conversion was incomplete. Nanak who was born a Hindu, opposed Hindu rituals and resisted initiation during the thread ceremony. A much higher sense of divine or a heightened insight into the secular nature of the divine was the guiding factor as well.

Some prominent symbols in the *yogi* text of signification are—(a) the reversal of man, (b) the inverted thousand petaled lotus from which the nectar of immortality drips, (c) the metaphor of the sky, and lastly (d) the reference to the 'three strand snare', meaning the three *gunas* (i.e., aspects of qualities) of *sattva* (goodness, calmness, and harmonious), *rajas* (passion, activity, and movement), and *tamas* (ignorance, inertia, and laziness), representing subtlety, action, and grossness, respectively. The term that Nanak uses most frequently for the divine is 'Hari', while for Kabir it is generally 'Ram'. His treatment of the yogic states of *pranayama* and *samadhi*, which is withdrawal from the physical reality, is also of the same nature. The reference to the "thunderbolt door" is a reference to the *kundalini* for awakening of the serpentine energy coiled at the bare of the spine.

Coming to the last metaphor, the symbol of the three *gunas* has its home in the *Samkhya* metaphysics which along with the Buddhist philosophy makes the foundation of the *nath* cult. According to the *Samkhya Upanishad,* reality has two aspects—the *purush* (male principle signifying the spiritual) and *prakriti* (the female principle signifying maternal reality, *maya*)

Reality

Purush:	*Prakriti:*
Represents Divinity.	Represents material reality which is made up of *sattva, rajas,* and *tamas.*

Kabir's name is synonymous with Hindu-Muslim unity. His vision of unity was rooted in the genuine religious belief of *bhakta*. The same ground was shared by his contemporary young Nanak. He went even further than Kabir in challenging the barriers of religious difference, declaring, "There is no Hindu or Muslim. So, whose path shall I follow? I shall follow God's path". The quest of Nanak led later to the formation of a third religion, *Sikh*. The *gunas* are the three qualities (essences) which permeate all matter in varying degree, *sattva* (means light and goodness), *rajas* (means action and passion), and *tamas* (signifies dullness, darkness, and sluggishness). In theological parlance, *gunas* occur most frequently in compounds (*Saguna* and *Nirguna*), and there is the perennial debate as to whether to perceive the supreme being as *Saguna* (i.e., having *gunas*—attributes), or as *Nirguna* (i.e., having no *gunas* or attributes of material reality).

The saint tradition, to which Kabir, Nanak, and Tukadoji belonged, distinguishes itself from the *Bhakti* movement at large by its orthodox denial of rituals and idol worship, its insistence on the formlessness of God, and its *Nirguna Bhakti* (which essentially perceives God as a formless and universal being/ spirit/essence).

> O *Nirgun,*
> To whom can I tell your tale?
> Who can be so wise?
> Kabir says
> Only those who ignite
> See the flash.
>
> (*Adi Granth*, 75)

He excludes the three *gunas* from his concept of the Divine Being, and orients to the term *Nirguna* when referring to Him. His poetic works have polyphonic aspect where each signifier (symbolic construct) signifies not just one, but a set of concepts. Among the remaining threads of influences are *sufism* and the saint Ramananda.

Kabir rejected the concept of *avatar vada* (incarnation) and denied recognition to Ram as a human form. He abandoned both Hinduism and Islam in favour of the pure essential Ram—the light of divine love in the heart.

> I abandoned all
> the written advice
> given me by pundits and mullahs,
> took none of it with me.
> If love is in your heart
> you can behold the Lord.
> Those who found him did so
> by first finding themselves, O Kabir.
>
> (*Raga Bhairav*, *Adi Granth,* 231)

Kabir debunked both the *Mullah* and the *Pandit*.

> Qazi, what book are you lecturing on?
> Yak, yak, yak, day and night.
> You never had an original thought.
> Feeling you power, you circumcise,
> I can't go along with that, brother.

If your God favoured circumcision,
why didn't you come out cut?
If circumcision makes you a Muslim,
what do you call your women?
Since women are called man's other half,
you might as well be Hindus.
If putting on the thread makes you *brahmin,*
What does the wife put on?
Hindu, Muslim—where did you come from,
who started this road?

(*Bijak, Shabda,* 84)

Hari in the east, Allah in the west
so you like to dream.
Search in the heart, in the heart alone;
there live Ram and Karim!
Which is false, *Koran* or *Veda*?
False is the darkened view
It's one, one in everybody!
How did you make it two?
Every man and woman born,
they're all your forms, says Kabir.
I'm Ram-and-Allah's foolish baby,
He's my *guru* and *pir*.

(*Bijak, Shabda,* 97)

Drop falling in the ocean,
  everyone knows.
Ocean absorbed in the drop,
  a rare one knows.

The Indian classification of knowledge *(jnana)*, works *(karma)*, and devotion (*bhakti*) is simple but basic. He pokes questions at the reader either to provoke us into thinking, or to chide us, taunt us, and laugh at us, and thereby arouse us out of the spiritual lethargy that lesser mortals tend to slip into.

It is uncanny ability of the mystic poet to utter sublime truths, speckled with flashes of insight and create great transcendental poetry that makes for a very sound basis. Indian *dhvani* theorists like Anandvardhana insist that a mystic poet's language is different than ordinary language, and connotes deep sound. It conveys more than what it says. Polyvalence is the way in which meaning works in these poems.

Kabir's Rama (as a reading of *dohas* reveals) is not Rama of Ayodhya in *Ramayana*. He debunks rituals and blind devotion of established opinion. He made no distinction between Hinduism and Islam. He was fond of oral teachings in the form of small poems, which were later collected in the *Bijak* in the sixteenth-century. Many of his poems are included in the *Adi Granth* of the Sikhs. Kabir was the poet and social reformist, and his poetry, in the tradition of Indian poetry, is predominantly characterised as being mystical, incantatory, and figurative.

Another advocate of Hindu-Muslim unity was Raidas, a cobbler. He was a poet and a singer, and hymns he sang had such a ring of truth that eventually the *brahmins* who came to hear him became his disciples. He views that lord is in the cells of his body as the drops of water are infused with fragrance of sandal, and he is filled with the fragrance. Lord is Lamp and Raidas is wick; Lord is pearl and he is thread. He writes "आरती कहाँ लो जावै" because 'He' pervades everywhere and in every direction.

As huge waves raised by the winds
In the great ocean
Are only water in water in water
What shall I say, O Lord,
About this delusion?
What we deem a thing to be,
In reality is not

(Raidas)

Raidas exemplifies the prevalance of universal spirit, and behind delusion reality operates.

Nanak's poetry reflects a deep love for nature and the cosmos, which can be perceived as an extension of the divine order:

A plate—like sky,
The sun and moon
Its prayer lamps,
The milkway, of pearls
Incense is the sandal-tree
Its fragrance the breeze fans, constantly.
And the lush green wealth of forests
Makes flower-offering at God's feet.
How beautiful is your prayer service!
....
Your soul, the soul of all life-form,
Your flame flickers bright
In all that lives
The *Guru's* guidance is the match-stick
Thus lit alone.

Kabir and Nanak both lived in north India and belonged to the generation that saw end of the fifteenth-century and the beginning of the sixteenth-century. "The river and its waves are one, where is the difference?", Kabir sang.

Guru Nanak was in the line of *Nirguna Bhakti* poets. Incidentally, he also became the founding saint of another religious tradition, Sikhism. Of his longer poems, the 'Japji', the 'Dakhni Onkar', and 'Siddha Goshti' are supposed to have been written by the older Nanak. In Kabir and Nanak, there is a confluence of *sufi* and *bhakti* mysticism. 'Japji' unfolds the fundamentals of Sikh–metaphysics and delineates means for the individual human soul to seek reunion with the Universal soul. 'Siddha Goshti' spells out Nanak's philosophy and argues the futility of the practices of the *karmakanda*, particularly the *yogis* who lay much stress on *hathayoga*. It advocates the path of *sahajayoga*.

In the poetic creations of Kabir and Nanak, the metaphors of Vedic system, conception, and the impact of yogic science are frequent. In his evolved conception, God is formless and omnipotent. Nanak defines the divine as the one who is omnipotent, omniscient, omnipresent, and immanent. In his addresses, he often uses terms like Hari, Rama, Gopal, Parameshwar, Jagdis, Prabhu, Allah, Khuda, Padshah, Sahib, Ruba, and Swami to refer to God, besides using innovations like O formless one, or O Immanent. The role of the *guru* in the process of salvation has been underscored by both Kabir and Nanak, for whom the *guru* is synonymous with the immediate representation of the divine.

Dadu Dayal (1544 A.D. to 1603 A.D.), like Kabir and Nanak, was also driven by the quest for pure spirituality and worked all his life towards unity between Hindus and Muslim. Dadu, like Kabir, worked towards religious syncretism, laying great stress upon Hindu-Muslim unity. With the help of his followers he compiled a book on religious literature which included devotional writings of various sects and several devotional hymns including those by *sufis* like Kazi Kadam, Sheikh Farid, Kazi Mohammad, and Sheikh Bahawad. Manjula Bhattacharya says in *'Medieval Bhakti Movements in Gujarat'*:

> It was perhaps the first anthology in the religious literature of the world in which the views of a great variety of religious sects had been collected. The second of this kind is probably the *Granth Sahib* which was complied in 1604 A.D., one year after Dadu's death.[21]

Dadu Dayal and Nanak had rendered monumental service to enrich the matrix of *Bhakti* Movements in India, by compiling religious and spiritual verses.

Chaitanya Mahaprabhu, Meerabai, Narsinh Mehta, Dadu, Ravidas, Vallabhacharya, Ramdas, and Tyagaraja

Another great saint of medieval India, though differing in some respects from the views of Ramananda, Kabir, Raidas, and Nanak was Chaitanya (1486 A.D. to 1533 A.D.) from West Bengal. He was a teacher running his own Sanskrit school; had migrated from Sylhet (East Bengal) and settled at Nabadwip in West Bengal.

Wrapped in mystic and emotional experience, he would repeat the name of Krishna, sing, laugh, weep, rave, and often fall into a trance. Soon a band of disciples including the famous Advaita and Nityananda had gathered around him. A new type of emotional and devotional singing, called *kirtana*, often consisting of merely recitation of the names of Hari and Krishna, and sung in chorus to the accompaniment of loud instrumental music, became a regular feature of religious life. Huge processions of *kirtana* parties paraded the streets of Nabadwip, with Vishvambhar and his prominent followers, singing and dancing wildly in a mood of ecstasy.

Vishvambhar took to *sanyasa* in January 1510 A.D. and came to known as Sri Krishna Chaitanya. He worshipped both Radha and Krishna as inseparable. The Vrindavana School of Sri Chaitanya made a profound mark upon the *bhakti* cult of Gujarat. It greatly influenced Meerabai (1504 A.D. to 1558 A.D.) and Narsinh Mehta (1500 A.D. to 1580 A.D.), the two exponents of *bhakti* in the sixteenth-century.

Krishna consciousness is conspicuous in Meerabai's verse. Meera was born around 1480 A.D. and visited Vrindavan and later settled into worship at Dwarka where she also breathed her last in 1546 A.D. Meera had lived in the midst of a great devotional renaissance. Among her immediate forerunner were Saint Ravidas, Kabir, Vidyapati, and Chandidas; and her contemporaries were Narsinh Mehta, Surdas, Nanak, and the early poets of the schools of Vallabhacharya (of Gujrat) and Sri Chaitanya (of West Bengal). Meera expressed a more personal association with the Lord Krishna.

As Kabir, Meerabai's poetry is an important manifestation of medieval Hindi poetry. She revolted against male dominance and deemed the Lord Krishna as her husband reversing the conventional Hindu set up. Her *Guru* was Ravidas.

> Mine is Giridhar Gopala, none else |
>
> Who wears the peacock crown, my husband, he |

Acceptance of a lower caste person as a *Guru* was considered as a revolt in the medieval period. Ravidas or Rohidas was from Kabir cult and in his poetry there are symbols of lotus. He says that without *Guru* it is impossible to visualise Lord and self also. In the poem, "फागुन के दिन चार रे", Meerabai's mystical experience is suffused with colour and rhythm. In the line "रोम रोम रंग सार

से" she experiences the display of colours, and her raiment also turns colourful and in the sky too there is the play of colours. She describes rhythm as "बिन करताल परवावज वजै, अणहत कि झणकारे रे।" In the poem "जोगी मत जा मत जा", Meerabai's mystical experience to merge with Lord is an ultimate stage. This is the peak of her devotion for Krishna.

Narsinh Mehta (1414 A.D. to 1480 A.D.), whose tradition regarded as the forerunner of Meerabai, was from a high caste *nagar brahmin* family. The desire for contact with the divine (whom he perceived in the image of Krishna) gathered momentum with passing years, until at a very age, an experience at Dwarka, completely transformed Narsinh and made him a "poet of genius, philosopher with a vision, and saint endowed with the overflowing love for God". Mahatma Gandhi would often sing his *bhajan*, "वैष्णव जन तो तेने कहिये रे।"

> O Hari, in the whole universe,
> You are the one reality,
> Varied and one infinite,
> You are the wind
> You are the water
> You are the earth, mountain,
> And the tree blossomed upto the sky.[22]

A married man with three children, the graph of Narsinh's domestic life (and domestic woes) echoes Tukaram's personal life too. Unlike Tukaram, Narsinh Mehta was born in a high caste and used to visit *pariahs*, for whom he had coined the term '*harijan*', meaning God's own people, which was extensively used and popularised by Mahatma Gandhi. He would often sing *bhajans* along with them. In this context, Meerabai and Sri Chaitanya were in the company of Narsinh Mehta. As Uma Deshpande exhorts:

> His direct perception of the supercosmic divine, the total mingling of his personality into the divine form of the Lord Krishna, and the experience of the divine grace in his life got him converged from a devotee to a philosopher, and from a philosopher to a mystic. (112)

Philosophical and mystical veins run in Narsinh Mehta's verse. Besides these *vaishnava* poets, there existed Pipa who lived around 1430 A.D. to 1435 A.D.; became the disciple of Ramananda and settled near Dwarka. Among the Hindu *bhakti* poets who existed in the sixteenth-century Gujarat and Rajasthan, were Bhan *Saheb* of Kathiawar (follower of Kabir) and Namdev from Marwar and Lalbag who inspired the Alakhnami sect in the Bikaner region. Laldasi of the Meo tribe of Rajasthan and the founder of the Laldasi sect was influenced by both Kabir and Dadu.

Vallabhacharya (1473 A.D. to 1531 A.D.), a theologian and philosopher, founded the Krishna centered *pushti* cult of *Vaishnavism* in the Braj region of India. The poet-saint Tulsidas belonged to the same sect. The leadership of the Vallabhacharya sect became the property of the descendants of the family of Vallabhacharya. This tendency of keeping the spiritual leadership with the family was avoided by the poet-saint, the first *Sikh Guru*, Nanak and his successors, the nine *Sikh Gurus* acquired the position on the basis of their spiritual greatness. This was the reason that the *Sikh* torch of faith grew strong and blazed deep enough to eventually become the only political strong arm in the north that could defend Islamic aggression in the form of Mughal oppression.

Ramdas (1608 A.D. to 1681 A.D.), a devotee of Hanuman and Rama, was a saint and a poet of Maharashtra. He established several *maths* and chose the leaders who were spiritual and able to work for society, but were also politically adept. In *Dasbodh,* he conjectured the life on the earth and transcendental—"First the earthly life to set well, then accept the conscience of transcendental (12.1.1)." The first eight sections of *Dasbodh* points at transcendental, and the next twelve sections at life on the earth and transcendental. He insisted on strength, organisation, efforts, and state of self religion.

Tyagaraja (1767 A.D. to 1947 A.D.), also known as Tyagayya, lived in Thiruvarur, Tamil Nadu and composed *bhakti* poetry in Telugu. He was prolific and influential in the development of Indian classical music, composed Carnatic music and Indian devotional poetry. He composed thousands of devotional compositions, mostly in Telugu and in praise of Lord Rama, and of special mention are five of his compositions called *Pancharatna Kritis*. Another source of qualitative spiritual poetry was poetry written in Bengali by *Brahmo Samajis*. Their songs were in line with the tradition of Kabir, Dadu, and Nanak, who shared the *Nirguna* concept of God.

In the pre-independence era, there were a significant number of mystics, saints, leaders, and intellectuals, marked by intense change and revolution in the Indian society fighting for independence. Large scale reform movements were the parts of this period and so were the social saints, reformers, and mystics, like Tarabai Shinde, Raja Ram Mohan Roy, Bankim Chandra Chatterjee, Ram Prasad Bismil, Subramania Bharati, Debendranath Tagore, Ramakrishna Paramahansa, Mahatma Jyotiba Phule, Dayananda Saraswati, Periyar Swami, Vivekananda, Rajashri Shahu Maharaj, Karmaveer Bhaurao Patil, Madan Mohan Malaviya, Vinayak Damodar Savarkar, Vitthal Ramji Shinde, Dhondo Keshav Karve, Vinoba Bhave, Surendranath Banerjee, Gopal Krishna Gokhale, Bal Gangadhar Tilak, Romesh Chunder Dutt, Aurobindo Ghosh, Rabindranath Tagore, Mahatma Gandhi, Gadge Baba, Tukadoji, Bhimrao Ramji Ambedkar, and Bhausaheb Deshmukh.

Along with participating in the heroic struggle for Indian Independence, the prophets and rebel-poets in the nineteenth-century and the first-half of the twentieth-century were the factors for shaping socio-political and moral-spiritual reality of the twentieth-century. Tukadoji projects the facets of twentieth-century socio-political, moral, and spiritual realities in *Gramgeeta* to view them in new constructive perspective.

Indian English Poetry: Nineteenth-Century to 1950's

The Indian poets writing in English in the late nineteenth-century were Henry Louis Vivian Derozio, Kashiprasad Ghosh, Michael Madhusudan Dutt, Toru Dutt, Manmohan Ghosh, and Vivekananda; and in the twentieth-century were Sarojini Naidu, Sri Aurobindo, and Rabindranath Tagore.

Toru Dutt

Toru Dutt's *A Sheaf Gleaned in French Fields* (1876) comprises 165 lyrics by the French poets, translated by her, and 8 lyrics by her sister, Aru, which are infused with lyrical strain. She has carefully avoided the classicists and chosen the Romantic poets. Victor Hugo, Soulary and de Gramont are the basis of this anthology. In the poems, 'Baugmare', 'The Lotus', and 'Our Casurina Tree' included in the book *Ancient Ballads and Legends of Hindustan* (1882), she is sensitive to nature, especially of sound and colour, which recalls the sensuousness of Keats and Shelley.

She sketches Indian social life and reflects on social problems, and to her, widowhood is the dreadful curse and a worse life.

> If sin there be
> But thou must make a different choice.[23]

In the rebellious spirit, she delivers the message of democracy.

> What is rank or caste?
> In us is honour, or disgrace,
> Not out of us..... (114)

She cherishes a passionate love of liberty in 'France', and is hopeful to rise from darkness.

Toru Dutta anticipated the themes from Hindu legends, epics, and ballads, and penned the poems, 'Savitri', 'Lakshman', 'Dhruva', 'Pralhad', and 'Sita', which nourish historical sense.

Manmohan Ghosh

Manmohan Ghosh's poems in *Primavera* (1890) unfold the hues of weariness, yearning, and the aesthetic approach of the 1890's. *Love Songs and Elegies* (1898) expresses the same strain, nostalgia, and longing for love; and celebrates the beauty of nature. *Perseus, the Gorgon Slayer*, an epic based on Greek myth Slayer, planned as a magnum opus, was begun in 1898 but abandoned in 1914 under official pressure, treating it as a political allegory. This fragment of six out of the projected twelve books runs to about 7500 lines of blank verse, and was to have for its central theme the idea of progress in human history and slaying of the spirit of stagnation and annihilation, which makes progress possible. Ghosh remained an alien, deviated from his native roots.

Vivekananda

Vivekananda's poetry is available in original and translated forms. The translated poems by Vivekananda include 'Nirvana Shatakam', 'Rudra Prayer', and 'Renunciation alone is fearless'; and by others, 'Shiva in Ecstasy', 'To a friend', and his 'Hymns.' The three significant themes running through his poetry which unravel his philosophic vision of life, are social, national, and metaphysical.

Social consciousness is mirrored in 'The Living God'. Vivekananda had firm faith in potentiality of man and depicts "Man is like an infinite spring, coiled up in a small box, and that spring is trying to unfold itself". He urges to worship living God, the man, and serve mankind. He is aware of social evils, and being conscious of dynamism of human power, encourages to fight and conquer in the poem 'Angels Unawares'.

> But stones and trees remain; that man alone,
> Is blest with power to fight and conquer fate,
> Transcending bounds and laws.[24]

Man's potential transcends contours and laws to create constructive new.

In the poem, 'To the Awankened India', he strongly condemns fancy for 'unreal dreaming'. This poem was written for the journal, *Prabuddha Bharata* or *Awankened India*, in August 1898, and it is addressed to India.

> Resume thy march,
> With gentle feet that would not break
> The peaceful rest, even of the roadside dust.
> That lies so low, yet strong and steady,
> Blissful, bold, and free. Awakener, ever
> Forward! Speak thy stirring words. (15-16).

Vivekananda knew that India's greatness had been built upon the concept of renunciation and sacrifice, and, therefore, he saw the necessity for service.

'My play is done' is a dramatic monologue. Vivekananda knew that life is a floating bubble having 'hollow form', and, therefore, he longed to 'know' light.

> Open the gates of light, O Mother, to me Thy tired son.
> I long, oh, long to return home! Mother, my play is done. (29)

These lines decipher Vivekananda's eagerness, longing to "return home". In *Gitanjali*, Rabindranath Tagore's heart longs 'to join thy song' (poem 13). He has addressed to mother, "Mother, I shall weave a chain of pearls for thy neck with my tears of sorrow". In the ballad, 'Nirvana Shatakam', the metaphysical poem, the focal line recurs in the poem six times and attributes musical quality to the poems.

> I am Existence Absolute, Knowledge Absolute, Bliss Absolute
> I am He, I am He ('Shivoham, Shivohari') (27).

The verse explicates *Nirvana* as formless and limitless in space and time.

Optimistic tone persists in Vivekananda's poetry, such as in his poem, "To the Fourth of July", where he says that the Sun, Lord of Light, emerges from behind the gloomy pall of dark clouds. The images of hope dominate the poem, "Hold on yet a while, Brave Heart". In 'Light', he has attained the sublimity of thought and is able to look at light in the deepest sorrows. The poem echoes the Shelley's optimistic voice in 'To the Skylark'. His poetry is in tune with philosophy, and in his poetry, intellect and emotions conjuct; and his poetry's appeal is universal.

Sarojini Naidu

Before entering into active Indian politics, she published *The Golden Threshold* (1905), *The Bird of Time* (1912), and *The Broken Wing* (1917); and then *Feather of Dawn*, anthology of poems, composed in 1927. Like romantics, she approaches to nature for beauty and solace, drifting away from weariness and strife in human life, and not to mystical vein. Izzat Yar Khan has viewed, "Sarojini Naidu's attitude to nature is nearer to Byron's and Shelley's than Wordsworth's".[25] To Byron, nature is the greatest consoler in the hour of the revolt against the folly of man. To Shelley, nature is more a personality but it is an ethereal and lovely presence. But, to Wordsworth, nature is a presence, capable of delightful ardour and elevating man by moral virtues.

Sarojini's poetry imbibes Indian ethos, the splendours of Indian scene, and traditional Indian life. 'Palanquin Bearers', 'Indian Weavers', 'The Village Song', 'Ode to H.H. the Nizam of Hyderabad', (*The Golden Threshold*), 'In the Bazaar's of Hyderabad', 'The Festival of Sea', and 'Raksha Bandhan' reveal myriad hues of Indian ethos. Her beggar woman is an old, bent and blind, sitting under banyan tree, and holding a battered begging bowl in her hand. She depicts the evening scene in an Indian village with picturesque quality in the poem, 'June Sunset':

> An ox-cart stumbles upon the rocks,
> And a wistful music pursues the breeze
> From a shepherd's pipe as he gathers his flocks
> Under the *pipal* trees.
> And a young *Banjara* driving her cattle
> Lifts her voice as she glitters by.[26]

In the poem, 'The Village Song', a rural woman goes to fetch water from Jamuna, and is lured by song. As the path is long and lonely, she prays for protection from dark storm, "Unless thou succour my footsteps and guide me". The poem, 'In the Bazaars of Hyderabad' is the recollection of the Mina Bazaar of Hyderabad. The poem, 'Ode to H.H. the Nizam of Hyderabad' is the tribute to the Prince, Mir Mahbub Ali Khan, whom she esteemed and honoured. She revolts against the attitude of fatalism, states social custom as *sutte*, and disapproves of the social convention for widowhood that deprives of fine clothes and jewellery. She has "the moonless vigils of her lonely night" (SF, 67), and so "Nay, let her be!"

Patriotic vein runs in her poetry, which depicts her love for India, and honour for freedom, liberty, and sacrifice. 'To India' is addressed to the Mother, India to rise from her sleep and open the prospects for her children. She reminds her of sovereign past which can awake her from gloom and darkness of slavery. Patriotic spirit binds the patriots, "One heart are we to love thee,

O our Mother" (SF, 180). The song bird experiences her wing to be broken, but her unflinching faith will rise her to see the country's freedom, "to scale the stars upon my broken wing" (SF, 145). The poem, 'In Gokhale's Garden' is a memorial verse on Gopal Krishna Gokhale who was the saint and soldier of our national righteousness. His sacrifice was for the unity of India. Sarojini Naidu proposes that the best homage is:

> And in a daily worship taught by thee,
> Upbuild the temple of her unity. (SF, 159)

The poem, 'The Gift of India' is salutation to the Indian soldiers who combated in the first world war. They fought in France, Flander, and Persian gulf, and sacrificed.

> And you honour the deeds of the deathless ones,
> Remember the blood of my martyred sons! (SF, 147)

In these lines, she makes the Britishers conscious to honour the sacrifices of Indians.

Her poetry reflects on life and death—the odyssey of finite towards infinite. She is not repulsive to the stark realities, and not indifferent to toil and trial in life. The forces of life do not subjugate her because of indomitable will to struggle and resist, and so she prays, "Give me to drink each joy and pain" (SF, 123). Almighty responded.

> Life is a prism of my light,
> And Death the shadow of My face.
>
> ('The Soul's Prayer', SF, 124)

In the poem, 'To a Buddha seated on a Lotus', she contrasts the serenity, peace of Buddha with ceaseless turmoil and burning wheel of desires. Man aspires and experiences the broken pride, defeat, and denial of fruit, but "not the peace, supremely won by Lord Buddha, of the Lotus-thorne" (SF, 61). She has also composed the poem 'The Prayer of Islam' converging on the conception of Allah.

In the poem, 'The Flute-player of Brindaban', Radha is irresistibly captivated to the flute-player, forsaking all the worldly shackles. No peril, no fear, she experiences:

Impede my heart that pants to drain,
The nectar of thy flute! (SF, 162)

The lines reveal the spell of the music of the infinite on an individual and the magnetic pull of the finite towards the infinite. In the poem, Lotika Basu observes, "the attitude of *Vaishnava* Philosophy with its mystic rapturous devotion".[27] It foreshadows the nuances with Rabindranath Tagore's lyrical poetry.

Sri Aurobindo

Aurobindo Ghosh had competent grasp of German, Italian, Latin, Greek, and French languages, and their classics. He found his roots in Indian culture and thought after his return to India from Cambridge. In India, he transformed himself by beginning with revolution, and then achieving revelation.

In his first anthology, *Songs to Myrtilla,* the echoes of Keats and Shelley are heard. The motif of *Urvasie* is love and it has classical blend, and in it, the Mighty Mother suggests the World Mother in *Savitri*. In *Love and Death*, indomitable love is presented as attaining victory over death. The legend in it recalls the Greek legend of Orpheus and Eurydice.

He was a political radical, and was arrested for having publishing political articles. He took the leading role in the deliberations of Nationalist (Extremist) party and resisted Lord Curzon's move to partition of Bengal. He met Yogi Lele and had the experience of utter silence of mind on 4th May, 1908. He was again arrested in link with the Muzaffarpur bomb blast and after detention of one year in Alipore Jail, he was acquitted. Soon after, he published *The Karmayogi,* a new weekly, but due to strong spiritual pull, he reached Pondicherry on 4th April, 1910. During the first years at Pondicherry, he was associated with the Tamil revolutionaries, V.V.V.S. Aiyar and Subramania Bharati. He paid tribute to Bankim Chandra Chattopadhayay in his poem. 'Baji Prabhu', is a long narrative poem, devoted to the valorous soldier, Baji, "a minstrel worthy of his imperishable sacrifice."[28]

Sri Aurobindo's poetry is suffused with meditative and mystic experiences. He expanded the cantour of Indian tradition of Upanishadic poetry and assimilated it into English. In the poem,

"Revelation", visionary flash is "like a startled bright surmise visible to mortal eyes", and "like a cheek of frightened rose" that glows with sudden beauty. In the poem, 'Transformation', he is not merely, "a vassal of flash" but an instrument of Almighty, tuned with the spirit of perpetual light.

> I am no more a vassal of the flesh.
> A slave to Nature and her leaden rule;
> I am caught no more in the senses' narrow mesh.
> My soul unhorizoned widens to measureless sight,
>
> (*Collected Poems and Plays*, II, 297)

The poem, 'Nirvana', speaks of a state of peace accomplished after detaching all allurements. *Nirvana* to Sri Aurobindo, is the deliverance from "the knot of the suffering, from the bondage of the ego; it is the state of Non-Being".[29] In the poem, 'Surrender', he prays to bend his mortal being in "Thy still glory of divinity", and to move "The rapture's streams" in his nerves and veins.

In the poem, 'The Mother of Dreams', the poet has drunk the wine of divine. The poem, 'Epiphany', speaks of two aspects of the Lord-Shiva—the bestower of bliss, and Rudra, the destroyer. The poem, 'Ahana', is an endeavour to humanise the divine. 'Moon of Two Hemispheres' is a poem surcharged with an individual's spiritual yearnings. The moon itself is a symbol of spiritual light. In Sri Aurobindo's poetry, 'Rose' is the supreme symbol of the essence and efflorescence of God.[30] The rose should bloom here in "Our heart of humanhood"; it is here on the earth that the Divine Life should be enacted.

Savitri, the epic in twelve parts spanning the earth and heaven, comprises diverse occult worlds, and projects the drama of life, death, and immortality on the cosmic stage. Savitri turns out to be the Aurobindonian Superman transforming the World of matter with her presence. She reveals her for the earth, "to change the earthly life to life divine."[31] In *Divine Comedy*, Dante fused poetry and philosophy in a massive magnitude, and here Sri Aurobindo repeats the same task. He operated poetry as the medium to imbibe his philosophy of evolution of race. His poetry involves the future of man and the lines on which the evolution of consciousness proceeds.

Rabindranath Tagore

Rabindranath Tagore, a bilingual, penned in Bengali and English, and translated in English, mostly from his writings in Bengali, besides the works of P.B. Shelley, Robert Browning, Ernst Mayr, and Victor Hugo. His anthologies of poems, *Gitanjali* (1912), *The Gardner* (1913), *The Crescent Moon* (1913), *Fruit-Gathering* (1916), *The Lover's Gift and Crossing* (1916), *Stray-Birds* (1917) and *Poems* (1943) center round the relation among man, nature, spirit immanent and spirit as mover, life, love, beauty, truth, and death. In his major poetry, crux of which he himself exhorted, the pivotal theme was "the relation between the finite and the infinite."[32]

Tagore's poetry has nuances with *Bhagavadgita, Rigveda*, the upanishadic philosophy, the tradition of Indian *Bhakti* poetry, and of Jaydeo, Kabir, Meera, Chaitanya Mahaprabhu, and the mystical Baul singers in rural Bengal. Tagore has individual talent in attributing lyrical cadence, meditative temper, and bridging transitory and eternal. His poetry is manifestation of his philosophic vision, nationalistic and humanistic approach, and search for spiritual reality.

His poetrty reflects that life and death are treated as twins, two shores of a river, as he has fear, "I shrink to give up my life", and in spite of it, he intends to welcome him.

> The night is dark and my heart is fearful-yet I will take up
> the lamp, open my gates and bow to him my welcome.
> It is thy messenger who stands at my door.[33]

Tagore will worship him and in his desolate house, his formless self will be his last offering to the Lord. In the poem anthology, *In Lover's Gift and Crossing*, he expounds that true love doesn't know any distinction of colour or caste. In the second part, 'Crossing', the poet is ready to cross the river of life and urges the Lord to grasp his hand to "deliver me from dispair". In *The Gardner*, the poet insists to trust love even if it brings sorrow, and "not to close up your heart". The lines, though human life is "full of sorrow, full of death, and pain of separation", it has "still bliss, happiness, and delight keep emerging with us", encapsulate his philosophical vision.

Nationalistic as well humanistic approaches are conspicuous in his poetry, such as "Jan, gan, man adhinayak jay he.....", the national anthem of India, celebrates masses and mind, highlighting diversity and honours for victory. In 1905, he fiercely resisted the partition of Bengal. In his essay 'Swadeshi Samaj', he discussed the facets of rural reconstruction, mass education, and co-operative movements. For agricultural and rural development, he established the organisation, *Sriniketan*, two miles away from Shantiniketan, which turned to realities of life, deviating from the British mode of education. Pearson, a philanthropist, and Leonard Elmhirst, an agricultural scientist, worked with him; and the schemes for developing animal husbandry, weaving, agriculture, and cottage industries were undertaken. The projects, such as village library, hospital, co-operative bank, irrigation, and industrial estate were also adopted. These ventures pace with Tukadoji's vision of rural reconstruction.

In the 35th poem, in *Gitanjali*, the poet prays:

> Where the mind is without fear and the head is held high;
> Where knowledge is free;
> Where the world has not been broken up into fragments by narrow domestic walls;
> Where words came out from the depth of truth;
> Where tireless striving stretches its arms towards perfection;
> Where the clear stream of reason has not lost its way into the dreary desert sand of dead habit;
> Where the mind is led forward by thee into ever-widening thought and action;
> Into that heaven of freedom, my Father, let my country awake. (162)

In his conceptual context of nation, citizens are dauntless and experience freedom, no discrimination by man's created compartments in truthful words. Conscience and reason are awakened, and thought and action have resonance. Tukadoji's *bhajan* (song), 'Let there be brotherhood in India', adopted as the university song by Rashtrasant Tukadoji Maharaj Nagpur University, reiterates the secular attitude, humanity, national spirit, and unity among human beings. Rabindranath Tagore was profoundly shocked by aggressive nationalism propounded by Benito Mussolini and Adolf Hitler. He advocated for the humanitarian values, freedom, unity, sacrifice, love, and universal brotherhood.

Search for spiritual reality and its realisation recur in his poetry. *Gitanjali* is a collection of 103 poems translated, transliterated, and transfused by him from his anthologies of poems in Bengali, i.e., 51 poems from *Gitanjali*, 17 from *Gitmalya*, 16 from *Naivedya*, 11 from *Kheya*, 3 from *Shishu*, 1 from *Chaitali*, 1 from *Smarna*, 1 from *Kalpana*, 1 from *Ustarga*, and 1 from *Achalayatana*.

Gitanjali, offering of songs, reflects on man's existence and longing for freedom, nature, death, spirit, and eternity. Poet's terrain is essentially meditative and mode is lyrical. W.B. Yeats observed that these lyrics "display in their thought a world I have dreamed of all my life long. The work of supreme culture, they yet appear as much the growth of the common soil as the grass and rushes."[34] It is indigenous in content, images, and symbols, and yet crosses the contour of Indianness to reveal cosmic vision. It is a spiritual therapy for an ailing being. While going through the book, the inner eye is opened and senses are purged. In it, the craving is to meet with the Lord, the flute-player, and experiences loneliness, separation, and desperateness. The poet's heart longs to join the song and realises, "Thou has made me endess" (31) and "The light of thy music illumines the world" (35). He lives in the hope of meeting but the meeting is not feasible. His desires are varied and his cry is pitiful, and earnestly he asks, "Ah, love, why dost thou let me wait outside at the door all alone?" (89). He humanises the infinite, "O Master poet, I have sat down at thy feet" (48). He deviates from the conventional approach of *bhakti* in temple and asks to leave chanting, singing, and telling of beads; and to meet him to toil for the poorest, lowliest, and lost. He prays with humility for "a shower of mercy" (174) and "joy to shine" (198) because God is "the King of Kings" (240) and "spotless and serene" (280). In his approach to the infinite, he orients from form to the formless, without attributes, and as thus, in the play house of infinite forms, the poet has "caught the sight of him that formless" (380) and realises "his touch who is beyond touch" (380). He salutes infinite "like a flock of homesick cranes flying night and day back to their mountain nests" (405).

In *Gitanjali*, there is precision of imagery and symbolism, and the disciplined rhythm as in Walt Whitman's poetry. The tone is quiter serene and the music is melodious. Ezra Pound has asserted that the charm of this work is "the subtle underflow,"[35] subsumed with the hues of life and the spirit of "curious quite"[36] enlivening it.

Tukadoji

After Namdev, Tukadoji penned poetry in Marathi and Hindi, with equal competence; both wandered in Maharashtra and out of it. His published anthologies of poems are, in Marathi, *Anubhavamrut Abhangavali* (Anthology of *Abhangas*), Part 1 (1940), Part 2 (1945), *Samaj Sanjivini* (1949), *Lokshahiche Powade* (*Ballads of Democracy*), *Rashtriya Bhajanavali* (Anthology of National *Bhajans*), *Kranti Veena* (*Veena of Revolt*), *Gramgeeta* (1955), and in Hindi, *Lahar ki Barakha* (*Downpour of Waves*), Part 1 (1934), Part 2 (1967), Part 3, *Rashtriya Bhanjanavali*, *Anubhav-Prakash* (*Light of Experience*), Part 1 (1930) and Part 2 (1942). He composed in the poetic forms, such as *ovi, abhang, slok,* and *powada* (ballad), and in various other meters.

He exemplifies, "I learnt literature from the sea of masses, the core of heart, and internal craving. The idea of literature I grasped in the sea of masses."[37] His approach to literature is mass oriented, and he prayed for the beauty in human life with the contention, "Let beauty be home to home as heaven". In a letter, he addresses:

> Art, beauty, the best singing, the best playing, not only this, but the best speaking, the best transaction, to write literature, all I like ..... no stance of nation enlightenment is before today's artist. Once that approach is imbibed,

> art will perform both, an entertainment and nation's development.[38]

He amalgamated the values of art and life. While desiring for entire progress of human beings, conscience, the art with the constrain of words is important to him.

> To elevate art, conscience is to be,
> One to be alert for the upliftment of all. ||81||[39]

His literary perception is to steer masses, realising the unison among masses and the divine, deeming "People as divine". His words, "I, the charity of words; with me all words" concern with his indomitable trust in words, not his self-conceit. "I, not poet, compassion I am" depicts that his poetry has blossomed from compassion, and compassion is humanity.

> No peace in me, the emotions of downtrodden, I am.
> Who walks to become human, their well wish I am.[40]

His poetry is compassionate to downtrodden, marginal, deprived, wretched, oppressed, and expelled who are at circumference. Humanity is the human essence in his literature; and it is life's value.

In the earlier poetry of Tukadoji, the pull towards the devotion to attributes operates. Later, devotion, expanding the level of reflection on life, attains collective consciousness, and then with the intuition of consciousness transports to transcendental. In spite of it, man, human society, environment, and world and its welfare retain centripetal position. Irresistible pull to meet, estrangement, unkindness, joy, downpour of bliss, and the myriad beams of devotion to attributes occur in his poetry. When comes with the faith, "none without you"[41], he is absorbed deep at the doors. He poses the questions, "How will I go, my lane is closed?" "How will I fetch water, small well is closed?"[42] (*Anubhav-Prakash*, Part 2, 91). "Estrangement is not tolerable to mind"[43] and it is restless, and "Why are away, though mine? Why unkind?" He urges, "Thou bless the humble" (*Anubhavamrut Abhanggatha*, 17).

Illusion in visible world, mortality, uncertainty, attachment to outer world, the shores of birth and death, strength, and the limitations of human existence are the core terrains of Tukadoji's reflection. "With ignorance, a rope seems a serpent"

(*Anubhavamrut Abhanggatha*, 169), and as this, the World to mind. Body is material and mortal, and mind is captivated by an oasis. Uncertainty lurks between the two shores, and as thus, "body, a glass tube, not certain when breaks" (*Anubhavamrut Abhanggatha,* 30). Who knows, which day will impede? Being the bondage of attachment and deeming appearance as reality, ego hikes up. He addressed to an attitude, "Where do you go abstaining from the external plodder?" (*Bhajanamruth Sagar*, 7). "Whether are you perpetual or temporal? raising this question, he elucidates, "You, not material, spiritual ever, illusion thy of material" (*Lahar ki Barakha*, Part 1, 63).

> A crore, crore lamps light in your heart,
> What do see outside, creative one?
>
> (*Bhajanamruth Sagar*, 413)

Light is inside, *Atta Dip Bhava* (Let light inner lamp). Musk is hidden inside, but man searches the fragrance of musk externally. Though, one has precious diamond, he worships stone. Divine experience is not attainable unless the dissolution of 'I' and 'you'. He doesn't experience divinity in stone, wood, and metal; and in temple, Murari (Krishna) with dark complexion is not seen. Service to downtrodden leads man to salvation. Being collectively conscious, he links himself with national life. Man has forgotten the nature of self and, by discriminating among Hindu, Muslim, and Christian, alienated from self. Alerting, "Leave enclosed at home, caste-cult, sect" (*Bhajanamrut Sagar*, 500), Tukadoji suggests to accept brotherhood and being Indian. He earnestly gives the call, "Render man, render me man" (*BS*, 317). He awakes youth by asking the question, "Is not thy village, a pilgrimage?" He is compassionate to those who succumbed to death or, are sufferers/victims of the Koyana earthquake catastrophe. He addresses youth to vitalise nation, and inspires them to activate in the wartime.

> Wake up nation, wake up nation, awake youth,
> Light the lamp of valour, awake youth.[44]

He advocates the values of freedom, equality, and brotherhood in his ballads on independence, democracy, and voting by citizens.

His stance of reformation is constructive and pragmatic, and asserts that revolution is not for devastation, but for peace.

> Valorous serviceman! awake, awake, listen to *tutari* of revolution.
>
> With peace, begins war home to home. (*BS*, 524)

He is gayful due to the blossom of freedom, but his heart is pained because of bloodshed in partition. He listens the melodious voice of the *Veena* of new revolution. In his salutation to nation, "Let our nation, India, be happy, in body mind-wealth", he longs for nation's happiness, unity in diversity, dauntlessness, truth, character, qualitative progress, eradication of discrimination, and national security. It recalls Subramania Bharati's poems, striving for freedom and breaking the shackles of slavery. His patriotic poetry has perpetual place in the saga of Indian freedom struggle. In 'Thirst for Freedom' he asks:

> When will this thirst for freedom slake?
> When will our love of slavery die?
> When will our Mother's fetters break?
> When will our tribulations cease?[45]

He bows to worship *Bharat*, the Mother. It is pertinent to observe that this vision extends beyond the confines of India. Unity and righteousness are essential to endure victory. Bharati projects the unified vision of India with her geographical intellectual and spiritual qualities. Nation's religion is the base for World because in his perspective, it crosses the contours and moves beyond to embrace universal brotherhood.

Cosmic consciousness mirrors in Tukadoji's poetry. Man plays a part in the world play, but to call the world one's home, needs "the intellect of the world" (*BS*, 431). He prays to the Mover to render "the consciousness of the world". In the collective prayer, he writes about the energy infused in the cosmos, "We, varied in bodies, but one in the principle". In the *bhajan*, composed in Tokyo on 4th July, 1955, and rendered in the World Religion Conference, he reiterates, "You in every nation, You in every attire, Your names many, You One." (*Rashtriya Bhajanavali*, 53-54)

> Let difference cease; let peace pertain for every,
> Being cleaned miscreant-denigrator, left no trace of hatred.
> (*BS*, 208)

He hopes for human welfare and elevation, and to move beyond differentiation towards unison with the cosmic vision, "let happiness be for the whole world". His poetry has the ascending steps for self elevation, mass elevation, and world elevation.

R.G. Jadhav has exhorted, in his presidential speech, at Rashtrasant Tukadoji Maharaj Second Literary Conference in Pune, in the context of mass elevation, that Gadge Maharaj and Tukadoji Maharaj, "these modern saints have accomplished more mental involvement and more activation in the work of mass elevation, which is to be deemed as the greatness of time. Medieval saints didn't have such generous companionship."[46] Tukadoji's poetry has cosmic consciousness, transcending location, time, caste, sect, cult, race, and class; and his creativity, which has humanity as life value, becomes suffused with cosmic value.

Tukadoji asks, "Learnt you the knowledge of *Vedas*, but will you not learn 'mass language'". He communicated with audiences in mass language and used the *vaidharbhite* dialects. His language has the capacity to address, rhetoric ability, frankness, fluid, and energetic. In syntax, inherent coherence is functional. He attributed direction to mass elevation, operating in expression simile, metaphor, allegory, irony, satire, and humour.

Majority of the poets exposed to an English education/ culture, hailed from the privileged background; there is very little reference to grass root reality in India. As D.P. Mukherji observes:

> The reformist zeal in literature had certain limitations, however, the lower castes not quite inside the pale of observation; and the social inequality was not further analysed into its essentials.[47]

Tagore and Aurobindo wrote poetry keeping pace with Indian traditional poetry and still maintaining their identities. They had affinity with Indian tradition and assimilated the foreign influences and emerged even richer. They were strongly rooted in the Indian poetic consciousness and had the courage to live up by their own convictions and with their life-long dialogue with mysticism. The water of the *Bhakti* poetry percolated in the nineteenth-century, and found expression in the poems by Aurobindo Ghose and Rabindranath Tagore. Sisirkumar Ghose's comment is relevant not only to Aurobindo but also to Meera, Nanak, Kabir, Tukaram, Akho, Tagore, and many mystic poets in Indian devotional poetry:

> To presume that visionary writers have a weak hold on life is part of the order of ideas that has to be left aside if we are to enter the world of Aurobindonian poetry. For it deals with, as it depends upon, experiences, "not very much frequented by common readers of poetry! An openness to these experiences and some knowledge of the conditions of their fit expression would seem to be the part of the reader's equipment."[48]

Despite national upheaval on the socio-political and economic fronts, the two world wars, and the crisis and plunder of partition, Indian English poetry in the Gandhian era (1920 to 1948) had a lull period. It was rare that the poets attempted to look beyond personal experiences, at a larger Indian reality, to hobnob with the spirit of the soil and to grow from within it. We find it happening in the poetical creations of Vivekanand, Sarojini Naidu, Aurobindo, Tagore, A.K. Ramanujan, Jayanta Mahapatra, Dilip Chitre, and Arun Kolatkar.

Indian English poetry has enjoyed an element of elitism and unlike the *bhakti* poets, it has maintained a distance from the rigours of the dust and sweat of Indian life. Indian English poetry has been alienated by fabricating it as an urban reality and distancing it from the cultural and emotional ethos of the uncultivated but potent native culture of India. Unless English is actively used to translate the Indian literature in regional languages, Indian literature in English will continue to undermine and misrepresent the picture of Indian creative writing.

Tukadoji's poetry has nuances with nationalistic fervour of Sarojini Naidu, Sri Aurobindo, and Rabindranath Tagore; its meditative blend and spiritual vein keep pace with the poetries of Vivekananda, Sri Aurobindo, and Rabindranath Tagore.

Without being influenced by English poetry, Tukadoji created the poetry, beginning from an individual and expanding to collective consciousness, and then to cosmic vision, rooted in Indian soil and moving beyond its contours too. In the post-colonial era, he has penned his magnum opus, *Gramgeeta*, which is multi-dimensional, multi-disciplinary, and polyphonic.

Gramgeeta: The Post-colonial Reality and its Facets

Even in the post-colonial era, the colonial apparatuses continue in the forms of language, such as English and French; colonial voices in British and French literature; and nomenclature of buildings and architectural styles.

In post-colonial, the hyphenated space connotes break or discontinuity or fissure from colonial in the context of power, knowledge, and cultural apparatus; focuses on freedom, justice, equality, human rights, native voices, multiplicities against homogeneousness, resistance against dominance, oppression in the garbs of political power, economic imbalance, social discrimination, gender divide and cultural hegemony; and as thus, the post-colonial studies encompass cultural studies, subaltern studies, and gender studies. In the post-colonial world, on practical level, paradoxes pertain, and so it is pertinent to pose the questions: Do freedom, equality, and unity prevail in the real sense of the word, 'post-colonial'? Are native voices heard or not? Is there differentiation on the tenets of class, sect, cult, race, and caste? Is the cleavage between 'have' and 'haven't' bridged or widen? Does national spirit culminate into narrow nationalism or aggressive nationalism? Is religion a medium for communal violence and bloodshed, though religion points at unison and the constitutional provision of the secular outlook? Paradoxically, in the post-colonial world, colonial reality persists with new hues, resulting into neo-colonial reality.

Bhakti poetry on the other hand, was an egalitarian literature of change, spanning through the entire gamut of social change. It enjoyed a large audience. Its poets, hailing from a cross section of Indian society, could be a weaver or a cobbler by profession, or even a *brahmin* or a king. The journey from the periphery towards the centre (represented by the vernacular and Sanskrit language of the lower castes and the *brahmins*, respectively) and the "displacement of the centre" are what make the *Bhakti* movement such an interesting and volatile area of study, historically, architecturally, linguistically, theologically, and sociologically in Indian literature and regional languages in the post-colonial era. Contemporary literature in regional languages share much better relation with their traditions rooted in rural and folk cultures. From this standpoint, Tukadoji's *Gramgeeta*, published in the post-independence and the post-colonial period in 1955, has significance, which on one hand has affinity with Indian tradition of *Bhakti* poetry and on the other points at multi-faceted contemporary reality in social, political, economical, ethical, and scientific terrains in the post-colonial era. In it, the axis of Indian poetry is oriented from elitism to masses.

> Let your labour receive dignity, all attention be converged on you;
> Let light of humanity be glittered in the world by this mean.
>
> (Dedication leaflet, *Gramgeeta*)

Tukadoji insisted on dignity of labour and humanity. *Gramgeeta* has 8 Quinates and 41 Cantos.

Quinate 1: Right Religion Reflection

Canto I	Vision of God
Canto II	Study of Religion
Canto III	*Ashram* Religion
Canto IV	Family and Transcendental
Canto V	*Varna* System

Quinate 2: Hypnotic Spell on People

Canto VI	Impact of Good Conduct
Canto VII	Impact of Conduct
Canto VIII	Significance of Propagation
Canto IX	Power of Service
Canto X	Strength of Unity

Quinate 3: Village Creation

Canto XI	Village Security

Canto XII	Village Purification
Canto XIII	Art of Village Creation
Canto XIV	Village Hygiene
Canto XV	Improvement of Cow Race

Quinate 4: Village Reformation

Canto XVI	Wealth of Garment
Canto XVII	Poverty–Richness
Canto XVIII	Labour Wealth
Canto XIX	Life Education
Canto XX	Women Elevation

Quinate 5: *Sanskar* Search

Canto XXI	Wedded Life
Canto XXII	Funeral *Sanskar*
Canto XXIII	Festival Celebration
Canto XXIV	Pilgrimage
Canto XXV	God Temple

Quinate 6: Foundation of Love Religion

Canto XXVI	An Idol Worship
Canto XXVII	Collective Prayer
Canto XXVIII	Prayer and World Religion
Canto XXIX	Service of Downtrodden
Canto XXX	*Bhajan* Influence

Quinate 7: Mean for Divinity

Canto XXXI	Saint Miracle
Canto XXXII	Saint Nature
Canto XXXIII	Incarnation Work
Canto XXXIV	Fatalism
Canto XXXV	Effort Influence

Quinate 8: Ideal Life

Canto XXXVI	Art of Life
Canto XXXVII	Spiritual Experience
Canto XXXVIII	Village Family

Canto XXXIX	Earth Paradise
Canto XL	Study of Books
Canto XLI	Significance of Books

Gramgeeta is progressive from an individual to village, village to nation, nation to the world, and the world to cosmos. The thoughts in *Gramgeeta* are pragmatic, inclusive, and irrespective of caste, race, creed, and religion; and have practical applications. Freedom, equality, and justice are the basic tenets of Tukadoji's humanitarian and cosmic vision. These voices are native, yet they cross their contours to resonate on global level.

By contextualising Vedic tradition, post-vedic tradition, and Upanishads, the exploration highlights the traditions of *Nirguna bhakti* and Indian devotional poetry, locating *Gramgeeta* in the literary, historical, and cultural frameworks. Retaining indigenous roots, the text has nationalistic spirit, as in the poetries of Sarojini Naidu, Rabindranath Tagore, and Sri Aurobindo; and reflective temper and spiritual realisation, as infused in the poetries of Vivekananda, Tagore, and Aurobindo. *Gramgeeta*, being the post-colonial text, imbues the post-colonial dynamics and projects myriad realities, which encampass multi-disciplines, and becomes polyphonic.

References

1. www.nap.edu., p. 4, accessed on 16th June, 2019.
2. Allen J., Haig Sir T. Wolseley, Dodwell H.H., and Sethi R.R. (1964), *The Cambridge Shorter History of India*, New Delhi: S. Chand and Co., pp. 5-6.
3. Rupa Goswami, (1965), 'The Bhakirasa', (tr.) Tridandi Swami, in *Indian Literary Criticism: Theory and Interpretation*, (2007), (ed) G.N. Devi, Hydrabad: Orient Longman Private Limited, p. 97.
4. Rupa Goswami, (1965), 'Bhava-Bhakti' (tr.) Tridandi Swami, in *Indian Literary Criticism: Theory and Interpretation*, (2007), (ed). G.N. Devi, Hyderabad: Orient Longman Private Limited, p. 98.
5. G.N. Devi, (2007), *Indian Literary Criticism: Theory and Interpretation* (ed), Hyderabad: Orient Longman Private Limited, p. 97.
6. *Ibid.*, p. 100.

7. Ramanujan A.K. (Tr.) (1973), *Speaking of Shiva*, New Delhi: Penguin Books India (P) Ltd., p. 40.
8. Ghosh, Siriskumar (1987), *Mysticism: Views and Reviews*, New Delhi: Clarion Books, p. 24-25.
9. Champakalaxmi, R. (1989), 'Religion and Social Change in Tamil Nadu', *Medieval Bhakti Movements in India*, Sri Chaitanya Quincentenary, (ed.), N.N. Bhattacharya, New Delhi: Munshiram Manoharlal Publishers Pvt. Ltd., p. 163-164.
10. Ramanujan A.K., Velcharan Narayan Rao, and David Shulman (Editors and Translators) (1995), *When Gold is a Customer*, Delhi: Oxford University Press, p. 49.
11. Ramanujan A.K. (1993), *Hymns for Drowning, Poems for Vishnu* by Nammaalvar, New Delhi: Penguin Books, p. ix.
12. *Sribhagvadgeeta* (2006), Gorakhpur: Gita Press, p. 163-165.
13. Dallmayr, Fred (1998), *Jnandev and the Warkari Movement*, Notre Dame: University of Notre Dame, p. 21.
14. Singh, Manmohan (1996), *Sri Granth Sahib*, Amritsar: Shiromani Gurudwara Prabhandak Committee, Vol. 5, 2846.
15. Bute, Shantaram (1990), *Sant Chokhamela Sarthgatha*, Akola: Sunanda Prakashan, p. 60.
16. Chitre, Dilip (Tr), (1980), *Says Tuka: Selected Poetry of Tukaram*, New Delhi: Penguin Books, xix-xx.
17. Raghavan, V. (1958), 'The Songs of the Saints of Medieval Hinduism', in *Sources of Indian Traditions: Introduction to Oriental Civilizations,* Vol. II, (ed.) Wm Theodre De Bary, New York: Columbia University Press, p. 79.
18. Shekhowat, Sant Singh and Kartar Singh Duggal (1982), *A History of Punjabi Literature*, New Delhi: Sahitya Academy, p. 64.
19. Ramanand, *Adi Granth,* (2004), Neethi M. Sadarangani, (tr.), *Bhakti Poetry in Medieval India*, New Delhi: Sarup & Sons, p. 112.
20. Dwyer, William S.J. (1981) *Bhakti in Kabir*, Patna: Associated Book Agency, p. 42.
21. Bhattacharya, Manjula (1989), 'Medieval Bhakti Movement in Gujrat', *Medieval Bhakti Movement in India,* (ed.) N.N. Bhattacharya, Delhi: Munshilala Manoharlal Publishers Pvt. Ltd., p. 103.
22. Deshpande, Uma (1989), 'Narsimha Mehta: Saint From Gujrat', *Medieval Bhakti Movement in India*, (ed.) N.N.

Bhattacharya, Delhi: Munshilala Manoharlal Publishers Pvt. Ltd., p. 107.

23. Dutta, Toru (1941), *Ancient Ballads and Legends of Hindustan* (ed.), Amarnath Zha, Allahabad: Kitabastan, p. 46.
24. Vivekananda Swami (1917), *Poems*, Almora: Advaita Ashram, p. 13. (All subsequent textual lines are from this edition.)
25. Khan, Izzatyar (1983), *Sarojini Naidu: The Poet,* New Delhi: S. Chand & Co. Ltd., p. 165.
26. Naidu, Sarojini (1943), *The Sceptred Flute*, Allahabad: Kitabistan, pp. 192-193.
27. Basu, Lotika (1933), *Indian Writers of English Verse*, Culcutta: Culcutta University Press, p. 91.
28. Sri Aurobindo (1942), *Collected Plays and Poems*, II, Pondicherry: Sri Aurobindo Ashrama, p. 101. (All subsequent quotation are from this edition.)
29. Sri Aurobindo (1939), *The Life Divine*, I, Culcutta: Arya Publishing House, p. 62.
30. Iyengar, K.R.S. (1961), *Sri Aurobindo: An Introduction,* Mysore: Rao Raghavan, p. 43.
31. Sri Aurobindo (1973), *Savitri,* Pondicherry: Sri Aurobindo Ashrama, p. 162.
32. Tagore, Rabindranath (1961), *Jeebansmitri*, quoted by S.K. Ghosh. *The Later Poems of Tagore*, Bombay: Asia Publishing House, p. 161.
33. Paul, S.K. (2009), *The Complete Poems of Rabindranath Tagore's Gitanjali,* New Delhi: Sarup and Sons, p. 346. (All subsequent textual lines are from this edition.)
34. Yeats, W.B. (1973), 'Introduction', *Gitanjali,* Madras: Macmillan Co. of India, p. xi.
35. Pound, Ezra (1961), *Tagore Centenary Volume* (Ed.), Mahendra Kulasresthu, Hashiarpur: Vishveshvaranand V.R. Institute, p. 114.
36. *Ibid.,* p. 111
37. *Sri Gurudeo*, February 1956, p. 9.
38. Mohod, Baba, (1966), *Rashtrasantachi Patre*, Gurukunj: Sri Gurudeo Prakashan, pp. 59-60.
39. Tukadoji, (2023), *Gramgeeta*, Ratnakar D. Bhelkar (tr.), Canto XXXVI, 'Art of Life', New Delhi: Atlantic Publishers and Distributors (P) Ltd., p. 325. (Subsequent textual lines are from this translated text.)

40. Tukadoji (2014), *Lahar Ki Barakha,* Bhag 3, Gurukunj Ashrama: Sri Gurudeo Prakashan, p. 41.
41. Tukadoji (2017), *Anubhavamrut Abhanggatha*, Gurukunj Ashrama: Akhil Bharatiya Gurudeo Sevamandal, p. 14.
42. Tukadoji (1942, reprint 2010), *Anubhav-Prakash Bhajanavali*, Bhag 2, Gurukunj Ashram: Sri Gurudeo Prakashan, p. 83.
43. Tukadoji (2017), *Tukadyadas Bhajanamrut Sagar,* Gurukunj Ashram: Sri Gurudeo Prakashan, p. 83.
44. Tukadoji (2011), *Samaj Sanjivani*, Gurukunj Ashrama: Akhil Bharatiya Gurudeo Seva Mandal, p. 11.
45. Nandkumar, Prema (2004), *Poems of Subramania Bharati,* New Delhi: Sahitya Academy, p. 73.
46. Jadhav, R.G., Rashtrasant Tukadoji Maharaj Second Literary Conference, the Presidential Speech, Pune, 10th June, 2007, p. 6.
47. Mukherji, Dhurjati Prasad (1948), *Sociology of Indian Culture*, Jaipur: Rawat Publications, p. 88.
48. Ghose, Sisirkumar (1973), *Aurobindo: A Poet as Seer,* (ed.) V.C. Joshi, Delhi: Viking Publishing House Pvt. Ltd., p. 44.

Chapter 2

Towards Cosmic Vision

Indo-Gangetic valley was occupied by Dravidian and Munda people before the Aryan came and pushed them further to south. Besides the Indian and Iranian, other branches of Aryans moved towards to West Asia and Europe. The Indian and Iranian Aryans were very close to each other with regard to language and religious beliefs.

A religion evolves from primitive beliefs. It evolves as language and civilization evolve. As the people separated and advanced culturally under different conditions, their religions also showed differences. In Indus culture, the principal deity seems to have been the Mother Goddess who is so prominent in all early cults; a three-headed deity seems to be prototype of Shiva. There is ample evidence of the cult of baetylus stones and phallic worship. Trees and animals also seem to have played their roles in the religion of these people. The culture of the Indus valley bears a general resemblance to that of Elam and Mesopotamia.[1] *The Rigveda* itself states that the religion was revealed. The vedic sages gave expression to the religious belief of the Indo-Aryans in the *richas* or *verses*. They received patronage of kings, like Divodasa and Sudas. The *richas* which they composed had royal backing behind them which gave them popularity and sanctity.

The seeds of the reforms which Jainism and Buddhism carried were already sown in the *Aranyak* and *Upnishads*, where distinction was made between *karmakanda* (ritual practices) and *jnanakanda* (knowledge practices). The protest against sacrifice and ritual (*karmakanda*) was made by Jainism and Buddhism.

Jesus Christ protested against the sacrifice of animals at the temple of Jerusalem and other malpractices prevailing there. Hazrat Muhammad propounded that Islam was not a new religion. It was a continuation of the old Hebrew religion of prophet Abraham, Moses and the other prophets of the Jews. His main protest was against the acceptance of the deities of the non-Jews and idols of whom had been installed in the temple in Mecca.

Approaches to Religion

The earliest attempt to define religion through the help of the etymological meaning of the word, was that of Cicero; the force of derivation appears to drive him to the conclusion that religion is the worship of gods. He divided the word into two parts, re and legere, meaning 'to take up, consider, ponder', i.e., having care for the God. Max Muller took it as the correct etymology and said that in its first conception the word meant respect, care, and reverence. The other derivation was supported by Servius, Lactantius, and others, who derived it from re-ligare, meaning 'bind to', i.e., forging a link between mankind and the gods.[2]

Spinoza says that the test of religious dogmas consists in their capacity to induce men to lead pious lives,[3] whereas Kant declares that 'religion is morality', i.e., according to him 'looking upon all moral duties as divine commands, constitutes religion'.[4] Fichte defines religion as knowledge[5] and Hegel, in opposition to Schleiermacher, defines it as freedom.[6] These are purely idealistic definitions of religion, what it ought to be in the views of these philosophers, rather than what it actually was when it conjugated.

According to Sir James Frazer, belief and worship are equally essential. By religion Frazer means a proposition or conciliation of powers superior to man which are believed to direct or control the course of nature to human life.[7] By 'power' he means 'conscious agents'.On the other hand, Professor Allen Menzies, by defining religion as "worship of unseen powers from a sense of need"[8], appears to give the first place to worship, perhaps thinking that there can be no worship without belief.

Professor Jastrow's approach is a combination of those of Frazer and Menzies. To him, religion comprises of three elements:

(a) The natural recognition of the Power or Powers beyond our control;

(b) The feeling of dependence upon the Power or Powers; and

(c) Entering into relation with the Power or Powers.

Amalgamating these elements into a single preposition, he defines religion as the natural belief in the power or powers beyond our control; and upon whom we feel ourselves dependent. The belief and feeling of dependence prompt to:

- organisation;
- specific acts; and
- regulation of conduct, with a view to establishing favourite relations between ourselves and the Power or Powers in question.[9]

Every religion is a social institution, followed by a group of persons who acknowledge their allegiance to that religion, explicitly or implicitly. It also determines the relation of the individual to the society of which he is a member. It is due to this social character of religion that ethics becomes closely associated with it.

Every religion has certain principles or doctrines, and certain beliefs which form a part of that religion. For example, Christianity and Islam believe in the existence of God and so every Christian or Muslim is expected and assumed to believe in God. Buddhism does not believe in the existence of God, but believes in the doctrine of retribution (*karma*); while Zoroastrianism believes in two spirits, viz. the spirit of goodness (Ahura Mazda or Ormazd) and the spirit of evil (Angra Mainyu or Ahriman). *Brahminism* believes in heaven (*svarga*), whereas Buddhism believes in 'extinction' (*nirvana*) and Islam in the day of judgement.

Every religion has some rules of conduct, which are based upon its principles, doctrines, and beliefs, and aim at furthering the happiness of individual in the present life or in the next or in both. This facet reveals the social character of religion as well because individual constitutes society. Buddha believed that life is a misery and attaining *Nirvana* means extinction of ego and with it of misery. He declared the eight-fold path, which leads to the extinction of misery or suffering. Hinduism believes that by knowledge, devotion, action, and love a man achieves salvation and by knowledge of *Brahma* one attains perfect life.

According to Zoroastrianism, it is the duty of man to uphold the forces of truth, while Christ taught to love and be merciful. Islam trusts on when a person says that he/she belongs to a particular religion and belongs to a community which professes that religion, holds those beliefs, and follows the rules of conduct which he/she believes to be conducive to his/her community's happiness.

The Sanskrit language has no word equivalent to what is understood by religion. Nor is there an English or even a European equivalent for the Sanskrit word *dharma*, which is the nearest term used to express the sense of the word religion. The word *dharma* is commonly described as '*dharayate iti dharmah*', that holds (together) or bears rules of morality, custom as well as regulation, which are supposed to form part of it.

The word *dharma* is not found in the *Rigveda*. There we have the word '*dharman*' which means 'bearer', 'preserver', 'maintainer', 'ordainer', 'support', 'foundation', or 'hold'. The above derivation is found even in the *Mahabharata*:

Dharanad dharman itya-huh dharma dharayate prajah
Yatsyad dharana samyuktam in dharma iti niscayah[10]

Origin of Religion

The various theories which venture to explain the origin of religion can be more or less correctly grouped under these answers.

(1) The first, the oldest and for a very long time the most commonly believed in, was the answer that man was created by some supreme being, at some definite period of time, possessing certain definite qualities, mental and physical, as a species distinct and differentiated from, and higher than, all the existing species. With this answer is associated the revelation theory of the

origin of religion, according to which a living God revealed to men a certain number of religious truths by supernatural phenomenon. Thus, a *prior* theory is found in almost all great religions of the world.

(2) The second answer is that man is a result of the process of evolution. As a consequence of revolution brought by this approach, the following theories were propounded:

(a) Fetishism by Charles de Brosses

(b) Animism by E.B. Tylor

(c) Ancestor-worship by Herbert Spencer

(d) Totemism by F.D. Jevons

(e) Frazer's theory of magic

(a) **Fetishism:** It is closely allied to and almost coexistent with animism. The term has been derived from the Portuguese word *feitico*, of uncertain meaning. It is often explained with meaning a 'charm' or 'something made by art' and is applied to any object large or small, natural or artificial and regarded as possessing consciousness, volition, and supernatural qualities, but especially magical power. According to E.B. Tylor:

> Fetishism is a doctrine of spirits embodied in or attached to certain material objects through which the spirits are believed to act and as a result to which each separate object being now treated as having personal consciousness and power is worshipped or ill-treated with reference to its past or present behavior to its votaries.[11]

Fetishism is indeed prevalent all over the world and its traces can be found in almost all religions, higher as well as lower; but as a theory, in explanation of the origin of religion, it is extremely unsatisfactory. Moreover, fetishism is much more magical in character than religious.

(b) **Animism:** The theory of animism is associated with the name of Tylor and means a belief that everything in nature has a soul or a spirit residing in it, which is distinct and different in quality from the physical object. The savage believes that the spirit can move away from the body and can perform acts like man himself. According to Tylor, animism arose as a result of two groups of biological problems present in the mind of the early man:

(1) What does make the difference between a living body and a dead one; what causes waking, sleep, trance, disease, and death?

(2) What are those human shapes which appear in dreams and visions?

This theory along with Tylor's great work where it has been propounded, attracted a great deal of attention. It certainly gives a correct explanation of many beliefs and practices of races both savage and civilized. It is also undeniable that it is a phenomenon of world-wide importance and constitutes an important factor in the making of religion. But, a careful study of animism as a form of human belief has also led authorities to the conclusion that animism as a theory of the origin of religion is inadequate.

(c) **Ancestor-worship or Ghost-worship:** This theory postulates that the worship of the dead ancestors forms the basis of all religion, and it is usually associated with the name of Herbert Spencer. According to him, anything which transcends the ordinary a savage thinks of as supernatural or divine, the remarkable man among the rest. The remarkable man may be a chief famed for strength or bravery; or powerful because he possesses some other quality to an extraordinary degree. For these powers of his, he is regarded with increased awe after his death and the propitiation.

(d) **Totemism:** Totemism as found in America and Australia, where it appears to be very highly developed, is a form of social organization composed of clans or tribes. These tribes are distinguished by the name of some species of animal or plant, or more rarely by some other natural phenomenon such as the Sun, rain, etc. The species or object which becomes the name of the clan is conceived as mystically related to every individual of the clan to whom the totem is considered as helpful. Thus, it becomes a subject of religious or quasi-religious emotion. The members of the clan, except in certain cases, as of ceremonial and self-defence, are forbidden to injure or kill it, or if an eatable to eat it. The members of the whole clan which has totem in common, regard themselves of one blood, as descendants from the same totem which is claimed as the common ancestor.

At present many anthropologists take the view that both magic and religion have a common root, and that they existed side by side in the most primitive times.[12] Thus, Marett holds 'that magic and religion are differentiated out from a common plasm of crude beliefs about the awful and occult'.[13] The mutual hostility of religion and magic, where it exists, is, in truth, the result of a later development.

It is clear from the above discussion that all the theories except that of Frazer are partially true. Neither fetishism, nor animism, ancestor-worship, and totemism can explain the whole complex structure of religion. They are important features of religious belief, but each of them is only a part and not the whole of religion.

Man is a product of both creation and evolution. This theory can be associated with the composite theory of the origin of religion, first systematically formulated by L.H. Jordan in his paper "Comparative Religion: Its Genesis and Growth", published in *Religious Studies*. Instead of maintaining with Max Muller that man is endowed with a special faculty in virtue of which he is compelled to seek after the divine, the representatives of the composite theory merely lay emphasis upon the fact that every man exhibits in himself the persistent operation of an impulse that turns his thoughts towards God. But, at the same time it is said that they perceive and admit that a man is a part of the nature, susceptible to its influences and governed by its laws.

All mankind must have passed through a savage condition of life before they were civilized. When the powers were conceived as coercible it led to magic; when they were conceived as uncoercible and their favour was sought by means of praising, praying, or offering gifts to them, it led to religion. In the *Rigveda,* we have a fire-god (*agni*), wind-god (*vayu*), a rain-god (*parjanya*), and a thunder-god (*Indra).*

Sir James Frazer, along with Professor Macdonell, is perfectly right in saying that the worship of nature is based on the assumption that natural phenomenon, whether animate or inanimate, are living personal beings analogous to man in their nature but far superior to him in power. In short, the worship of nature is based on the personification of nature.[14] Supporting the ideas of prayer and sacrifice to have derived from magical practices, which one assumed on the evidence of the beliefs and practices of the existing savage races to be of antiquity and very prevalent in primitive times, we would expect to find the very first prayers and sacrifices entirely of magical characters, but gradually growing more and more religious as time advanced. It is a well known fact that the vedic Indians, Iranians, as well as Greeks and Romans of historic times offered sacrifices in fire kindled on an altar, believing that through the smoke or the flame of it the gifts were carried to the gods. Taylor has expressed, "as prayer is a request made to a deity as if he were a man, so sacrifice is a gift made to a deity as if he were a man".[15]

It is quite certain that there were no temples and images in the Indo-European times as there were none even in the period of the *Rigveda*. The Indo-Iranian prayer may have been something like the following:

> O thou Ahurian one! grant me an offering manly and legitimate, who may promote my house, my village, my tribe and province and the authority thereof.... May'st thou hear our sacrificial chants... The good waters give to him who sacrifices, both spendour and glory, and health and vigour of the body and prominence of form...a long enduring life.

The prayer is addressed to Ahurian—water to flourish house, village, tribe, and province; water for enriching life with splendour, glory, health, and energy.

The *Rigveda* is the *veda* of hymns and prayers addressed to the natural powers such as the sky, earth, dawn, waters, etc. as gods; and they were meant for loud recitation. The *Samaveda* is the *veda* of chants and consists of hymns, mostly borrowed from the *Rigveda*, which are set of music and one meant to be sung by singers during the performance of the soma sacrifice. The *Yajurveda* is the *veda* of 'sacrificial prayers' and besides a great many hymns, borrowed from the *Rigveda,* it also contains original prose formulas. The *Atharvaveda* is a collection of quite a miscellaneous character. It contains, on one hand, several hymns borrowed from the *Rigveda* and especially the tenth book of the collection, and on the other, various magical spells and incantations directed against hostile agencies such as illness, demons, and enemies of man in general and on the whole this latter element of witchcraft and sorcery predominates.

The *Upanishads* are philosophical treatises in the form of dialogues, being the attempts of the early Indians at a systematic treatment of metaphysical problems. The third and the last stage of *Vedic* literature consists of *Sutras* or books which give a systematic and connected account of the *Vedic* ritual on the one hand and customary law on the other. Respect for global family is religion in essence and it is for upliftment of self and happiness to others.

The conflict is between faiths and the faiths, which were always there in the pre-Christian world, became intensified after the birth of Christianity in the form of constant intolerance, violence, and war between Christian and non-Christians, culminating in the long and bloody crusades in the Middle Age. After the reformation in the sixteenth-century, between the various denominations of Christianity itself, it culminated in the devastating Thirty-years' War between Catholics and Protestants in the next century.

Science and Religion

The conflicts between science and reason, on the one side, and religion and faith, on the other, have become prominent during the last four hundred years. The West holds that reason, which is the lifeblood of science, is the death knell of religion. That is how religions developed in the West, and its science also treated religion as outside the pale of reason. But, in recent decades, the Western people themselves are not happy over this conflict, and are in search of a new approach and a new reconciliation. Man in this technocratic civilization is feeling inwardly impoverished and empty in an environment of wealth, power, and pleasure; he is full of tension and sorrow, and doubt and uncertainly. Social distortions are on rise because man is not inwardly satisfied; he is smitten with ennui and boredom arising from the limitations of his sense bound world.

Today there is a paradigm shift in understanding, valuing, and knowing our world. Human culture, religion, spirituality, and nature were the crucial factors governing the mode of life but since the seventeenth-century, discoveries and inventions had brought the changes in human perception. Galileo's astronomical view about the motion of the Sun and the Earth, discoveries of Hydrogen and Oxygen by Cavendish and Priestley respectively, Theory of Evolution in *Origin of Species* (1859) by Charles Darwin, Socio-Economic Theory in *Das Capital* by Karl Marx, analysis of psyche, analysis of dream by Sigmond Freud, analysis of collective consciousness and myth by Carl Jung, the philosophical findings by Nietzsche and Sartre, Global Economics (Liberalisation, Privatisation, Globalisation), researches in Genetics, Nuclear Science, Energy fields, and Grand Unification of Forces (GUF) in Quantum Mechanics, had changed our approach to life and the world.

The end of the nineteenth-century and the middle of the twentieth-century saw the eclipse of religion in the West. But, there was an uneasy feeling in the minds and hearts of the thinkers, such as Emerson, Thoreau, Romain Rolland, Max Muller, and Albert Einstein that something of deep value to man and his civilization had been overthrown, and they attempted reassessment of the meaning and scope of religion with a view of making it in accord with the spirit and temper of science.

Science is a verified knowledge. Objective and precision, both as to thought and its verbal formulation, are two important characteristics of scientific method. In his lecture on 'Religion and Science', Vivekananda expounded:

> Experience is the only source of knowledge. In the world, religion is the only science where there is no surety, because it is not taught as a science of experience. This should not be. There is always, however, a small group of men who teach religion from experience. They are called mystics, and these mystics in every religion

> speak the same tongue and teach the same truth. This is the real science of religion. As mathematics in every part of the world does not differ, so the mystics do not differ. They are all similarly constituted and similarly situated. Their experience is the same; and this become law...
>
> 'Religion deals with the truths of the metaphysical world, just as chemistry and the other natural sciences deal with the truths of the physical world. The book one must read to learn chemistry is the book of nature. The book from which to learn religion is your own mind and heart.[16]

There are two areas in which man lives and functions—one, the external world and the other, the internal. The exploration of one alone does not investigate the whole range of experience and something lies beyond one discipline. When religion refuses to take the help of reason it weakens itself. Indian religions' thoughts emphasise upon *sadhana*, experiment, as the dynamics of religion; they have turned to *jijnasa,* or inquiry, for the formulation of their views.

When we go deeper into the nature and scope of science, its limitations become apparent. With the invention of microscope, a man came to know that besides the organisms visible to naked eyes, there are also bacterias and viruses. In the twentieth-century, with researches in radioactivity and spectroscopy, the nature of nucleus of the atom was investigated. It has been realised that there is a severe limitation placed on our knowledge regarding the truth of external world. Science is dealing with the phenomenon revealed by the sense or by approaches helpful to sense. These senses reveal little, and what they reveal only tells us that there are realities behind the sense world, determining it and controlling it. Man reveals dimensions that cannot be reduced to merely physical or merely material. There is transcendental, which cannot be reduced to material. If science is to progress, it has to take cognisance of this aspect, and also of the mystical facet of human life besides the exploration of the unknown reality of external world. This is a vast field of study—the terrain of man's self-awareness, elevation of consciousness, sublime consciousness, self-elevation, self-realisation, and welfare of the world.

Upanishads discover the finite man as the outer crust of infinite and immortal man within. If a man does not acquire the strength of spirituality from within, he will have to depend more and more on the external sources for stabilising himself.

In a lecture on 'The Evolutionary Vision', delivered in 1959 at the closing session of the Chicago University Symposium on 'Evolution after Darwin', held to commemorate the centenary of the publication of Darwin's *On The Origin of Species*, the noted biologist, Sir Julian Huxley, gave a spiritual orientation to the evolutionary process:

> Man's evolution is not biological but psycho-social; it operates by the mechanism of cultural tradition, which involves the cumulative self-reproduction and self-variation of mental activities and their products. Accordingly, major steps in the human phase of evolution are achieved breakthroughs to new dominant patterns of mental organisation of knowledge, ideas, and beliefs—ideological instead of physiological or biological organistaion...
>
> All dominant thought organisations concerned with the ultimate, as well as with the immediate, problems of existence or, I should rather say, with the most ultimate problems that the thought of the time is capable of formulating or even envisaging. They are all concerned with giving some interpretation of man, of the world which he is to live in, and of his place and role in that world—in other words, some comprehensive picture of human destiny and significance.[17]

To him, man's evolution is not only biochemical but also pyschosocial which leads man to reflect on the human existence in the world and its role and purpose.

Firstly, discovery of path leading to the processing of raw experience into knowledge, of knowledge into power, and power into control and manipulation of the environment constituted of the not self-aspect of experience. Secondly, a faint awareness of the reality of himself as the subject, as the self, behind the fleeting images in his mind, and the discovery of the road leading inward to the total comprehension of this new dimension of reality result in the increasing liberation of moral, aesthetic, and spiritual values in his life, action, and behaviour. Swami Ranganathananda asserts that in a moral or an ethical man, a man with culture and mind expands and moves beyond the limitations of physical consciousness and enters into other psyches of the social *milieu*. This is the outcome of psychosocial evolution to which the service of religion calls ethical awareness and social consciousness.[18]

The disparity between man's knowledge of self and control over inner nature and inner exploration, on the one hand, and man's knowledge and control over the external nature and outer exploration, on the other; and between moral efficiency and technical efficiency, confronting with the most serious problems of evolution has so far seriously posed a danger for the human civilization. If neglected and unsolved, this problem may destroy culture and civilization.

The only solution lies in the deepening and strengthening of inner exploration in moral and spiritual awareness. Biological evolution achieved a measure of this in the life of earliest man in his rudimentary knowledge of his own self. Social evolution, guided by human intelligence, advanced it still further, by which a physical and organic self separated from all other selves—a social self and a moral self. Referring to dire need to rise from knowledge to wisdom, Bertrand Russell states:

> We are in the middle of a race between human skill as to means and human folly as to ends. Given sufficient folly as to ends, every increase in the skill required to achieve them is to the bad. The human race has survived hitherto owing to ignorance and incompetence; but given knowledge and competence combined with folly, there can be no certainty of survival. Knowledge is power, but it is power for evil just as much as for good. It follows that, unless men increase in wisdom as in knowledge, increase of knowledge will be increase of sorrow.[19]

In dynamism of human evolution, from biological evolution to psychosocial evolution, a man must rise from egocentric to ego-transcendence and from knowledge to wisdom.

A religiously enlightened person is liberated from his selfish desires and preoccupied with thoughts, feelings, and aspirations to which he clings because of super-personal value. Religious person is a devout in the sense that he has no doubt of the significance and loftiness of those super-personal objects and goals which neither require nor are capable of rational formulation. From this prospective, conflict between religion and science appears impossible. Albert Einstein has analysed the terrains of science and religion as:

> For science can only ascertain what is, but not what should be, and outside of its domain value judgments of all kinds remain necessary. Religion, on the other hand, deals only with evaluations of human thought and action: it cannot justifiably speak of facts and relationships between facts.[20]

Science analyses and interprets facts and relationship between facts; and religion focuses on values outside the domain of science.

A conflict arises when a religious community insists on the absolute truthfulness of all statements recorded in the *Bible*. This means interference of religion into the terrain of science and this is where the struggle of the Church against the doctrines of Galileo and Darwin belongs. On the other side, representatives of science have often made an attempt to arrive at fundamental judgments with respect to values and ends on the basis of scientific method. These conflicts have sprung from fatal errors. Albert Einstein asserted:

> But science can only be created by those who are thoroughly imbued with the aspiration toward truth and understanding. This source of feeling, however, springs from the sphere of religion. To this there also belongs the faith in the possibility that the regulations valid for the world of existence are rational, that is, comprehensible to reason. I cannot conceive of genuine

> scientist without that profound faith. The situation may be expressed by an image: science without religion is lame, religion without science is blind.[21]

To him, the conflict between science and religion cannot exist but the practical reality in the context of historical religions differs. He viewed, "Though I have asserted above that in truth a legitimate conflict between religion and science cannot exist, I must nevertheless qualify this assertion once again on an essential point, with reference to the actual content of historical religions."[22]

This assertion has to do with the concept of God. During the youthful phase of mankind's spiritual evolution, human fantasy created gods in man's own image, who, by their will, were supposed to determine or influence the phenomenal world. Man sought to change the dispositions of these gods in his favour by means of magic and prayer. The idea of God in the religions taught at present is a sublimation of that old concept of the gods. Its anthropomorphic character is shown and men appeal to the Divine Being in prayers and plead for the fulfillment of their wishes. The main source of the present day conflicts between religion and science lies in the concept of a personal God. It is the aim of science to establish general rules which determine the links of objects and events in time and space. In their struggle for the ethical good, teachers of religions must have the stature to give up the doctrine of a personal God, that is, to give up that source of fear and hope which in the past placed such power in the hands of priests. It is true that scientific results are entirely independent from religious or moral considerations but those individuals with creative achievements of science were imbued with truly religious convictions that this universe of ours is something perfect and comprehensible to rational striving for knowledge. He earnestly insisted on the ethical values in the technocratic civilizations:

> I believe, indeed, that overemphasis on the purely intellectual attitude, often directed solely to the practical and factual, in our education, has led directly to the impairment of ethical values. I am not thinking so much of the dangers with which technical progress has directly

> confronted mankind, as of the shifting of mutual human considerations by a "matter-of-fact" habit of thought which has come to lie like a killing frost upon human relations.
>
> Fulfillment on the moral and aesthetic side is a goal which lies closer to the preoccupations of art than it does to those of science. Of course, understanding of our fellow-beings is important. But this understanding becomes fruitful only when it is sustained by sympathetic feeling in joy and in sorrow. In this sense, religion forms an important part of education, where it receives far too little consideration, and that little not sufficiently systematic.
>
> The frightful dilemma of the political world situation has much to do with this sin of omission on the part of our civilization. Without "ethical culture" there is no salvation for humanity.[23]

Intellectual attitude is to be coupled with ethical values and without ethical culture human civilization has no hope and salvation.

Science prolongs life and religion deepens it. For the production of food, clothing, and shelter, man has to resort to science. But, for the creation of love, kindness, compassion, dedication, peace, and joy, a man has to resort to science of inner life which is religion. Meditation is a unique technique of the science of spirituality. The challenge to human search for knowledge and truth comes not only from external physical nature but also from something deep within man himself. Both these worlds are to be investigated; reason and faith are to be used in such investigation. We need to have faith in ourselves, in other human beings, and in the ultimate meaningfulness of the universe. In the science of religion, such investigation is done by life itself, and not by mere intellectual cognition. But, this faith (*sraddha*) is different from the usual idea of faith as mere static belief, swallowing everything that is said by any authority without subjecting to evidential test. Man can see and experience the known world with senses but he cannot see or know the unknown world, and yet he experiences that it is there. This basic positive attitude to the unknown dimension of reality is called *sraddha*. *Sraddha* in religion is the basic reverential attitude that the unknown, the unseen, and the imperishable exist behind the known, the seen, and the perishable. Reality as revealed by five senses is little, yet it is fascinating to human mind. When we come to religion, we get the intimation that these are profound truths hidden beyond the perishable and behind the psycho-physical organism and the fleeting ego.

The structural construction in *Gramgeeta* has scientific approach which encompasses consequence, reason, remedy, and subsequently logical consistency. Tukadoji's presentation is in discourse form between the narrator (the writer) and audiences, in which he vehemently resists superstitions in society and insists on human efforts; and in this context, his stance is pragmatic. He has practiced the cleanliness drive for rural hygiene and inculcated environmental awareness among masses. He expounds that research aptitude is to be developed in youth for welfare of the society for global competence.

> Fascination of youth in other nations, relentless new research much;
> Spell of it to be experienced by educated village youth. ||56||[24]

Besides the requisite of research temper in masses he is conscious of the progress in science and technology.

> Flew to the Mars; climbed Himalaya's peak completely;
> Searched fire-weapons, nuclear-weapons, massive hydrogen too. ||112||
>
> Listen from crores of miles, singing-lecture of each other;
> Bringing within reach the world made home to inhabit. ||113||
>
> (Canto XXXV, 'Effort Influence')

Though the advancements in science and technology are important for the material evolution in human society, Tukadoji reflects that knowledge is to be muted with wisdom and ethical values. Religion expands from individual to family, family to village, village to nation, and nation to world for peace.

Individual religion, family religion, social religion, rural religion;
Empowers national religion, for road of success. ||16||
Individual to nourish family, family to society;
Village to nation, nation to world for people. ||17||
(Canto II, 'Theological Study')

The basis tenets of religion are sacrifice, non-violence, truth, and restrain. Religious vision is to make entire world happy and benefactor, and it is to be nourished in every villagers.

Nation, an element of world, village of nation;
Man, foundation of village, he to be religious. ||22||
Individual religion is to know all, family religion to behave;
Rural religion is to follow with national spirit. ||23||
(Canto II, 'Study of Religion')

Village beings an element of nation and nation of world. It is to be progressed materially and spiritually. Individual religion here means practice of an individual, infused with virtues. Religion forms *sanskar* to lift up others and advocates four *ashrams—Brahmacharya-ashrama* (Celibacy), *grihasthashrama*, *vanaprasthashrama* (seclusion in forest), and *sanyasashrama* (renunciation). Religion is humanity and it relates to justice which remains same to anyone for ever.

Religion is humanity, relies humanity one on justice;
Remains justice, same to anyone for ever. ||22||
(Canto XXIX, 'Service of Downtrodden')

Krishna says, "समं हि ब्रम्ह" and, thus, equality is divine religion.

To treat equal man by man, to elevate others;
To infuse joy in society, real service of religion it is. ||98||
(Canto XXIX)

The real service of religion is to elevate others and to infuse joy and peace in society. Mahatma Gandhi, Mahatma Phule, and Babasaheb Ambedkar understood the need to uplift downtrodden, that is, those who are deprived of rights. Human idols are cracked, and in their service, devotion is to God. Sajan (butcher), Ravidas (cobbler), Dadu (weaver), Gora (potter), Banka (Mahar), and Kanhopatra came from peripheral strata of the society and served the humanity. Coordination of all religions through mass prayer is essential for the school of people reform. Though religions are many, they have single kernel. It is a narrow viewpoint that God of Hinduism is for Hindus; of Islam for Muslim, and of Christianity for Christians. God is trust in sublimity, conception of World guardian. Though the names, Allah, God, Drahat, Ahura Mazda, Nirvana, and Shiva are different, but Supreme *Gurudeo* is one. As P.B. Shelley says, "One remains, many change".

> The One remains, the many change and pass;
> Heaven's light forever shines, Earth's shadows fly;
> Life, like a dome of many-coloured glass;
> Stains the white radiance of Eternity.
>
> (LII, 'Adonais', 460-61)

The eternal spirit remains while many beings came into this world and went. The poet stresses the eternal nature of One and transient nature of temporal. Tukadoji asks the questions in Canto XXVIII, 'Prayer and World Religion', if the core motto is one, why to differentiate on the tenets of sects, religion, devotion, and kinds. The poet highlights misconception about religion:

> Hindu-Muslim not in religion; Parsi-Christian not in religion;
> At core when looked into no Sikh-Jain in religion. ||31||
> People's amnesia for the crux of religion; turned Hindu, Muslim;
> Lost they humanity their located at core. ||32||
> Wore masks of nation, language; changed custom due to weather;
> To exterior religion they call, less knowledgeable. ||33||
>
> (Canto XXVIII, 'Prayer and World Religion')

Basically there are no differences in religions but man has created those differences. In all religions, unity and humanity are at core and with conscience it is to be understood. No religion permits an act which rebels against humanity. Hindu, Islam, Christian, Jain, Sikh, and Mahanubhava are the external names of religion. Human beings organised on the grounds of religions set rules, and because of attachment and entanglement of ego, the real motto of religion is kept aside. Politics enters in religion and chaos is created in all nations. Anger and hate have become the means of wish fulfillment and the revengeful minds have caused the outbreak of wars.

> Contentment of anger, hate, mean of wish fulfillment;
> So with revengeful mind outbreak of war, repression. ||73||
>
> This not thought of religion, use of power it is;
> Destruction of human beings, innocent, not acceptable to religion. ||74||

Destruction of human beings or blood shed in war is not acceptable to religion. The fundamentalist forces and aggressive attitude or blind adherence to religion culminate into communal riots; on the contrary, any religion, at core, has importance for human values, like peace, love, justice, non-violence, and sacrifice. It is not possible to end conflicts without love, and mass prayer is a practical mean to bring people together from all religions.

> Quarrel of religion-sect-nation, not possible to end without love;
> To attain that love, no level best than prayer. ||91||
>
> Principle of prayer in every religion; equality perpetual in good;
> Understanding importance of it, all to bring at one place. ||92||

In village to village, equality in religions makes the world happy, which attributes the honour of heaven to the earth. In the inaugural speech at the Parliament of the World's Religions for World Peace, Shimizu, Japan, on 23rd July, 1955, Tukadoji said:

> A true essence of religion is kept aside. People from Japan, Hong Kong, Burma, and India, who are advocators of the religions of love; whose hearts are filled with belief in God; who earnestly wait for the door of heart to open, seem same to me. But, they can't

> understand each other. They breath the same air, the same light, and live on the same earth, but they fight for individualism and nationalism. They are ignorant of the real principle of religion, and magnanimity of the heart of the great souls. As a consequence we see the prevalance of dissatisfaction, strife, and struggle in the world. Every religion is created for upliftment of man. Does sea water differentiate between man and man? Do the sunlight or the moonlight discriminate?[25]

People combat for individualism and nationalism because they are ignorant of the real principle of religion. Religion is created for upliftment of man and doesn't differentiate between man and man.

> Narrow mindedness in our heart sprouts and blossoms in the form of ignorance and selfishness. Responsible person in the families, in the towns, and nations have abandoned their duties towards their families, towns, and nations; and as a result, we have numerous quarrels and biting worries. How can they know religion wearing the garb of politics? Religion is basically to create peaceful world and such creation is possible by those who know cosmic nature of God, who tell how man has to behave with man. God's voice has origin in pure man's heart.[26]

Tukadoji observes discordancy between religion and politics. The prime motto of religion is to create peaceful world, and it is possible by knowing cosmic nature of God.

> Only blessed one can give a message of harmony and peace. Pure mind can't divert religion for selfish means. The sword, the atom-bombs will not render any solution to this explosive situation. Rapid development in science and technology has brought people from the different corners of nations close and near. In such an atmosphere helping hand to each other will have to be proved the best possible access for establishing peace in the world. I heartly pray to save this world from destructive tendencies and shower the world with

> understanding and cooperation to create the kingdom of peace, by propogating this religion of truth and love.[27]

He discerns that religion doesn't concern with selfish means. To wipe out destructive tendencies, understanding and cooperation are imperative by nourishing the religion of love and peace. He exhorted in his speech on 24th July, 1955:

> An individual who thinks of others can have such constructive vision. Man's cordial objective is to protect the harmonious relationship in the world for his own self. We have to adopt humanitarian attitude to feel that mankind is one to create the world family. We have to follow the ways of non-violence and truth to keep away the barriers which creep in the way of peace. If man is cruel and not kind, can we call him 'man'? We will have to say him 'devil' who does not understand others. We must surrender before saints who insist on the value of brotherhood.[28]

Saint trusts in humanitarian attitude, non-violence and truth, and equality and unity to create world family. The founder of Ananai-kyo, a religious organization, St. Yonosuke Nakano, at the Second World's Religions Conference, Shimizu, Japan expressed:

> In the world, verbal intellectuals are many but the persons with spiritual power and self-motive are rare. In *Rashtrasant,* we experienced the vision of inclusive investigative thought based on religious foundation. His innocent attitude, brotherly behaviour, and high philosophy witness his forefront position in India.[29]

To Younosu-kyo, Tukadoji's vision has cosmic dimension, which is accentuated by the Valedictory discourse at the World's Religions Conference in Tokoyo, on 5th August, 1955, which discerns that religion can establish peace in the world by elevating humanity. The religion's true road imbibes love and co-operation, and to follow religion means to love human beings in the world, and to resist anger and greed. He is conscious that "...people are fearing for an ensuing world war, however the avenue to dispel it is resurgence of love among them."

At the World's Parliament of Religions, Chicago, on 11th September, 1893, Swami Vivekananda explicitly stated:

> We believe not only in universal toleration, but we accept all religions as true. I am proud to belong to a nation which has sheltered the persecuted and the refugees of all religions and all nations of the earth... Sectarianism, bigotry, and its horrible descendant, fanaticism, have long possessed this beautiful earth. They have filled the earth with violence, drenched it often and often with human blood, destroyed civilization, and sent whole nations to despair. Had it not been for these horrible demons, human society would be far more advanced than it is now.[30]

Sectarianism and fanaticism had fragmented human society and they caused violence and bloodshed. To curb it, Vivekananda accepted not only universal tolerance but also all religions as true. At the final session of the World's Parliament of Religion on 27th September, 1893, he harped on religion's unity and yet retention of individuality.

Much has been said of the common ground of religious unity. But, if anyone here hopes that this unity will come by the triumph of any one of the religions and the destruction of other, to him, Vivekananda says, "Brother, yours is an impossible hope. Do I wish that the Christian would become Hindu? God forbid. Do I wish that the Hindu or Buddhist would become Christian? God Forbid".

> The seed is put in the ground, and earth and air and water are placed around it. Does the seed become the earth, or the air, or the water? No. It becomes a plant. It develops after the law of its own growth, assimilates the air, the earth, and the water, converts them into plant substance, and grows into a plant.
>
> Similar is the case with religion. The Christian is not to become a Hindu or a Buddhist, nor a Hindu or a Buddhist to become a Christian. But each must assimilate the spirit of others and yet preserve his

> individuality and grow according to his own law of growth.
>
> If the Parliament of Religions has shown anything to the world, it is this: It has proved to the world that holiness, purity, and charity are not the exclusive possessions of any church in the world, and that every system has produced men and women of the most exalted character. In the face of this evidence, if anybody dreams of the exclusive survival of his own religion and the destruction of the others, I pity him from the bottom of my heart, and point out to him that upon the banner of every religion will soon be written in spite of resistance: "Help and not fight", "Assimilation and not Destruction", "Harmony and Peace and not Dissension".[31]

In spite of resistance, he insists on cooperation, assimilation, harmony, and peace for the survival of every religion. Sarvepalli Radhakrishnan, in his speech at Rishikesh on 12th August, 1954, stressed:

> The goal of religion is the opening of a new realm of consciousness. When this consciousness arises, we see that the individual parts of the universe derive their significance from the central unity of spirit. This renewal of consciousness ... is the goal of the religious quest.[32]

To him, the goal of the religious quest is the renewal of consciousness which experiences the presence of all pervading spirit in the universe. As air can't be seen, it can be experienced; similarly, spirituality, ideal, faith, and sensitivity can't be seen, their repercussions can be seen. The repercussions of implementation of spirituality in life is seen in implemention of ideal in life. Spiritualism in one sense is called as the highest state of consciousness. E. Kirk, a delegate from Britain for the World's Parliament of Religion, exhorted that the verdicts of this great person are able to provide the plan for world peace and spiritual vision.[33] His knowledge is not verbal, but self-inspiring. For this, the religious leaders of all nations have to operate the thoughts of this Indian saint.

Our sages were the scientists of consciousness. They made their own body the laboratory to conduct experimentation and devised disciplines adopting which human beings can develop super-mental powers. Religion is explained on three levels—Metaphysics, ethics, and spirituality. Spiritual power, all pervading spirit in the world, infuses life in religion. Spiritual presence is the base of religion, and it is perpetual. But, now religion has become ritual centred and not spirit centred. Scientific spirituality is the need of time, and it is the religion of twenty-first century. Science and religion point at the different facets of reality.

Science	Religion
Everything is made up of matter and can be demonstrated through experiments.	Spirit is reality and can be experienced by consciousness.
Science is one of the means of pursing knowledge.	By transcending the limitations of senses, true knowledge is experienced.
Denies the existence of supernatural, superphysical, and extra sensory.	Life is manifestation of sublime consciousness.
Life or Being is manifestation of biochemical and biophysical matters.	Human life has definite purpose, self-realisation, self-elevation, and welfare of the world.

Thus, science concerns with biochemical, biophysical, and cosmic matters whereas religion focusses upon spirit, self-realisation, self-elevation, and welfare of world.

The Perception of God

Like art, religion has been an attempt to find meaning and value in life, despite the suffering that flesh is heir to. Through the history, men and women have experienced a dimension of the spirit that seems to transcend the mundane world. Indeed, it is an arresting characteristic. All the major religions, however, would agree that it is impossible to describe this transcendence in normal conceptual language. Despite the secular tenor of much western society, the experience of God still affects the lives of millions of people. Recent surveys have shown that ninety-nine percent of Americans say that they believe in God, and the word, God has shaped the history of human culture. Things come and go in meaningless flux. Nothing has permanent significance. Religion starts with the perception that something is wrong.

Human sacrifice was common in the pagan world and it was cruel. The first child was often believed to be offering of God. Abraham decided to trust the God. Abraham and Isaac set off on a three-days journey to the Mount Moriah, which would later be the site for the Temple in Jerusalem. It was not until the very last moment, when Abraham actually had the knife in his hand and God relented and told him that it had been a test. Yet, to modern ears, that is horrible story because it depicts God as a despotic and capricious sadist. That is a brutal, partial, and murderous God; a God of war who would be known as Jehovah Sabaoth. The prophets of Israel developed their own traditions to meet the changing conditions with the result that Yahweh eventually became the only God. The Jews had not yet begun to philosophise but during the fourth-century they came under the influence of Greek rationalism. Some Greeks came to know the God of Israel and decided to worship Yahweh (or Iao as they called him) alongside Zeus and Dionysus. But, over the centuries Yahweh had became an idea that could help people to cultivate a compassion and respect for their fellow human beings.

Jews expected the Messiah, the anointed one, to be a descendant of King David who, as king and spiritual leader, had founded the first independent Jewish Kingdom in Jerusalem. The Psalms sometimes called David or the Messiah 'the Son of God' but was simply expressing the intimacy with Yahweh.

Mark's Gospel, the earliest and the most reliable, presents Jesus as a perfectly normal man with a family that included brothers and sisters. John, the Baptist, had recognised Jesus as the Messiah. After leaving his corporeal frame, Jesus being a God in human form was not finalised until the fourth-century. The development of Christian belief was a gradual and complex process. Jesus himself certainly never claimed to be a God. At his baptism he had been called the Son of God. But, that was simply a confirmation that he was the beloved Messiah.

The Gospels

The Gospels tell us that God had given Jesus certain divine 'powers', which enabled him to perform the God like tasks of healing the sick and forgiving sins. People also noted that Jesus had never claimed that these divine 'powers' were confined to him alone. Again and again, Jesus had promised his disciples that if they had 'faith' they would enjoy these 'powers' too, by cultivating inner attitude of surrender and openness to God. This type of incarnational devotion had been fairly constant theme in the history of religion. In both Buddhism and Hinduism, there had been a surge of devotion to exalted beings, such as the Buddha himself or to Hindu Gods which had appeared in human form. This kind of personal devotion known as *bhakti* seemed to be a perennial human yearning for humanised religion. The development of *bhakti* answered a deep rooted need in human culture for same kind of personal relationship with the ultimate. St. Paul, the earliest Christian writer who created the religion that we know as Christianity, believed that Jesus had replaced the Torah as God's principal revelation of himself to the world. He certainly believed that Jesus had been the Messiah and the word 'Christ' was a translation of the Jewish Massiach; the Anointed one. The early Christians felt that Jesus was in some mysterious way still alive and the 'powers' that he had possessed, were then embodied in him, as he had promised. In his letter, he tells his converts that they must have the same self-sacrificing attitude as Jesus.

The emperor Constantine became a Christian himself after the battle of Milvian Bridge in 312 A.D. and legalised Christianity the following year. Even though paganism flourished for another two centuries, Christianity became the state religion of the empire and began to attract new converts who made their way into the Church. Christianity would have not succeeded without the support of the Roman empire.

Arins of Alexandria had issued a challenge, how could Jesus Christ have been God in the same way as God, the Father?

Jesus had specifically said that the Father was greater than him. The Cappadocians had taken the stance that Athanasius had used in his dispute with Arins; God has a single essence (*ousia*) which remained incomprehensible to us but three expression (*hypostates*). Father, Son, and Spirit should not be identified with God himself. They are the only terms that we use to speak of the *energiai* by which he has had himself known. The Trinity, therefore, should not be seen as a literal fact but as a paradigm that corresponds to real facts in the hidden life of God.[34]

The Trinity reminded Christians that the reality that we called 'God' could not be grasped by the human intellect. The idea of a personal God or a personalised Absolute has been important in the history of God. But, the paradigm or symbol of Trinity suggests that personalism must be transcended and that it is not enough to imagine God as man, behaving and reacting in much the same way as we ourselves.

The doctrines of the incarnation can be seen as another attempt to neutralise the danger of idolatry. Once 'God' is seen as wholly other reality, 'out there', he can easily become a mere idol and a projection which enables human beings to externalise and worship their prejudice and desires. By making Jesus, the incarnation, Christian would adopt an exclusive notion of religious truth that Jesus was the first and the last word of God on the human race.

Islam

A prophet arose in Arabia during the seventh century who claimed to have received a direct revelation from their God and to have bought a new scripture to his people. The new version of monotheism, which eventually became known as 'Islam', spread with astounding rapidity throughout the middle east and North Africa. Only two generations earlier, the Quraysh had lived a harsh nomadic life in the Arabian steppes, like other Bedouin tribes. During the last years of the sixth century, however they had become successful in trade and made Mecca, the most important settlement in Arabia. They were now rich and the old tribal values had been superseded by a rampant and ruthless capitalism. People felt disoriented and lost. Muhammad knew that the Quraysh were on dangerous course and needed to find an ideology that would help them to cope with their new condition. Muhammad was convinced that, unless the Quraysh learned to put another transcendent value at the center of their lives and overcome their egotism and greed, his tribe would tear itself apart morally and politically in strife. In the rest of Arabia the situation was bleak.

The Quraysh loved to make the ritual circumambulations around the shrine but when they put themselves and their material success into the center of their lives they had forgotten the meaning of these ancient rites of orientation. Consequently, Muhammad made his converts bow down in ritual prayer (*salat*) twice a day. This external gesture would help Muslims to cultivate the internal posture and reorient their lives.

In practical terms, Islam meant that Muslims had a duty to create a just equitable society where the poor and vulnerable are treated decently. The early moral message of the *Koran* is simple. It is wrong to stockpile wealth and build a private fortune, and good to share the wealth with society fairly by giving a regular proportion of one's wealth to the poor.[35]

Alms-giving (*zakat*) accompanied by prayer (*salat*) were two of the five essential pillars (*rukh*) or practices of Islam. Muhammad preached an ethic that we might call socialist as a consequence of his worship of one God. The *Koran* is meant to yield a sense of divine:

> [Know], [that] God is sublimely exalted, the Ultimate Sovereign (a/-Malik), the Ultimate Truth (a/-Hqq): and [knowing this], do not approach the *Koran* in haste, ere it has been revealed unto there in full, but [always] say: 'O my Sustainer, cause me to grow in knowledge.[36]

By approaching the *Koran* in the right, Muslims claim that they do experience a sense of transcendence of an ultimate reality and power that behind the transient and fleeting phenomena of the mundane world. The *Koran* sees God as the Absolute, who alone has true existence: "All that lives on the earth or in the heaven is bound to pass away but, forever will abide thy sustainer's self, full of majesty and glory."[37]

In the *Koran,* God is given ninety-nine names or attributes. These emphasise that he is 'greater', the source of all positive qualities that we find in the universe. Thus, the world only exists because 'He' is *al-Ghani* (rich and infinite); 'He' is the giver of life *(al-Muhyi)*, the knower of all things *(al-Alim)*, the producer of speech *(al-Kalimah)*; without 'Him', therefore there would not be life, knowledge, or speech. It is an assertion that only God has true existence and positive value.

Islam has two sects—sunnah and shiah—on the basis of interpretations and leadership. The shiah gradually evolved ideas that seemed even closer to Christian incarnation. Gradually, the Imams revered as *avatars* of the divine. Each one had been 'proof' (*hujjah*) of God's presence on earth and in some mysterious sense, made the divine incarnation in human form. As Christians had seen Jesus on the way, the truth and the height that would lead man to God, shiahs revered their Imams as the gateway *(bab)* to God, the road (*Sabil*) and the guide of each generation.

The Muslims who attempted to apply rational arguments to the *Koran* were known as *mutazilis*. Karen Armstrong viewed that like the shiahs, the *mutazilis*, declared that justice is the essence of God and 'He' cannot do wrong with anybody; 'He' cannot enjoy anything contrary to reason. Here they came into conflict with the traditionalists who argued that by making man the author and creator of his own fate, the *mutazilis* were insulting the omnipotence of God. They complained that the *mutazilis* were making God too rational and too like a man.[38]

Western Perspectives

In his *Critique of Pure Reason* (1781), Immanuel Kant argued that, in order to live a moral life, men and women needed a governor, who would reward virtue with happiness. In this perspective, God was simply tracked on to the ethical system as an afterthought. The centre of religion was no longer the mystery of God but man himself. God has become a strategy which enables us to function more efficiently and morally.

Hegel (1770–1831) had asserted that 'God' was not separate from mundane reality, an optional extra in a world of his own, but was inextricably bounded up with humanity. Like William

Blake, he expressed this insight dialectically, treating humanity and Spirit, finite and infinite, as two halves of a single truth which are mutually interdependent and involved in the same process of self-realisation. Instead of pacifying a distant deity by observing an alien, unwanted Law, Hegel had in effect declared that the divinity was a dimension of our humanity. Indeed, Hegel's view of the kenosis of the spirit, which empties itself to become immanent and incarnate in the world, has much in common with the incarnational theologies that have developed in all faiths.

Paul Tillich (1868–1965) was convinced that the personal God of traditional Western theism must go but he also believed that religion was necessary for humankind. A deep-rooted anxiety is part of the human condition; this is not neurotic, because it is ineradicable and no therapy can take it away. We constantly fear loss and the terror or extinction, as we watch our bodies gradually but inexorably decaying. Tillich agreed with Nietzsche that the personal God was a harmful idea and deserved to die.

Instead we should seek to find a 'God' above this personal God. There is nothing new about this. Ever since Biblical times, theists had been aware of the paradoxical nature of the God to which they prayed; personalised God was balanced by the essentially transpersonal divinity. Tillich preferred the definition of God as the ground of being.

Martin Heidegger (1899–1976) saw 'being' in rather the same way as Tillich, though he would have denied that it was 'God' in the Christian sense—it was distinct from particular beings and quite separate from the normal categories of thought. Some Christians have been inspired by Heidegger's work, even though its moral value is called into question by his association with the Nazi regime. *What is Metaphysics?*, his inaugural lecture at Freiburg, Heidegger developed a number of ideas that had already surfaced in the work of Plotinus, Denys, and Eriugena. Since 'being' is 'Wholly Other', it is in fact nothing—no thing, neither an object nor a particular being. Yet, it is what makes all other existent possible. The ancients had believed that nothing came from nothing but Heidegger reversed this maxim: *ex nihilo omne qua ens fit.* He ended his lecture by posing question to question asked by Leibniz: 'Why are there beings at all, rather than just nothing?' It is a question that evokes the shock of surprise and wonder that has been a constant in the human response to the world, why should anything exist at all? In his *Introduction to Metaphysics* (1953), Heidegger began by asking the same questions, "Why there essence; why is there anything at all, rather than nothing?"[39] Theology believed that it had the answer and traced everything back to something else, to God. But, his God was just another being rather than something that was wholly other.

The idea of personal God seems increasingly unacceptable at the present time for all kind of reasons—moral, intellectual, scientific, and spiritual. Feminists are also repelled by a personal deity who, because of 'his' gender, has been male since his tribal, pagan days. Yet, to talk about 'She'—other than ín a dialectical way—can be just limiting, since it confines the illimitable God to a purely human category.

The God of the mystics might seem to present a possible alternative. The mystics have long insisted that God is not an Other Being; they have claimed that 'He' does not really exist and that it is better to call 'Him' Nothing. This God is in tune with the atheistic mood of our secular society with its distrust of inadequate images of the absolute. Instead of seeing God as an Objective Fact, which can be demonstrated by means of scientific proof, mystics have claimed that God is a subjective experience, mysteriously experienced in the ground of being. This God is to be approached through the imagination and can be seen as a kind of art form, akin to the other great artistic symbols that have expressed the ineffable mystery, beauty, and value of life. Mystics have used music, dance, poetry, fiction, stories, painting, sculpture, and architecture to express the reality that goes beyond concepts. Like all art, however, mysticism requires intelligence, discipline, and self-criticism as a safeguard against indulgent emotionalism and projection. The God of the mystics could even satisfy the feminists, since both *sufis* and *kabbalists* have long tried to introduce a female element into the divine.

The Indo-European Phase

So far as the conception of God in the Indo-European period is concerned, we have five philological equations which bear upon it:

(1) SK. *deva*, Lat. *dues*, Lith, *diewas*, Ir. *dia*, O.N. *tivar*, Nom. Pl. celtic *devos* (in the Gallic proper name *Devognata*), derived from some such root as *div* or *dyu* 'to shine' and meaning 'the shining one', 'god'.

(2) SL. bogu, Old Persian *baga* 'god', Av. *bagha* 'god' SK *bhaga* 'god of fortune'.

(3) Av. *spenta*, Lith, *szventas*, 'Pure', 'holy'.

(4) SK. *yaj*, AV. Yaz, 'to reverse', thence 'to worship'.

(5) SK. sraddha, Lat credo, 'to believe'.

Firstly, the heavenly phenomenon had made a great impression upon and had attracted the attention of I.E.s. Secondly, these were thought to be beneficent and not inimical. Thirdly, the I.E.s regarded their powers with awe and reverence, as a result of which they wished to propitiate and please rather than coerce them into obedience. Fourthly, however much they might have been entangled with lower beliefs such as magic, fetishism, ancestor-worship, etc. I.E.s had at last taken a definite step in rising higher than these.

The various powers of nature were conceived as the guardians of the universal law and order, and their favour was sought through poetic praises and gifts. But, gradually the sacrifices were becoming more and more complicated and more gifts were coming to be offered more regularly. The class of poets composed the praises or the hymns and who offered the gifts on a 'carpet of herbage' probably already existed.

The Indo-Aryans possessing a genius for language soon developed an admirable phonetic system and a rich vocabulary. The singing of the praises of the 'heavenly ones' was considered to be an important part of the worship of the natural powers and, thus, the composition of religious poetry was cultivated as a sacred art.

Moreover, the Vedic literature clearly shows not so much the separation of magic and religion as their coming closer and closer together till at last, the one can hardly be distinguished from the other. The magical character of both the prayers and sacrifice, since the later part of the *Rigvedic* period, does not diminish but manifests clear signs of being on the increase. Macdonell, who shares the view of Oldenberg, himself states the position quite clearly:

> In the creative age of the *Rigveda* new prayers were produced for ritual purposes; but in the age of the later Vedas... prayer was nothing more than the mechanical application of ready-made formulas', and the adds, that the idea of the efficacy of prayer, even in the *Rigveda*, shows that 'magic is already beginning to encroach on the domain of religion. A similar tendency is observable in regard to the sacrifice which accompanied the prayers to the gods. The conception of the effect of sacrifice which prevails in the *Rigveda* is that the offering wins the favour of a God and induces him to fulfill the accompanying prayer....
>
> Even in the *Rigveda*, however, traces are already to be found of the notion that the sacrifice exercises compulsion not only over gods, but also over natural phenomena without requiring the co-operation of the gods. Here again we have the intrusion of magic into the domain of religion.[40]

He deciphers how magic began to intrude the domain of religion. Magic and witchcraft formed an essential part of religion; they had penetrated and become intimately blended with the holiest Vedic rites.

The Indo-Europeans: Their Home and Culture

On philological and other grounds it is commonly assumed that Indians, Iranians and Armenians of Asia, Slavs, Lithuanians, Greeks, Romans, Celts, and Germnas of Europe were at some distant age, about 3,000 to 2,500 years before Christ, originally one people, living common life and speaking a common language or more probably different dialects of essentially the same language. Professor G. Sergi thinks that it is an error to maintain that the Germans and the Scandinavians are Aryans; they are what he calls 'Eurafricans of the Nordic variety', and further:

(1) That the Aryans are of Asiatic origin; and

(2) That the two classic civilization, Greek and Latin, were not Aryan, but Mediterranean.

According to Prof. Sergi the Aryans were savages when they invaded Europe. They destroyed in part the superior civilization of the Neolithic population, and could not have created the Greco-Latin civilization.[41] Keith expresses the same opinion.[42] Among others, Max Muller and J. Muir supported the Asiatic origin of the Indo-Europeans. There are indeed many powerful arguments in favour of a European than an Asiatic home, but the view that it lies partly in both the continents appears to us to be more probable.

The Indo-European Conception of God, Vedic God, and Aftermath

In the Indo-European Religion, the Indo-European gods are: *dyeus*, *varuna*, the mother earth, the god of thunder, the sun, the moon, the dawn, the stars, the day and night, the *asvins*, the fire, the wind, the water, and the lightning.

These powers of nature, which we have now enumerated, i.e., the sky (*dyeus*), together with the phenomena appearing in it or coming from it, 'the heavenly ones' (*deivos*), is certainly the real kernel of the old Indo-European. The primitive Indo-Europeans thought was that these natural powers were great conscious agents possessing human characteristics such as will and desire, but being of superhuman power, capable of helping or hindering men in their lives. The instinctive craving of the mind, after simplification and unification of ideas, may be a psychological fact, and it may also be granted that the current opinion that animism is a very primitive form of belief, is correct.

It is a well known fact that the vedic Indians, Iranians, as well as Greeks and Romans of historic times offered sacrifices in the fire kindled on an altar, believing that through the smoke or the flame, gifts were carried to and reached the gods. It is quite certain that there were no temples and no images in the

Indo-European times as there were none even in the period of the *Rigveda*.

The poets of different families, at different times, going back at any rate to Indo-Iranian period, had been in the habit of composing poems addressed to the higher natural powers and phenomena as gods, and being supposed to be the products of an inspiration which was later believed to be divine. These poems continued among the members of the same family from generation to generation by an immemorial oral tradition.

The celestial vedic gods are *Dyaus* (heaven), *Varuna, Surya, Savitr, Mitra, Vishnu, Vivasvat, Pusan, Bhaga, Adityas, Aryaman, Amsa, Daksa, Usas,* and *Asvins*. The atmospheric vedic gods are *Indra, Maruts, Vayu, Vata, Rudra,* and *Parjanya;* and other atmospheric gods are *Apah, Trita Aptya, Ahibudhnya,* and *Ekapad*. Terrestrial gods are *Fire, Som,* and *Brhaspati;* and other terrestrial deities are *Prithvi* and rivers.

The immediate generations of the separated group of Indo-Aryans continued to compose poems in praise of the Nature—gods, which were meant to be sung with the *soma*-sacrifice. The need of these praises and sacrifices so far as they were the product of the feeling of dependence, fear, and reverence of the uncontrollable natural forces, began to decrease. On the other hand it was felt more deeply because they came in contact with the human foes, the *Dasyus*. This necessitated the innovations as the means of self-preservation, and this nature poetry was maintained in the late Indo-Iranian period. The whole of the *Rigveda* is full of innovations to gods to destroy the *Dasas,* or to give more power over the dark-skinned, or to bestow wealth and strong sons. These prayers are exclusively addressed to Indra. The sort of sublime nature of religion which consisted in believing that the natural phenomena alone were the gods, and in which the pressing of the *soma* and offering smaller sacrifices to the various gods were the important religious ceremonies, could never had continued to exist much longer in the same healthy condition.

With the growth of the practice of sacrifices, a legendary power of compelling the gods to do the worshipper's bidding was attributed to it. This was accentuated by the conscious selfishness of the priests who devoted themselves solely to make the sacrifices more and more complicated, to exaggerate the purpose and the utility of the sacrifice, and to sing the praises of the liberality of their benefactors. It is true that it was the same approach of asking blessings from the gods that assumed the disgusting nature of *dakshina*.

The nature religion of the Indo-Iranian period reached its pinnacle in the middle of the Rigvedic period but began to degenerate owning to contact with *Dasyus*, settled life, and the increase of population. As Dr. P.S. Deshmukh alias Bhausaheb Deshmukh pointed out in *The Origin and Development of Religion in Vedic Literature:*

> The phase of religion which begins to appear in the latest portions of the *Rigveda* and which begins to receive a more or less definite form in the *Yajurveda* and the parts of the *Atharveda*, culminates in the *Brahmanas*. In the *Sutras* it receives a little more systematic treatment, but from the point of view of innovations or drastic modifications, the religion in the older *Sutras*, at any rate, remains essentially unchanged. The religion in the *Brahmanas* is predominantly ritualistic, and as distinguished from the nature religion of the *Rigveda*, it may be conveniently called *Brahmanism.*[43]

As thus ritualistic religion is the phase, aftermath of nature religion. To Jacobi:

> The word 'Brahmanism' seems originally to have been used, and popularly still to be understood, to denote the religion of those inhabitants of India who adored Brahma as their Supreme God, in contradistinction to those who professed Buddhism, and in more recent times, Muhammadanism. (p. 349)

This ritualistic spirit of religion continued to pervade and dominate, not only literature, but both life and thought, till the rise of Jainism and Buddhism. Thus, Brahmanism may be taken to denote the form of religion which existed in India from the end of the Rigvedic period of about the sixth-century B.C.

Gramgeeta's Perception of God

Three Upanishads—*Mandukya, Katho,* and *Prashno*—speak about the concept of *Om* (*Aum*), which Nanak has incorporated in the invocation of the *Japji*. The great tree with leaves representing the songs of the Vedas, described in Chapter fifteen of the *Bhagavad Gita*, is also mentioned in the *Granth Sahib*. The philosophy of the Vedas and the Upanishads was later elaborated into six systems *(Samkhya, Yoga, Nyaya, Vaisheshika, Mimansa,* and *Vedanta),* to which Nanak often refers in his compositions—one such reference is like this, "six the sacred texts, six the *gurus* who wrote them, and six messages they left". Nanak's poetry has allusions and references to *Vedas, Upanishads,* and the yogic practices. Nanak defines the divine as the one who is omnipotent, omniscient, omnipresent, and immanent. In his address, he often uses terms like Hari, Ram, Gopal, Parmeshwar, Jagdis, Prabhu, Allah, Khuda, Badshah, Sahib, Rubba, and Swami to refer to God, besides using innovations like "O formless One," or "O Immanent".

Nanak was a *Sufi* and a Saint, a hardcore iconoclast and his forerunner Kabir was a humanist, spiritualist, and a social reformer.

> मौको कहा ढुंढता बंदे, मैं तो तेरे पास में।
> ना मैं देवल ना मैं मस्जिद, ना काबे कैलास में।
> Where you search me, I am within you.
> Not I in a temple, a mosque, Kaba, a heaven.

To Kabir, God is not in a temple, a mosque, or a heaven, He is in man himself and He is to be searched within.

Gramgeeta reveals Tukadoji's approach to concept of God and its relevance in the individual and social contexts. It opens with traditional conception of God but then it attributes pragmatic significance to it. Tukadoji addresses God as the Mover of Universe, the Master of Cosmos, and the Guardian of the World, who appears in myriad forms. While meeting with Him, all doors of knowledge are opened. He manifests in heart as the sun rises in the sky and darkness vanishes, and as *chakora* regales when the moonlight shines. His embrace relieves pain, and as lotus in the sunlight smiles and blossoms, He blesses.

> Water and milk separate by swan's bill;
> Realises virtue, flaw as mind grasps Your knowledge. ||25||
>
> Flashes lightening in inky darkness, sees one at distance;
> Prevails peace when Your presence is experienced. ||26||
>
> (Canto I, 'Vision of God')

Tukadoji experiences the vision of God as "lightening flash in inky darkness", and as Alighieri Dante experiences the light, enlightenment, and the vision of God after his turbulent odyssey through inferno and purgatorial fire, in *The Divine Comedy*. The difference is that Dante seeks the guidance of Beatrice as the guide to lead to the path.

The Divine Comedy starts from the conviction that the contemporary world is morally corrupt; and in historical and cultural contexts *Gramgeeta* keeps pace with *The Divine Comedy*, being conscious of contemporary reality and dwindling of ethical values. Dante and all his fellow men are on the road to damnation. Divided into three *cantiche* and a hundred cantos, *The Divine Comedy* begins with the account of Dante, the character's frustrated attempt to escape from the dark wood that represents his own state of sin; the way towards virtue is blocked by three beasts, of which the third, the wolf, apparently representing avarice, is cast as the most dangerous. Rescued from the wolf by the soul of the Roman poet Virgil, sent by his dead beloved Beatrice, Dante is taken on exceptional personal journey—first through the ten circles of Hell; then up the mountain of Purgatory to the Earthly Paradise, where at last he meets Beatrice; then with Beatrice replacing Virgil as his guide, up through the heavens, until he reaches the true seat of the blessed; and at the very end of the poem has a vision of God himself.[44] It is a journey of individual salvation, grounded in Dante's own personal history, and above all in his love for Beatrice, but the personal continually merges with or exemplifies universal values.

Tukadoji employees beautiful smiles to decipher the relationship between God and devotees:

> Though immerse we, fall we, Your look as of black kite;
> To provide happiness by all means, will extract out of ignorance. ||36||
>
> Moos a cow for calf path-forgotten, guards an egg a bird;
> Cares for kid though performs mother household work. ||37||
>
> Nourishes a black-bee worm, makes like oneself;
> Likewise embraces God devotees spreading a web of means. ||38||
>
> (Canto I, 'Vision of God')

He is like a soaring eagle; a cow who directs to calf, path forgotten; a bird who guards an egg. An audience asked: Doesn't work function without utterance of God? Does work infect without shower of blessing? Why should be indulgence in religious stories? Why does believe in God? It is a reality that belief in God has become feeble in people and villages are becoming bankrupt.

> Story of the world some narrate, concentrate some on nation;
> We have to pen *Gramgeeta,* focusing on village. ||68||
>
> (Canto I, 'Vision of God')

He has meditated deeply not to make people coward and lazy. To him, God is valorous, seat of justice, moral, and spring of rebellious work. He is a Superman and an Ideal of human beings. His work is to inspire new generations. He views non-conventionally that he who makes other happy is not atheist though he doesn't utter the word 'God'. To place the ideal of boundless knowledge with genuine faith, the name 'God' is choosen. Great souls have created books with pious motto for self contentment, and with cosmic motive, *Krishnageeta, Ramgeeta, Hansageeta, Hanumangeeta, Shivgeeta, Avadhootgeeta, Gurugeeta, Ganeshgeeta, Pandavgeeta, Bhagwatgeeta, Devgeeta,* and *Devigeeta,* all have been written and their essence is:

> Essence of all to purify the temple of heart;
> All beings are to make happy for righteous course. ||71||
>
> (Canto I, 'Vision of God')

It resonates with "सर्व भूर्ते हितेरत:" (Let welfare be of all beings).

Tukadoji makes the stance of *Gramgeeta* clear that knowledge is futile which doesn't comprehend rural service, and in a social structure, village is an important unit.

> Nation to be judged from village being a map of the world;
> Nation dwindles down when village devasts. ||49||

A nation's heath collapses if its village succumbs of disease. A conscious person has to diagnose this symptom. Bearing in mind these aspects, *Gramgeeta* is penned and Tukadoji approaches literary creativity as service:

> Realise literary service as service to channelise masses;
> Deeming man as divine, one has to work. ||63||
>
> (Canto I, 'Vision of God')

He employees the conventional smile to illustrate the concept of God, but there is a shift in his interpretation when he views:

> Instead of immersing nose in temple, better to pick up thorns on a road;
> To provide water to a sufferer, the best pilgrim place. ||19||
>
> (Canto XVIII, 'Labour Wealth')

In these lines he deconstructs the traditional set of notion and orients towards a living human being. He doesn't see 'Murari' in a temple.

> What are doing in temple? See with eyes focused;
> See shaking bells, see bowing down;
> What is there? waste-stones, Lord not there;
> He is toiling in poor's home.[45]

He further asks to a person who disdains hungry and sufferer, "whether He is fool to salivate you?"

Rabindranath Tagore's conception of God is human oriented and directs to leave chanting, singing, and telling of beads and search Him in a labourer who is toiling in a dusty soil on the road.

> Leave this chanting and singing and telling of beads! Whom dost thou worship in this lonely dark corner of

> a temple with doors all shut? Open thine eyes and see thy God is not before thee!
>
> He is there where the tiller is tilling the hard ground and where the pathmaker is breaking stones. He is with them in sun and in shower, and his garment is covered with dust. Put off thy holy mantle and even like him come down on the dusty soil![46]

He says a worshipper to come out of temple and put off holy mantle to see Him on dusty soil. His stance on deliverance has flavor of it and views that God is bound with the bonds of creation, with us.

> Deliverance? Where is this deliverance to be found? Our master himself has joyfully taken upon him the bonds of creation; he is bound with us all for ever. Come out of thy meditations and leave aside thy flowers and incense! What harm is there if thy clothes become tattered and stained? Meet him and stand by him in toil and in sweat of thy brow.[47]

Tagore exhorts to come out of meditations and keep aside flowers and incense to meet Him in toil and in sweat. He attributes importance to dignity of labour. In *Gramgeeta*, Tukadoji writes:

> To dig a land of hand length, worship better than others;
> Effect its, more, than hundred lectures. ||20||
>
> What makes food available to labourer, work is the best than *yagnya;*
> Otherwise something else not to support by mentioning *Geeta.* ||21||
>
> (Canto XVIII, 'Labour Wealth')

To dig a land is better than worship. The work which provides food to labourer is better than *yagnya*, or any other rituals. In his perspective, he reiterates that common man is not alienated from religion and God. Labour for welfare of common man is better than rituals. The rift among common man and worship, ritual, religion, and God is not to be supported by mentioning *Geeta*. It exemplifies the counter discourse of worship in enclosed temple, pilgrim place, orthodox concept of God, and superstitious rituals, and converges on dignity of labour for welfare of common man and service for humanity.

> All religions same principally where humanity in religions;
> *Geeta*, not against this of socialist Krishna. ||33||
>
> Says Krishna 'all is Brahma', equality is divine religion;
> Visionary with equality, an intellectual best; equality, the essence of *yoga*.||34||
>
> (Canto XXIX, 'Service of Downtrodden')

The conceptions of Reality of God, perceived by Tagore and Tukadoji, are common man oriented; and consequently in their conceptions of religion and God, common man is not excluded, which decipher their humanitarian vision. Tukadoji treats an idol worship as a medium and not an end to know an abstract conception of God.

> Idol worship, chant, penance, no harm when principle attained;
> Verified it when peeped into experience by saint people. ||82||
>
> To make of *bhakari* of clay to prepare the best *bhakari* in practice;
> As showed idol worship a road to an abstract Lord. ||83||
>
> (Canto XXVI, 'An Idol Worship')

He satirises fixing of gold and diamond in a crown of an idol but not providing a strip of cloth to a labourer. "God is basically inside (XXVI: 84)" and no differentiation exists after realisation. When one assimilates righteous knowledge to perform righteous work, a function of idol worship is over for a devotee.

> Says, manifest me in all, became cosmic in cosmos;
> Began to perform all work for inner reality. ||96||
>
> (Canto XXVI)

Corporeal ego melts when one realises the vastness of God, step by step. Entire world becomes uniform sea as salt merges.

> One principle, compactness of spirit as fragment of snow;
> Variations embedded on it, this sign of experience. ||49||
>
> I, the cause of all, vastness this of my spirit;

> When familiar, realised in totally, non-duality, in all. ||50||
> (Canto XXXVII, 'Self-Experience')

In a new realm of consciousness, one experiences that spirit pervades everywhere and variations are manifestation of one principle, which leads to cease duality in all.

> No differences of caste, cults; no sense of I-other, joy, sorrow;
> Manifests *Sacchidananda* bliss, in all, same forms. ||62||
> (Canto XXXVII)

One realises that Supreme Bliss, *Gurudeo*, exists in all myriad forms and differences of caste, sect, I and you, joy and sorrow, end; and one travels towards cosmos.

> Viewed cosmos in oneself who realised spirit inner;
> As the light of divine vision grappled by Arjuna. ||85||
> (XXXVII)

In the divine vision, one experiences that I is merged in you, you in we, and we in cosmos. Now, we understand what Tukaram has to assert, "Tuka became like the sky", and only left for service.

> As the sky, no fragments but appears due to clouds;
> Likewise being ignorant, not separate when experienced. ||88||
> (XXXVII)

Because of clouds, the sky appears in fragments; likewise when experienced, a being is not separated or alienated from cosmic presence. This illumined phase of human existence is transcendental, level of self-development, and fruit of human efforts. When one attains transcendental level, it elevates consciousness and "people will be lords".

> Such people to create, the new world will merge;
> With glory, village, world will exist, all time, Tukadya says. ||103||
> (XXXVII)

New world will emerge, in which people will be lords and odyssey will begin from I to you, you to we, and we to cosmos, for welfare of all.

Human beings cannot endure emptiness and dissolution for longtime; they have to fill the vacuum by creating a new focus of meaning. The idols of fundamentalism are not good substitutes for God. A man has to ponder the history of God for some lessons and warnings in the world religions as Islam and Hinduism. To *Gramgeeta*, God is a flash in inky darkness, transcendental. In mystical and spiritual experience, one experiences elevated consciousness, Supreme Bliss, *Gurudeo;* duality ceases and equality, irrespective of caste, creed, and sects prevail in the vision. In Tukadoji's approach, the vision of God doesn't alienate man from self but elevates self. He deconstructs the traditional faith in God and orients it towards man and constructive human values to rebuild society.

Saint—Nature and Function

The individual experiences the futility of human desires, sublimity, and marvelous order which reveals in nature. The religious geniuses of all ages have been distinguished by this kind of religious feeling. We find men who were filled with this highest kind of religious feeling and were in many cases regarded by their contemporaries as atheists, and sometimes as saints. In this context, Democritus, Francis of Assisi, Spinoza, Buddha, Vivekanand, and Tukadoji are closely akin to one another.

Saints are spiritual seekers to eradicate evil and nourish good. For welfare of the world, their visions are not fragmented by narrow wall but encompasses cosmic consciousness. They are the best ideal of humanism, whose narrowness has gone and heart has become vast. A saint's heart though kind and pure with justice and moral, is harder than *vajra*, the mythical weapon especially one wielded by the God Indra.

> One religion with all saints, welfare work of all beings;
> Humanism, core religion for all time. ||49||
>
> No caste bar for saint, world family, his ancestor;
> Whoever will meet, close to him, kind hearted. ||50||
>
> (Canto XXXII, 'Saint Nature')

Saint has self-power, work-power, knowledge-power, love-power, pious-art, and elevated all aspects, inside and outside.

All to turn to equality, oneness to implement practically;
Entire world to harmonise at Supreme, thinks saint. ||75||

(Canto XXXII, 'Saint Nature')

Saints are blissful and affectionate to both animals and human beings; unravel the essence of books and end illusion with their experience; enhance the glory of truth, forgetting one's greatness; and don't succumb to dignity, glare, and off-way.

Becomes an eye for blind, pours spirit everywhere;
Inroads becoming formula of equality inside contradiction. ||98||
All human beings to elevate, contentment everywhere to reach;
To each other everyone to be complimentary, advise such. ||99||
Downpour from a cloud, no *guru*-disciple there;
Self-spirited see all, saint, righteous one. ||100||

(Canto XXXII, 'Saint Nature')

Miraculous practices misguide people and an ignorant ones falls pray to them, leaving mode of efforts. A saint has potential which manifests in the magnificent mission for welfare of society, and fulfills herculean task with consistency, patience, and devotion, that is a sense of commitment.

Lord of an elephant to an ant, wondrous it seems;
But happens it by progress of power as saint's work to people. ||92||
Deeming it miracle, forget people the base of work;
Inactively with blindness they run after it. ||93||

(Canto XXXI, 'Saint Miracle')

No importance is to be assigned to miracle but to a spring of knowledge and inspiration for work in right-work tradition. Saints have done a miraculous work to transform the darkness of ignorance into the light of knowledge.

Their miracle one only, less knowledgeable being moulded cosmic;

> Perceived God in all beings, everywhere by these eyes. ||97||

Saints transcend self to cosmic level and perceive divine presence in all beings, everywhere. They keep aside their selfish motto and trust in welfare of the world; they are incarnation of service. Their service is to elevate human beings and teach self-religion and nation-religion.

The Conception of *Guru*

The conception of sacred, non-sacred, and their practices has root of inequality in human society and is the product of human mind. Vedic *sanskar* was denied to *vaisyas* besides *shudras* and treating नन्दान्तं क्षत्रियकुलम *kshatriya* too were pushed into the category of *shudra*. It means the right of *upanayan*, twice born was confined to *brahmin* only. To attain-divinity and treating themselves as "pure *kshatriya*", rulers had to procure the right of *upanayan* or new divine birth by experiencing embryonic process in '*hiranyagarbha*'.

Upanayan is *sanskar* of symbolic end of material birth and emergence of new divine birth. After *upanayan* only, entrance was for Vedic studies. Initiation of *upanayan* was indispensible to enter in the area of sacred knowledge. This condition, inevitable for the right to knowledge, is also found in primordial tribes for tribal initiation.

> The (initiated) young man learns not only the behavior patterns, the techniques, and the institutions of adults, but also the myths and the sacred traditions of the tribe, the names of the gods, and the history of their works; above all, he learns the mythical relations between the tribe and supernatural beings as those relations were established at the beginning of time.

Condition for the right to knowledge was found in primordial tribes. But, in Vedic period, the right to knowledge was restricted and others, such as rulers, *vaishya, shudra,* and *kshatriya* were dislocated from the centre and pushed to periphery.

Initiation by *yagnya* is limited to a person who practices *yagnya* and *upanayan* is deemed as necessary for persons confined to three varnas, at puberty level. In A.M. Hocart's words, "Initiation ceremonies through the world are usually an introduction to adult life and occur at, or about puberty".[49] '*Deeksha*' whose English alternative is 'Initiation', is defined by Mircea Eliade as:

> The team initiation in the most general sense denotes a body or rites and oral teachings whose purpose is to produce a decisive alteration in the religious and social status of the person to be initiated. In philosophical terms, initiation is equivalent to an ontological mutation of the existential condition. The novice emerges from his ordeal with a totally different being: he has become another.[50]

The proof of prevalence of such initiation rituals in human society from primitive time is made available by anthropologists.

The truth of aspiration to birth of new and divine life, and then end of life given by nature manifests in the conception of initiation, and Mircea Eliade stresses this truth in *Myths, Dreams and Mysteries*:

> Let us come back once more to the primitive mysteries of initiation. Everywhere we have found the symbolism of death as the ground of all spiritual birth that is, of regeneration. In all these contexts death signifies the surpassing of the profane, non-sanctified condition, the condition of the 'natural man', ignorant of religion and blind to the spiritual. The mystery of initiation discloses to the neophyte, little by little, the true dimensions of existence; by introducing him to the sacred, the mystery obliges him to assume the responsibilities of a man. Let us remember this fact, for it is important that access to the spiritual is expressed, in archaic society, by a symbolism of death.[51]

It is assumed that one who has not performed the initiation of *upanayan* is *shudra* though born in *brahman* family. Likewise one who is not initiated by *Guru* is low, though spiritual oriented. The concept of *Guru* is composed of mother and father, both. *Guru* system is born out of beliefs of collective consciousness, carried out from era to era. It has given happiness and contentment to human society but its distorted form provided unhappiness to it. Primordial deities were androgyne, at once male and female. As Eliade viewed that "Androgamy is an archaic and universal formula for the expression of wholeness".

मां हि पार्थ व्यपाश्रित्य येऽपि स्युः पापयोनयः।
स्त्रियो वैश्यास्तथा शूद्रास्तेऽपि यान्ति परां गतिम्।

Arjuna, women, *vaisyas* (members of the trading and agriculturist classes), *sudras* (those belonging to the labour and artisan classes), as well as those impious birth (such as the *pariah*), whosoever they may be, taking refuge in me, they attain salvation. Here Krishna keeps aside the lines of stratification to seek refugee for devotee.

Jnaneshwar had given a striking blow to the society which was accepting *varnadharma* proposed *Vedic* religion by saying that *Vedas* were miser. His attack on some directions given in *Vedas* has historical significance in the history of religions scripts. *Vedas* had given rights to three *varnas* to read and study. *Vedas* had deprived women and *shudra*; and so Jnaneshwar called *Vedas* as miser and his verdict has historicial significance from the standpoint of the period, which was the *varnashramdharma* proposed social system in the medieval period, i.e., in the thirteenth-century. How had Jnaneshwar attempted to bring changes in the practice of devotion? What is his contribution to the practice of devotion? It will be fruitful if we evaluate Jnaneshwar's stance:

एवं सकल साख्य सिंधु। श्रीभगवत्‌गीता प्रवंधु।।
हा औदार्ये आगला वेद्। मुर्त जाण।।1456।।
वेद संपन्नु होय गई। परि कृपण ऐसा आनु नाही।
जे कानी लागला तिही। वर्णा चाचि।।1457।।
येरा भवव्यथा ठेलिया। स्त्री शूद्रादिका प्राणियां।
अनवसरू मांडूनिया। राहिला आहे।।1458।।

(Canto 18, *Jnaneshwari)*

Material deterioration and psychic slavery masses were inactive and inartistic. Saint movement emerged as a consequence of it. The nature of movement to the most extent was religious and cultural. Jnaneshwar turned to Marathi because of mass orientation. His contention was that 'mass institutes' are to be secured. All saints anticipated the vision to make these 'mass institutes' as the source of new vigour. G.B. Saradar pleads that mass orientation of *Warkari* saints was not only confined to spiritual practices.[52] It hammered on orthodox practices, superstition, and social inertia; and this is the social outcome of saint literature.

Warkari cult opened an avenue to women and downtrodden for self-development. The movement had provided an assurance that spiritual elevation can be attained by *warkari,* person from any caste by *bhakti.* In *Warkari* cult, people from different castes, *brahmin, kunbi, mali, teli,* carpenter, goldsmith, potter, and *mahar* were involved. Jnaneshwar and Eknath had rendered philosophical base to it. They introduced new tendencies by assimilating tradition. Buddhism made it clear that knowledge for salvation is to be percolated to the lower strata.

Jnaneshwar and Shivchhatrapati are heroes with differences in temparament and time; they were meant for self-enrichment of Marathi culture. In people, conception of Hero and Saint's conception of Hero are polar. The former is courageous, valorous, and fighter; and another is self elevated and elevates society and nation too. Though both heroes are not attached to body at the phase of departure, heroicness pertaining to saint is to create sanctity of world. Critics take the cognisance of the concept of hero from archetypal point of view. 'Archetype of hero' is encompassed in ancient epics in the world and folk tales in the world as in saint literature. In saint literature, *'Sadguru'* is 'saviour archetype' as well as 'archetype of hero' which overcomes calamity.

The role of the *guru* in the process of salvation has been underscored by both Kabir and Nanak, for whom the *guru* is synonymous with the immediate representation of the divine. A *guru* (which would translate as master, in English) was someone who had arrived at the perfected state and who in turn helped others to achieve that state of perfection. They had settled with their inner voice to guide them and be their light/*guru.*

In compositions of both Kabir and Nanak, there is a good deal of emphasis upon the absolute need for the *guru* and the *guru* is grace. The *guru* more often is, the *shabda*, the inner voice, the illuminated conscience of the fearless champion of truth. Therefore, the mystics stress upon inner cleaning and purging so that grace can be received when it is given. Nanak emphasises the aspect of *bhakti* as:

The wandering mortal staggers and strays
In eighty four lacs of births
Blind to the Guru inside, bound.
In the noise of Yamadut......
Man you must end this inner strife,
sing the Lord's praises
and merge in the sahaj
through the satguru ...
Rare is the one that washes
The inner fiflth with thy Name
Rare the one that practices truth.
Only then, by the Guru's grace
his comings and goings end.

('Prabhati', *GS* 4437-4438)

The *shabda* as the vehicle of salvation enables man to wash off ego (*haumai* is the term Nanak used) and acquire detachment from *maya*. In Nanak's system of theology, the practice of truth (*sachh*), meditation on the word (*shabda*), and upon the essence (*nam*) are the essentials for reaching the state of the *sahaj*—the perfect union with the Divine.

To categorise and distinguish between the *shabda* and *nam* are not easy, for often they are used interchangeably. *Nam*, an esoteric term for essence, seems to refer to the object of salvation and *shabad* is the medium to salvation. Another concept which is integral to Nanak's theology is that of *hukam* (command) or will of the divine order. The *hukam* as conceived by Nanak is an all embracing principle. It is the subject of the very first stanza of Nanak's *Japgi*:

By His *hukam* the universe comes to be—
it is difficult to say, how?
By His *hukam* the living beings came to be
and by His *hukam* they receive merit.
By His *hukam* exist the high and the low,
and by His *hukam* obtain their share of joy and woe.
Some receive gifts by His *hukam*, some toil in vain.
All that is, is by His will, nothing beyond it.
Who understands His *hukam* alone finds freedom from *haumai*.

(Tr. Neeti Sadarangani, 'Japji' *GS* 1)

Entire saint literature is influenced by honour of *Guru*. They have firm faith that without *Guru* it is difficult to proceed for salvation. Eknath writes about *Guru:*

- Give new birth after initiation by *Guru;*
- Complete form of mother and father; and
- Birth giver, performing *upanayana*, saviour from fear, death, and *sadguru*.

In a broad sense, mother and father are different. Father injects semen and mother takes it in her uterus, but *Gurumother* embraces a child from outbid and showers love and so *sadguru* gives divine birth.

Say Father as *Guru*, thou for single birth I
This mother father ancient, creator of whole world II

Look after as mother, *Guru*, her love for thy embryo I
Secures stay in uterus, *Guru*; more love for offspringII

To come out of uterus, rises mother with love for, offspring I
Embraces outside, with love, beautiful *Guru* Mother II

(Eknath, *Bhagvat* 12, Tr. myself)

Guru, as father and mother, loves and cares for an offspring.

Vedic tradition has given power of *upanayana* to three *varnas* and *shudras* were deprived of it. "जन्मना जायते शूद्र! संस्काराद् द्विज

उच्चते।" reveals that everyone is *shudra* and by *upanayana sanskar* attains divinity. Ramdas pens:

> मुजी बंधनविरहित। तो शूद्रचित निभ्रांत।
> द्विजमी हमणोनि सतंत। द्विज लेसे नाम।।

Ramdas, *Dasbodh, 5.1.9*

Upanayan sanskar is a purification process for new birth. Tulsidas and Ramdas directed towards Rama, an archer, and Chaitanyaprabhu and Meerabai to Krishna, for devotion. Depending upon nation and time, a centre for organisation and the mode are to be selected, keeping pace with the reality. Tukadoji selected *Gurudeo*, Supreme Guide, who is for welfare of all, not confined to any sect and party, and a witness for all nations. In all religions, Hindu, Islam, Christianity, and Sikhism, respect is for *Gurudeo* and perception of *Gurudeo* in *Gramgeeta* is inclusive.

> Be it in Vedic or others respect for *Gurudeo* in all sects;
> Devotion to *Gurudeo*, immense in Islam, Christanity. ||33||

(Canto XXVII, 'Collective Prayer')

A sect propagator's *guru* is different and dualism exists there. A *guru* should be an experienced person having sublime knowledge and sublime consciousness.

> *Guru*, not of bones, flesh; *Guru* not caste-cults;
> *Guru*, pure knowledge principle of experienced. ||35||
> One who receives this knowledge, cosmic his mind becomes;
> Cease sect-party-religion; all merge there. ||36||

The knowledge of *guru* elevates man to cosmic level where sect-party-religion end and merge. Tukaram experienced this sublime level as he realises "Tuka became as sky." Tukadoji writes:

> Melted corporal ego as realised God consequently;
> Merged salt in sea water; uniform sea has become. ||94||

(Canto XXVI, 'An Idol Worship')

Subjectiveness ceases as stepwise a man proceeds towards objectiveness. Self manifests in all and becomes cosmic in cosmos. When one experiences the presence of self everywhere, one transform into complete *yogi*. As thus, one has not to stick to an image but to ascend stepwise dynamically to realise Lord in the World. A new realm of consciousness creates cosmic vision:

> All people, our Lord; all villages, our temples;
> To render service relentlessly, worship ours. ||104||
>
> Work with honesty, chanting of Lord's *nam* ours;
> Unified love in all beings, religion our. ||105||
>
> Transcendental not great than this when deeply determined;
> Essence this of transcendental of those who experienced. ||106||
>
> (Canto XXVI, 'An Idol Worship')

This experience of underlying principle in external diversities is cosmic God, comprehended by knowledge and perceived as *Gurudeo* in collective prayer.

When one sees outwardly, one alienates from self, and when one reflects to know 'What is the world?', 'Who am I?' one's consciousness turns inward to know nature of self. God is sublime consciousness of self. God is not alienation from self but projection of self at enlightened level and sublime level.

In *Gramgeeta*, Tukadoji prays, "Let differentiation in the world be ended", and "litte being has become cosmic". Echo Tukaram's words, "Tuka became as sky". *Guru* is a companion, a supporter of humanity, and not alien to any language, who creates right emotion, guards deprived and sorrowful, and eliminates evil. *Guru* is Supreme who has encompassed everything. The great person, irrespective of caste, creed, and religion, becomes *guru*, dissolving personal and transforming into impersonal, with cosmic consciousness.

> His worship not with *tilak*; His temple vast;
> Limit to vastness but *Guru* infinite than it. ||42||
>
> (Canto XXVII, 'Collective Prayer')

How can there be hate when we understand him? And to know this the medium is structured with an open mind for collective prayer for unity of masses. In collective prayer, collective God is to conceptualise and then to experience in work and visualize in cosmic form, *Gurudeo*. Tukadoji penned, "We as birds, our life new ever", "Tukadya says Thou nest, become, then gratifies wish". No illusion was in his soaring, every renewing. Ashok Kamat has asserted that he wandered wilfully but also entered in masses, enlightening human mind. Adopting the approach of saints, he rendered devotional songs. In it, the consciousness was not only about the power of cosmic spirit, but also of reality in vicinity.[53] In Tukadoji's *Gramgeeta*, the experience is of organic merging of tradition, cosmic vision, and reality.

S.D. Pendse, the scholar on *Jnaneshwari,* has aptly pointed out that Jnaneshwar's marvelous efforts to eradicate evil, to eliminate darkness, and to experience cosmic consciousness are to be turned into reality. Social system manifesting equality is to be existed and he poses a pertinent question: Are the directions mirrored *in Smruti, Bhagavadgeeta*, and Saint literature sufficient? If they are insufficient, operation method is outdated, and if it seems to be meaningless, our present problems are not in its ambit; and therefore, it is not indispensable to keep aside that framework.[54]

Gramgeeta is the counter discourse of traditional conception of orthodox religion, fanaticism, sectarianism, aggressive nationalism, excessive individualism, selfish motives, the notion of sacred and non-sacred to divide, superstitious ritualistic practices, and dominance to refrain from reading and studying. It resists social stratification and cultural hegemony; and converges on dignity of labour and accepts the conception of *guru* and the practice of *nam*, which are inclusive to open doors to those who are excluded, and asserts that religion at core nourishes human values, and collective prayer is pragmatic mode to bring together all from various religions.

Gramgeeta's stance of *Gurudeo,* an experience of *Gurudeo* keeps pace with the tradition of *Nirguna* devotion of Kabir and Nanak, and it is operable without discrimination to infuse spirit of unity, equality, and justice in human society which is divided on the tenets of language, race, caste, creed, cult, sect, and religion. The vision in *Gramgeeta*, irrespective of caste, creed, race, and religion is cosmic, which converges on life on the earth and transcends towards cosmic.

References

1. Allen J., Haig T. Wolseley, Dodwell H.H., Sethi R.R. (1964), *The Cambridge Shorter History of India*, Delhi: S. Chand & Co., p. 4.
2. Muller, F. Max, (1898), *Origin and Growth of Religion*, London: pp. 10-12.
3. Jastrow, M. Jr. (1901), *The Study of Religion*, London: pp. 133.
4. *Op. cit.*, p. 14.
5. *Ibid.*, p. 14.
6. *Ibid.*, p. 19.
7. Frazer, J.G., (1911), *The Golden Bough*, Vol. I, London: p. 63.
8. Frazer, J.G., (1915), *History of Religion*, London: p. 16.
9. Frazer, J.G., (1914), *The Study of Religion*, London: pp. 171-72.
10. Karna, LXIX, p. 59.
11. Taylor, E.B., (1873), *The Primitive Culture*, London: p. 145.
12. Marette, R.R. (1914), *The Threshold of Religion,* London: p. 36.
13. *Ibid.*, p. XI.
14. Cited in Frazer J.G., (1926), *The Worship of Nature*, Vol. I, London: p. 19.
15. *Op.cit.* p. 375.
16. Vivekanand, 'Religion and Science', *Complete Works of Swami Vivekananda,* Vol. VI, Kolkata: Ramkrishna Mission, p. 81.
17. Huxlay, Julian, *Evolution After Darwin*, Vol. III, pp. 251-52.
18. Rangnathananda, (2000), *Science and Religion*, Kolkata: Advaita Ashrama, p. 35.
19. Russell, Bertrand (1985), *Impact of Science on Society,* London: Routledge, pp. 120-21.
20. Einstein, Albert (2009), *Ideas and Opinions,* New Delhi: Rupa Co., p. 46.
21. *Ibid.,* p. 46.
22. *Ibid.*, p. 46.
23. *Ibid.,* p. 53.
24. Tukadoji, (2023), *Gramgeeta,* (tr.), Ratnakar D. Bhelkar, Canto XVIII, 'Labour Wealth', New Delhi: Atlantic Publishers

and Distributors (P) Ltd., p. 165 (Subsequent Canto numbers, titles, page nos. are indicated in parentheses).

25. Tukadoji, 'Inaugural Speech in World Religion Parliament', in *Voice of Saint Tukdoji*, (tr.), Ratnakar D. Bhelkar, Vol. I, No. I, July 20, 1997, p. 1.
26. *Ibid.*, p. 2.
27. *Ibid.*, p. 3.
28. *Ibid.*, p. 3.
29. *Sri Gurudeo,* Japan Travel Special Issue, Nov. 1955, p. 26.
30. Swami Vivekananda, (2010), *Chicago Address*, Kolkata: Advaita Ashrama, pp. 20-21.
31. *Ibid.*, pp. 59-60.
32. Radhakrishanan, Sarvapalli, (2007), '*The Speech at Reshikesh' in The World's Greatest Speeches*, (ed.), Vijayalaxmi Iyer, Delhi: GNOSIS, p. 169.
33. E. Kirk, *Shri Gurudeo,* Nov. Issue, 1955, p. 26.
34. Armstrong, Karen (1999), *A History of God*, London: Vintage Book, p. 141.
35. *The Koran*, 92: 18, 9: 103, 63: 9, 102: 1.
36. *Ibid.*, 20: 115.
37. *Ibid.*, 55-26.
38. *Ibid.*, p. 196.
39. Heidegger, Martin (1999), *An Introduction to Metaphysics* (tr.), Ralph Manheim, Delhi: Motilal Banarasidass Private Ltd., p. 1.
40. Deshmukh P.S., (1998), *The Origin and Development of Religion in Vedic Literature*, Amravati: Amravati University, pp. 58-59.
41. G. Sergi, (1901), *The Mediterranean Race*, London: p. 1-27.
42. Cited in Frazer, James, (1926), *The Worship of Nature*, Vol. I, London: p. 18-19.
43. *Op. cit.*, p. 349.
44. Hainsworth, Peter and Robey, David (2012), *Italian Literature: A Very Short Introduction,* New York: Oxford University Press, p. 65.
45. Tukadoji (2012), '*Lahar Ki Barkha*', Part I, (tr), Ratnakar D. Bhelkar, Gurukunj: *Atmanusadhan* Tekdi, p. 88.

46. Tagore, Rabindranath, (1999), *Gitanjali*, New Delhi: Macmillan India Ltd., p. 6.
47. *Ibid.*, p. 40.
48. Eliade, Mircea, (1969), *The Quest: History and Meaning in Religion,* Chicago: University of Chicago Press, p. 113.
49. Hocart, A.M., (1927), *Kinship*, London: p. 135.
50. *Op.cit.,* 120.
51. Eliade, Miracea, (1972), *Myths, Dreams and Mysteries*, (tr.) Philip Mairet, New York: Harper and Row, Torch books, p. 200.
52. Sardar, G.B. (2004), *Sant Vangmayachi Samajik Falsruti*, Mumbai: Lokvangmay Griha, pp. 21-22.
53. Kamat, Ashok (2003), *Sant Sahitya: Kahi Anubandha*, Pune: Padmagandha Prakashan, p. 241.
54. Pendse, S.D. (1961), *'Marathi Sant'*, quoted from, in *Santachi Samajik Drusti*, Shankarrao Kharat, Pune: Kantinental Publication, p. 45.

Chapter 3

Utopia and its Practicability

The practitioners of the mimetic mode narrates the familiar and usual known experience, strictly adhering to facts; and faithfully represents the outside reality. A stream of consciousness writers, such as Virginia Woolf and James Joyce asserted that reality is in a state of flux, and tried to give a moment to moment record of changing reality. To them, reality is not static but dynamic. The psychological novelists like D.H. Lawrence used traditional techniques to explore psychological reality by focusing on that part of human personality which is submerged in the subconscious. To them, reality is internal. We have learned to doubt interpretability of what we see or learn. Scientists have to reconcile themselves to one kind of uncertainty. They cannot fix both position and momentum of an electron anymore but can pin a butterfly to a cork and still expect to study its flight patterns. Ultra-violet rays are not visible without the help of a spectrometer. Science has made it hard for us to ignore the illusionary nature of our sense data. From the standpoint of psychologists, reality is a name that we give to something which emerges out of the interaction between the inner and the outer, and the subjective and the objective. Our normal day to day experiences can be very well narrated in the "realistic terms" ('realism' being understood in the usual sense). Fantasy does not copy empirical world but creates a world which follows its own laws.

Approaches to Fantasy and Reality

The term, fantasy mode, needs not to be viewed reductively as it cannot be understood in the same sense. Various researchers have approached fantasy in diverse ways. Utopia is a fantasy of welfare society and so let us examine the diverse approaches to fantasy.

The term 'fantasy' did not enjoy the same status which it does now. As we know, Coleridge uses the term in a slightly disparaging sense, considering it as an inferior mode. The change in our attitude towards fantasy is reflected at the turn of the century when T.E. Hulme said in a clear and unambiguous term that "Fancy will be the necessary weapon"[1] of the new age. Our view of fantasy underwent a change when we contrasted it with reality as distinguished from imagination. These new insights were available due to the Freudian approach.

Freud's approach to fantasy is psycho-analytical and takes into consideration the role of unconscious desire in relation to fantasy. Freud postulated the wide ranging influence of the unconscious in human behavior and, thus, laid the groundwork for psycho-analytic theory which does not deny but stresses the role which fantasy plays in the apprehension of reality. In the essay 'Formulations on the Two Principles of Mental Functioning' (1919), Freud presents his theory of the primacy of fantasy. The sovereign tendency of the primary mental process which governs the larger part of the unconscious, is to seek pleasure, that is, this process either strives independently and immediately towards the satisfaction of some need, or flees from some pain. Initially fantasy in the form of hallucinatory wish fulfillment is the sole form of mental activity. The aim of the first psychic activity is to produce a repetition of the perception which is linked with the satisfaction of a need. The psychic activity produces a "perpetual identity" between the hallucination and the activity which previously brought satisfaction.[2] Thus, hallucination turns away from reality and generates a metaphor—the thought is like the external object which satisfies the need. We turn from fantasy towards reality not in conflict but in accord with pleasure principle; and we learn that to satisfy desires we must plan, act, and defer immediate gratification. Nonetheless, a residue of hallucinatory activity is split off, and kept away from reality-testing, remaining subordinate to the pleasure principle alone. This residual activity, which functions as a compensation for the normal dominance of the reality principle, is fantasy, and it is the artist's special function to indulge in this compensatory activity. Art's special relevance to the relation between fantasy and reality links it with the central issues of psychoanalysis, and makes Freud's assessment of the artist's motives and the function of his products, particularly provoking. He writes:

> An artist is originally a man who turns away from reality because he cannot come to terms with the renunciation of instinctual satisfaction which at first demands, and who allows his erotic and ambitious wishes full play in the life of fantasy by making use of special gift to mould his phantasies into truths of a new kind which are valued by men as precious reflections of reality. Thus, in certain fashion, he actually becomes the hero, the king, the creator, or the favourite he desired to be, without following the long round about path of making real alterations in the external world. But, he can only achieve this because other men feel the same dissatisfaction, which results from the replacement of the pleasure principle by the reality principle, in itself a part of reality.[3]

In the Freudian sense, an artist does not confront reality but turns away from it into the world of fantasy to gratify his unconscious desires. He identifies an artist's work with imagined gratification, a pretence of actual satisfaction, as in primary fantasy. He equates fantasy with dream which is an alternative, a substitute, a safety-value to reality, and views it as an escape from reality.

Besides Freud, Rosemary Jackson and Harold Bloom have approached fantasy in psychological terms. Rosemary Jackson speaks of fantasy as "a literature of desire, which seeks that which is experienced as a absence and loss." Further she writes:

> In expressing desire, fantasy can operate in two ways (according to different meaning of "express"): it can tell or manifest or show desire (expression in the sense of portrayal, representation, manifestation, linguistic, utterance, mention, description) or it can expel desire

> when this desire is a disturbing element which threatens cultural order and community (expression, getting rid of something by force). In many cases fantastic literature fulfils both functions at once for desire can be expelled through having been told to and, thus, vicariously experienced by author and reader. In this way, fantasy literature points to or suggests the basis upon which cultural order rests for it opens up for a brief moment onto disorder, onto illegality, onto that which lies outside the law which is outside dominant value systems. The fantastic traces the unsaid and the unseen of culture that has been silenced, made invisible, covered over, and made "absent."[4]

Jackson stresses fantasy as subversion and as a means for dealing with that which has been repressed and, hence, unexpressed. She expresses her belief that fantasy, because of its subversive qualities, "may lead real social transformation."[5]

Harold Bloom focuses on elements, namely, on world-one, in which a writer lives and writes:

> Fantasy as belated version of romance promises an absolute freedom from belatedness, from the anxieties of literary influence and originations, yet this promise is shadowed always by a psychic over-determination in the form of fantasy that puts the stances of freedom into severe question. What promises to be the least anxious of literary modes becomes much the most anxious, and the anxiety specifically relates to anterior powers that is to what might call the genealogy of our imagination. The cosmos of fantasy, of the pleasure/pain principle, is revealed in the shape of nightmare, and not of hallucinatory wish-fulfilment.[6]

He thinks that fantasy should free the writer from his sense of being a dwarf following giants, although, paradoxically, promised freedom usually elicits extreme anxiety from the writer.

To Tolkien, fantasy is natural human activity and as such, it engages both the writer and the reader. He defines the term 'fantasy' as embodying both and views, "the sub-creativity Art in itself and a quality of strangeness and wonder in the expression... Fantasy (in this sense) is not lower but a higher form of Art, indeed, the most nearly pure form, and so (when achieved) the most potent."[7] Tolkien, who applied the phrase, "the sub-creative art" to the writing of fantasy, saw such literary creation as the natural outcome of man's natural creative capacity, in no way conflicting with the exercise of his other principle faculty, his reason. As he asserts:

> It (fantasy) certainly does not destroy or even insult Reason; and it does not either blunt the appetite for, nor obscure the perception of, scientific verity. On the contrary, the keener and the clearer is the reason, the better fantasy will it make...For creative Fantasy is founded upon the hard recognition that things are so in the world as it appears under the sun; on a recognition of fact, but not a slavery to it.[8]

He envisages that fantasy is not opposed to reason, and reason helps to create better fantasy. Here is a paradox, lying in the heart of fantasy, that is, to be able to create an imaginary world, and what an author relates consistently seems 'true' and accords with the laws of that world, and the reader, too, believes in it.

Thomas D. Clareson also views that fantasy is not opposed to rational thought.

> Fantasy, other side of realism, of which SF is the latest expression, has existed side by side with what has come to be called the mainstream the "realistic", the representational-throughout literature and certainly throughout the history of modern fiction.[9]

To Clareson, fantasy is not a polar opposite of realism, but other side of realism. It has existed side by side with what has been called as 'realistic'.

John H. Timmerman views that the chief distinguishing trait of the *genre* of fantasy is perhaps an evocation of other world:

> First, the world matches our world in reality. It is not a dream world, a never-never land, but a world in which characters confront the same terms, choices, and dilemmas we confront in our world...second, this

> world is "evoked", or called forth for us, and we have to cross the threshold to it in our minds.... Third, the world of fantasy, however, should not be considered an escapist world, but a world in which we live. There is always this reciprocating action in fantasy, an interchange between two world.[10]

Timmerman wants to assert that the world of fantasy if evoked, purposefully created, provided for human beings to apprehend the known world in new perspectives. Readers have to cross boundaries of 'this' world, the known world, to enter into 'other world', the unknown world, that is, the world of fantasy. The world of fantasy is not to be considered as an escapist world which has no relation with the world of factual reality in which human beings live. The reason for creating the world of fantasy is to confront more openly and daringly the reality too often ignored in our world.

Ann Swinfen approaches fantasy in relation to the primary world and the secondary world. In a popular type of fantasy set in the primary world—animal fantasy in which animals are given anthromorphic characters and occasionally human beings are metamorphosed into animals—Swinfen writes:

> From such fantasy located entirely in the primary world, the move is logically to the next stage in obstruction beyond the normal space-time continuum, where the primary world and other world are juxtaposed. The secondary world of such pairs of 'worlds in parallel' still maintains close contact with normal experience in the real world and as such it may be distinguished from the secondary world which is no way directly linked with primary experience.[11]

Superficially, at least, the secondary world of fantasy is remote from everyday life. Such distancing may alienate the reader or at any rate fail to involve them, may not awake that deeper level of sympathy which the writer intends to create. However, the reader can be involved if that basis of sympathy and identification can be established. The secondary world of fantasy offers unique advantage. The main advantage of the secondary world for such writer is a freedom from the restricting assumptions and realities of the primary world. Moreover, in the context of an independent secondary world, a new corpus of values may be more easily presented. When a writer of fantasy is in full control of his imagination, and not simply soaring off into the void, he uses these marvelous elements for specific purpose for imaginative enrichment derived from exploring an experience beyond everyday reality, for the realisation of some serious intent which lies behind his fantasy.[12]

As it has been already pointed out earlier while approaching fantasy, Timmerman concenrtrates on 'other world' and Ann Swinfen on 'the secondary world'. Kathryn Hume approaches fantasy laying emphasis on world-1 in which the author selects and manipulates materials. World-1 from which the author selects and manipulates materials provides the author with assumptions about reality and meaning. She proposes that fantasy is the desire to alter reality out of boredom, longing for something lacking, or need for the metamorphic images that will bypass the audience's verbal defences.[13] She writes:

> Fantasy is any departure from consensus reality, an impulse native to literature and manifested in innumerable variations, from monster to metaphor. It includes transgressions of what one generally takes to be physical facts such as human immortality, travel faster than light. Telekinesis and like Telepathy....[14]

She makes it clear that since departure from consensus reality can only be registered from its appearance in the text, one might at first class her inclusive definition as work-oriented, but "consensus" immediately refers us to both the world of the author and that of the audience. Here 'consensus reality' means reality which is accepted by the inhabitants of world-1. She includes in fantasy some technical or social innovations which have not yet taken place, even though they may well happen in the future. She also includes in fantasy the alternative worlds and universes, and those stories whose marvel is considered 'real' although not in the same fashion that a chair is real.

These diverse approaches to fantasy reveal that we cannot approach the relation between fantasy and reality in a fixed way.

This theoretical discussion about the inter-relation of fantasy and reality is indeed illuminating and valuable, however there is no fixed theory which can account for the way in which fantasy and reality become operative in different literary works. There is no reason why we should follow the preconceived notion about the inter relation between the two.

Utopia and Historical Perspective

Utopia is fantasy of welfare society and on contrary, dystopia is fantasy of subvert value, dark world. Utopia is not an escape from consensus reality but the projection of consensus reality to create utopian world which unfolds his vision of reality. The utopian writer looks at his society first and tries to see what, for his purposes, its significant elements are. Utopia itself shows what society would be like if those elements were fully developed. Plato looked at his society and saw its structure as a hierarchy of priests, warriors, artisans, and servant, much the same structure that inspired the caste system of India. *The Republic* shows what a society would be like in which such a hierarchy functioned on the principle of justice, that is, each man doing his own work. Thinking within a Christian framework of ideas, it is assumed that the significant elements of society were the natural virtues, justice, temperament, fortitude, and prudence. Thomas More's *Utopia* shows what a society would assume to its natural form. Francis Bacon, on the other hand, anticipates Karl Marx by assuming that the most significant social factor is technological productivity, and his *New Atlantis* constructs accordingly.

Plato's *Republic* is a city-state, Athenian in culture and Spartan in discipline. It was inevitable that the utopia, as a literary genre, should be revived at the time of the Renaissance, the period in which the medieval social order was breaking down again into city-state units or nations governed by a capital city. Again, the utopia, in its typical form constructs implicitly or explicitly, the writer's own society, with more desirable one, he describes. The desirable society, or in proper utopia is essentially the writer's own society, transposed into conscious equivalents. The contrast in value between the two societies implies a satire on the writer's own society and the basis for the satire is the

or anarchy. Examples of the former in the literature of the last century include Edward Bellamy's *Looking Backward*, William Morris's *News from Nowhere*, and H.G. Wells's *A Modern Utopia.* Wells is one of the few writers who have constructed both serious and satirical utopias which include Zamyatin's *We*, Aldous Huxley's *Brave New World*, and George Orwell's *Nineteen Eighty-Four.*

The nineteenth-century utopia had a close connection with the growth of socialist political thought and shared its tendency to think in global terms. When Friedrich Engels attacked "utopian socialism and contrasted it with his own 'scientific' kind, his scientific socialism was utopian in the sense in which we are using that term but what he rejected under the category of 'utopian' was the tendency to think in terms of a delimited socialist society". For Engels, as for Marxist thinkers generally, there was a world-wide historical process going in a certain direction; and humanity had the choice either of seizing and directing this process in a revolutionary act or the drifting into greater anarchy or slavery. The goal, a classless society in which the state had withered away was utopian; the means adopted to reach this goal were 'scientific'. Northrop Frye stated:

> The Utopia, the effort at social imagination, is an area in which specialised disciplines can meet and interpenetrate with a mutual respect for each other, concerned with clarifying their common social context.[18]

For More, as for Plato, utopia is the kind of model of justice and common sense which, once established in mind, clarifies its standards and values. The 'Republic' built by Plato is derived from his ability to see society on two levels, a lower natural level and an upper ideal level. What gives them the ability to perceive this upper level is education. The vision of the *Republic* is inextricably bounded up with a theory of education. The bodily senses perceive the 'actual' or objective state of things.

Although, not all utopia writers are Platonists, nearly all of them make their utopias depend on education for their permanent establishment. It is a theory of education that connects a utopian myth with a myth of contract. This is abundantly clear in Plato, and later in Rousseau whose *Emile* is the utopian and educational counterpart of his social contract. In the sixteenth-century, Machiavelli's *The Prince*, Castiglione's *The Book of The Courtier*, and More's *Utopia* form a unified Renaissance trilogy—the first two providing a contract myth and an educational structure respectively, based on the two central facts of Renaissance society, the prince and the courtier.

The utopian writer looks at the ritual habits of his own society and tries to see that society would be like if these ritual habits were made more consistent and more inclusive. The Lilliputian society is essentially the society of Swift's England, with its rituals looked at satirically. In Samuel Butler's *Erewhon*, we have an early example of the contemporary or technological utopian satire. Erewhonians are afraid of machines and their philosophers have worked out elaborate arguments to prove that machines will eventually take over if not suppressed in time.

Trends in utopia are found in the studies like Lewis Mumford's, *The Story of Utopias* (1922), J.O. Hertzler's *The History of Utopian Thought* (1926), V.F. Calverton's *Where Angels Dread to Tread* (1941), Marie Louise Berneri's *Journey Through Utopia* (1950), and Negley's and Patrick's *The Quest for Utopia* (1952). The scope and spirit of these studies are apparent by what Hertzler states to be the purpose of his book, namely that it "attempts to give an unprejudiced, systematic treatment of the Social Utopias as a whole". David Riesman opens an essay on community planning with the assertion, "A revival of the tradition of Utopian thinking seems to me one of the important intellectual tasks today".[19] Martin Buber devotes his *Paths in Utopia* to the demonstration that of the two, Marxist (or scientific) and Utopian socialism, it was the latter which may well be clearing the way for the structure of society to be.

Utopian Communities

Utopian communities have their characteristics and emphasise upon cooperative mode. Cooperative communities search for 'better society' neither by slipping away into an imaginary 'nowhere' nor by relying on an equally utopian Marxist leap. Instead, they explore, in a pragmatic fashion, the possibilities of a more satisfying mode of social and economic relations. Following the methods of socio-political-economical relations, they see as their ultimate goal, the discovery of more consistent and at the same time viable norms of behaviour. Like Saint Exupery, there are some who feel that in the world of today they are in fact exiles, who have not built yet their homeland. Yet, they may well find themselves to be at home where men and women, like those of the co-operative communities are actively searching for the ways of working in living together in peace and harmony.[20] According to their origin, we can distinguish three basically different types of cooperative communities—(1) the religious, (2) the socio-reformistic, and (3) those predominately motivated by economic considerations.

The religious and the socio-reformistic communities, frequently characterised as 'Utopian', were predominant in the past. They made their appearance at different times since the early sixteenth-century in the New World of 130 'utopia' community enterprises, representing 236 community units, which are known to have existed in the United States of America and in Canada. Only the religions have survived for a longer period. The modern cooperative community in its main types, synonymous with the cooperative farm, has developed into a new socio-economic kind of organisation, used by government or semi-government agencies as an instrument of rural rehabilitation. The growth of interest in the practical possibilities of cooperative farming has been very marked, particularly since the end of the World War II, in many countries of Asia and the East. The soundness of this trend was affirmed at a meeting of the food and agriculture organisation of the United Nations held in Lucknow, India, from 24th October to 2nd November, 1949. At its conclusion, the meeting, attended by 38 delegates, observes, and the representatives of the FAO from Australia, Ceylon, France, India, Pakistan, Thailand, and the United Kingdom resolved that "Cooperative farming provides an ideal solution for the pooling of resources of the cultivators in land, labour, and capital". Accordingly, the meeting recommended, "that Government should actively encourage cooperative farming societies with financial and technical advice."[21]

The Anna Community (founded in 1714), the Doukhobors (organised about the middle of the eighteenth-century), and Hutterite colonies (first formed in 1528) are still in existence.[22] The most significant of the 'Utopian' communities are Hutterite colonies. According to a census taken in 1951 (published in *The Mennonite Quaterly Review* of January, 1951), Hutterite colonies are found today in addition to South Dakota, in North Dakota and Montana of the United States; and in the Canadian provinces of Alberta and Monitoba. There are some newer colonies in Ontario (Canada), England, and Paraguay.

The Hutterite community is typical of all the 'Utopian' communities founded on religious principles and practicing all-inclusive or comprehensive cooperation. It offers all the advantages of doing things together, such as economic security, a high degree of work satisfaction with the ensuring economical and mental health, and a strongly developed we-feeling. Frugality and isolation, fostered for the sake of purity and preservation of these creed, enable them, however, to attract only small numbers of participants.

The 'Utopian' communities were motivated by religious creeds or social-reformistic zeal. Mahatma Gandhi reiterated on the dire need to reconstruct the villages of India in *Harijan* on March, 1935:

> It is profitless to find out whether the villages of India were always what they are today. If they were never better it is a reflection upon the ancient culture in which we take so much pride. But, if they were never better, how is it that they have survived centuries of decay which we see going on around us.... The task before every lover of the country is how to prevent this decay or, which is the same thing, how to reconstruct the villages of India so that it may be as easy for anyone to live in them as it is supposed to be in the cities.[23]

Tukadoji observes consensus reality, and being dissatisfied with it, projects it in *Gramgeeta* in a magnified form to create the utopian world of social, economical, political, ethical, educational, hygienic welfare, and development in science and technology.

Gramgeeta attempts to create better world envisaging evils in existing society.

> Friends, we have to create such human society which steps to comprehend vastness of universe and relieve others from pain. We can reach higher goal of human society when it strives for welfare of others. Saints have sacrificed and experienced the fruits of self-knowledge. They have searched the perpetual principle and contributed human culture with the light of self-knowledge. Man's ultimate goal is to know vastness of soul and its practical mean to serve living being. *Seva* means to activate those lag behind. I believe that persons who perform their duties honestly, have minimum needs, can help others, and fulfill the cherished dream of human society.
>
> Friends, if the entire world follows these guidelines, everything in the world belongs to all, and to be honest to one's duty to maintain beauty, harmony, and peace in the world is man's most cordial aim.[24]

By creating utopian world he comments on real world and views that equality, unity, secular approach, self-reliance of villages, democratic approach, cleanliness, collective prayer, no exploitation of labour, no orthodox rituals, knowledge of *guru*, and self-realisation are important to human life.

He treats village as a unit of nation and a nation's progress rests on villages.

> Nation to be judged from village being a heart of nation;
> Nation dwindles down when village devasts. ||49||[25]
>
> (Canto I, 'Vision of God')

His vision of reality expands from individual to family, family to village, village to state, state to nation, nation to world, and at cosmic level.

Social Approach

Chaturvarna system is basically based on qualities to work and not on caste. *Brahmanya* is an attitude and aptitude to work, a quality which sees equality in all beings. *Brahman* has foresight, purity of heart, killer of evil mind, love, and sacrifice.

In Indian context, human society has vertical caste hierarchy, and there are sub-castes. Internal and intra-compartments make Indian social structure more intricate. Buddha, Saint poets, Kabir, Phule, Periyar, Vitthal Ramji Shinde, Shahu Maharaj, and Dr. Ambedkar resisted the discrimination among human beings, with the voices of protest.

Varna System

Conceptually, *brahman* is not caste but an attribute of vastness and with politeness serves and sees *brahma*, divinity in all. All are equal to him and so *Brahman varna* is deemed as the best and Tukadoji urges to create this *brahmanya* to experience happiness and peace by all. *Brahmanya* is righteous mind which nourishes other qualities. *Varnashrama* is for convenience and distribution of work for mass education, security for justice, nourishment of people, and labour. One has to work as per human nature to beautify village. But, in reality, on practical level, the ideal in the concept had deteriorated due to the attitude of dominance. Conceptually, to *brahman*, untouchable, *kshatriya*, and *vaishya* are equal but in practice it had not operated.

> Not paid heed to quality but birth decided *varna;*
> Profession gave birth to caste in society. ||24||
>
> Tradition this discontinued, divided by power, greed;
> Discrimination increased to avail power. ||32||
>
> Pride of *varna* persisted, qualities crushed;
> *Sanskar* moulded in these ways, setting difficult. ||47||
>
> (Canto V, '*Varna* System')

Power and greed had corrupted mind and discrimination entered which had given a jolt to *varna* system, basically meant for welfare of the society. In the course of time, watertight compartments were formed among *varnas,* which had culminated into caste system.

For work, *varna* was formed but ego entered and the motto of *varna* was kept aside. Ignorance created differences and those

discrimination which formed cleavages, watertight compartments, and led to caste system in India. The core motto was good but evil entered in the garb of the practitioner and fouled the social scenario.

The basic incantation for village welfare is to unite all gentlemen. Organisation is a formula of energy to create village state. The present time is of people power and intrinsic energy is in people. People's determination and action can bow down empire.

> Time this of mass strategy, energy all in people;
> Can bow down empire, the power of people determination. ||14||
> Basic incantation of village welfare, to assemble gentlemen;
> Organization, formula of village, energy to create village state. ||17||
>
> (Canto XI, 'Village Security')

The enlightened people have responsibility to curb superstitions and create awareness about delusionary views. The rural youths have to make organization strong for village state.

> Ready to be all rural youth if impends any calamity;
> Keeping aside their work all have to run for. ||105||
> For fire, drowning in well, cholera, fainting;
> To run everytime, there duty is. ||106||
> Planning this for village service, enlighten village army;
> There in heaven's paradise, blossoming with ease. ||107||
> By such organizations luminant glory village will experience;
> Village state, treasure of happiness, Tukadya says. ||108||
>
> (Canto XI, 'Village Security')

In the speech delivered at Chandurbazar, he asserted, "Our village, our city are big pilgrim places and every one has to work hard. Our energy is to be directed to make it ideal. Nation is to be rebuild...for it everyone has to be conscious".[27]

Village State is *Ramrajya* and self-reliance is self-rule. *Panchayati Raj* is democratic in nature. He stressed upon the real signs of ideal village state.

> All to work for all, in the welfare of all our welfare;
> Great one to reveal lesson practicising with determination. ||123||
> In it greatness, village life will be self-reliant;
> This only real sign of ideal rural state. ||124||
> (Canto XXXIX, 'Earth Paradise')

Gramgeeta has pulse of democracy in its veins.

Woman Elevation

Education is the base of village development. Today's offsprings are the creator of tomorrow's nation. Mother instills *sanskar* on children from embryo formation. Hand that rocks a cradle upgrades the world. The best mother looks after her home with mission and makes her children ideal beside attributing warmth of love for all. Annasaheb Karve, in the essay 'Woman Education and its Calamity', alleged:

> Especially women forgetting higher, lower untouchability, different castes, have to sow the seeds of nationality. Women of different castes and different religions have to organize programs to exchange thoughts. For this there is need of proper education for them.[28]

In September 1945, *Sri Gurudeo* Women *Mandal* was founded and Vimalatai Thakar, Prabhatai Deshmukh, Radhadevi Goyenka, Venutai Wankhede, Narmadabai Sapkal, Renukadevi Birle, Sarajabai Malgujar, Hirutai Boke, and Rukminibai Goswami were active members. There were 700 branches of Woman *Mandal* and 75 women propagators. *Gramgeeta* refers to Prahlad's mother Kayadhu, Shivaji's mother Jijabai, Rama's mother Kaushalya, and Krishna's mother Deviki. Nowhere we finds light of love like mother. In sainthood, a form of mother prevails.

Some view that woman is slave and has no right to uplift but this verdict is blind, selfish, and doesn't suit to wise people. A woman has polar facets.

Fascinating unlike woman, renounced unlike woman;
Soft unlike woman and iron-hearted *Ranchadika.* ||53||
(Canto XX, 'Woman Elevation')

Some girls take physical education and become brave, so that others have no courage to attack them. With self power women can kill evil forces.

How ugly widow women look with tonsured head? Tukadoji poses the question, how does it attain renunciation? There is not to be gender discrimination and family planning is to be applied for both.

Respect which for male in society, same to be for female;
More thought to be given to it in society. ||78||
(Canto XX, 'Woman Elevation')

But, in practice, former is lifted up and another suppressed.

This is to be changed, education to be given everywhere;
Woman's life to be enlightened to survive village state. ||81||

Wise persons not to forget, arrangement in village for all;
Which will cause elevation of male as well as female. ||82||

Village will beautify on both sides of male and female;
Heaven will descend with the progress of work. ||83||

Inner qualities of woman will flourish by education special;
When given to her to change world in future. ||84||

Higher education of woman, place of life in education to be;
In life, importance of peace, kindness to be. ||85||
(Canto XX, 'Women Elevation')

He understands the importance of woman education to nourish self-confidence and honour. Higher education is to be provided to girls as boys.

Educate consciously, both to make like two wheels of a chariot;

Village to be infused with power, tact. ||94||

(Canto XX, 'Women Elevation')

As organised army of boys, organisation of women is to be constituted to give vent to expression of happiness, sorrow, and disgust. The birth-death anniversaries of holy and reformative women are to be celebrated. Library facility is to be opened for women. Whatever the means of freedom, happiness are for male, they are to be for female too. In XI plan, UGC has directed universities and colleges to operate Women Cell to develop individuality and identity to reflect on woman related issues. UGC has stressed the formation of Task Force Committee and Women Harassment and Grievances Committee in the XII and XIII plans for freedom and security of women.

As organised army of boys, organisation of women to be;
To express our happiness, sorrow in meeting, conference. ||102||

(Canto XX, 'Women Education')

Organisation has potential to face questions and search solutions for hindrances.

Books are to be made available in library to mould and ignite women's minds against injustice. Independent seminars and conferences for women are to be organised for their honour to create consciousness for resistance. The means of freedom and happiness are to be provided for women without differentiation. Simone de Beauvoir aptly remarks, "The situation of the woman is that she—a free and autonomous being like all human creatures—nevertheless finds herself living in a world where men compel her to assume the status of the other."[29] She argues that woman is other to man, and defined and differentiated with reference to man; "She is not born, but rather becomes woman". She is being an individual and capable of, through trial and error, finding her own way to identity. The both wheels of chariot are to be strengthened to flourish village. This is the thought for women' salvation and freedom, and the feminist approach stresses on gender studies.

Wedded Life

Wedded life being crucial, turning, and channelising. Tukadoji reflects on man-woman relationship. He viewed in his essay 'Enogressive Development of Half Nation':

> The cooperative venture of men and women is indispensable and apt to involve in social and religious works.... The system of wedding is born to link with social work by balancing individual attitudes of both. Man and woman are two wheels of a chariot, without which a chariot can't run. The symbol of the chariot of human society is inherent in it. When the chariot of nation has to face challenges which creates disturbances, it is beneficial for these two wheels to run with equal speed.[30]

Marriage being social institution plays significant role for social harmony. Before wedding, a boy and a girl have to see each other and freedom of thought is to be provided to them. With the consent of both wedding is to be arranged to make family happy. Tukadoji comprehended the distinction between animal instinct and human instinct, pondering on human role to play. Animal instincts of dogs give birth to puppies and once birth given, they are left over after sometime. It is not with human being who has to carry responsibility of offspring. In some cases, in the short span of wedded life, husband demises and bride turns widow. Widow marriages are to be encouraged and evil practices are to be abandoned.

> Tells ritual not to marry; mind disturbed, how to control?
> Secretly inclination towards sin, sorrowful it is. ||43||
> Such evil customs whatever are to be discarded;
> Again new creation of special rules ought to be. ||44||
> Widow who intends to marry has to speak with elders;
> With kind heart marriage to arrange treating it nature of life. ||45||
>
> (Canto XXI, 'Wedded Life')

The negative social custom of dowry is to be eradicated and Tukadoji asks the pertinent question, does bond of love operate with cost for anyone?

Some arrange marriage, takes dowry as one desires;
Not seen whether matched or unmatched for sake of money. ||48||

Though bridegroom old or diseased, nice bride given;
Evil transactions of different types for wealth. ||49||

Accepting wealth of boy-girl, despair they nourish;
Does the trap of love operate with cost for anyone? ||50||

(Canto XXI, 'Wedded Life')

To him, greed is evil in man-woman relationship. He directs to keep aside the insistence on numerical in astrology because an astrologer manipulates numerical to incur benefit.

Bargaining with an astrologer manipulates numerical;
Telling alternative name increases unreality seriously. ||77||

Observe planets in the sky, here in nature different insistence;
Revulsion which rises in life, not seen by them. ||78||

Says the best of bride, bridegroom, matched thirty-six numerical;
Here rivalry or polarity full, spoils life. ||79||

The virtues of bride, bridegroom, ornamental for each other;
Though marriage performed gloriously without them, unholy. ||80||

(Canto XXI, 'Wedded Life')

The best qualities of bride-bridegroom are to be taken into cognisance. In marriage celebration, excess money is not to be poured and taxing rituals are to expelled out. In the celebration, Tukadoji assigns priority to healthy environment, simplicity, religion, *sanskar*, and the warmth of love. To him, fresh air, water, and season are apt for wedding, and other interferences are meaningless. Time, money, and labour are to be saved by planning well, and more importance is to be given to qualities leaving aside caste and wealth illusions. In the wedding *sanskar* (ritual), initially, introduction of bride-bridegroom and expression of determination for good work should be included. Then, holy work is to be performed by uttering *mangalashtaka* which contains motto of wedding, besides advice by a virtuous person. Blessing of elders is to be sought to behave with love for all.

> *Sanskar* of marriage, its importance the greatest;
> On its base social temple, so make it beautiful. ||101||
> Female, male, two wheels, complementary to each other really;
> With heavenly joy village will flourish, Tukadya says. ||103||

To him, female and male are not polar opposites but complementary to each other to flourish family, village, and society.

His approach to man-woman relationship recalls Tarabai Shinde who has penned *Stri-Purush Tulana* (1875), Mahatma Fule's revolutionary thoughts, reformative zeal of Maharshi Dhondo Keshav Karve and Mary Wolsoncraft, which has triggered off the thought and action in man-woman equality.

Political Facet

The Village State

The system of the self-governing village community was the basic feature of ancient Indian Policy. But, the village was not merely a primary unit of political administration. It was free and synthetical communal order in which the community found fulfillment of its economic and social needs as well as its religious and cultural urges. An ancient Indian village has been described as a village republic which was autonomous, self-sufficient, and governed by its own elected officers, satisfying its own needs. Such village system provided management for its own education, police, tribunals, all economic necessities, and functions.

The institution through which the village expressed its self governing and autonomous characters was the *gramsabha*. It was an assembly of elders and heads of families representing the entire population of the village. It was supreme administrative and judicial authority in the village.

The head of the assembly was called *'gramini'*, and was generally chosen by the people themselves but was sometimes nominated by the king. He was helped by a council of two, three, or five persons; or by committees elected for different purposes. *'Gramini'* and the council were ultimately responsible to the people who regularly met in the assembly hall to administer their affairs.

Gram Sabha and Gram Panchayat

Gramgeeta has the pulse of democracy and emphasises upon ideal system in the village.

> Ideal system to be of village, so narrated *Gramgeeta;*
> Expanded from village to become cosmic. ||49||
>
> Not understood village religion, what can be for world religion?
> To know this simply, the mean is of village. ||50||
>
> (Canto XXXVIII, 'Village Family')

'Rural Family' is the name attributed to *Gram Sabha* in *Gramgeeta,* which functions through *Gram Panchayat. Gram Sabha* or village assembly is formed for village upliftment, and it formulates laws. It is also termed as rural self-government. Every village has its own right to solve problems pertaining to village. Village assembly has power to formulate rules and plan for welfare of village. It is a supreme body in the village. Mahatma Gandhi contended,

> My idea of village *Swaraj* is that it is a complete republic, independent of its neighbours for its own vital wants, and yet interdependent for many others in which dependence is a necessity.[31]

To him, *Swaraj* means self-rule, self-restrain, and self-government, and depends entirely on our internal strength. In Article 40 of the Constitution of India, it is explicitly stated, "The state shall take steps to organise village *panchayats*, and endow them with such powers and authority as may be necessary to enable them to function as units of self-government." Constitution of India has empowered village assembly as Supreme Governing Body in the territory of a village. Right to give in village is confined to village assembly.

In *Gram Panchayat,* members are elected among villagers. If elected members don't function properly, *Gram Sabha* has power to change them. Government may direct to dissolve *Gram Sabha* but can't dissolve, being self-reliant. *Gram Panchayat* is a body of government officers whom *Gram Sabha* governs. It implements decision taken by *Gram Sabha.* In state, state assembly operates and in village, village assembly functions. Village being state, whatever lies within the limit of village is owned by village.

> Village rules village state, no over indulgence of anyone;
> In village, we will live by all means. ||83||
>
> (Canto XIX, 'Life Education')

Village rules village state and there is no indulgence of anyone. Village is to be self-reliant. Forest, pasture, lake, and land lie in the jurisdiction of village. Villager's attention is to be directed to make village self-reliant. Villagers have to train to make footwears from leather obtained from dead animals, obtain phosphorus from bones, prepare manure from waste and urine, and cultivate plants in farm. By becoming self-reliant with respect to food, clothes, and shelter, village can be self-governed.

> All to work for all, in the welfare of all our welfare;
> Great one to reveal lesson practicing with determination. ||123||
>
> In it greatness, village life will be self-reliant;
> This only real sign of ideal rural state. ||124||
>
> Village state, *Ramrajya*; self-reliance, this self-rule;
> Spoke universely honoured great ones; progress fine this. ||125||
>
> Our village one state, mother home of all indispensable;
> Whenever such ideals are, our relations there. ||126||
>
> (Canto XXXIX, 'Earth Paradise')

Village *swaraj*, village self-government as conceived by Mahatma Gandhi, is strengthening of *Panchayati Raj,* and Tukadoji conceptualises village as the welfare state, which is self-reliant, empowering *Gram Sabha.* Village is everyone's mother home. He associates with everything whatever is an ideal and during his life, he ventured to create ideal villages as Amgaon in Gondia district of Maharashtra.

Secular Spirit

Secularism has been and continues to be a central issues in our political and public life. From the pre-independence developments, centered on the question of Hindu-Muslim unity, the post-independence secular concept has evolved in a broader perspective.

There was originally no specific or explicit mention in Constitution which declared that India was a secular state. The forty-second constitution Amendment Act, 1976 inserted in the preamble the word 'secular', though even the earlier provisions regarding religion were implicitly pointing towards a secular state. During the last two decades, we are witnessing an increasing shift to religion in the sphere of Indian Politics. At the heart of the problem lies the issue of how to keep politics aloof from religion. Secular approach to Indian Society is mirrored in Tukadoji's verses:

(a) No party, no sect; no discrimination, opposition any;
Our village will live joyfully as family. ||3||

(Canto XXXIX, 'Earth Paradise')

(b) Let there be brotherhood always in India;
Render us blessings.

(c) Come people of any sect, any religion;
Open to all our temple is.

The concept of secularism is essentially Western. It is a product of struggle between the state and the church. It was propounded by the church as an assertion of its independence in its religious affairs from the control and regulation by state. Its constitutional and institutional manifestation is the separation of the state and the church. It was George Jacob Holyoake, in 1850, who coined for the first time the term and explained the meaning of the word 'secular', stating that it has no connection with religion and is concerned with the worldly things, no relation to the church or religions' rule. It was to him a non-religious term.

History reveals that secularism signifies the separation of the state and church. Secularism has necessarily not conflict with religion. In recent times, a new understanding of secularism has been emerging. Secularism does not mean no faith in religion or philosophy or life but indicates a spirit of tolerance and understanding of other person's religious faith. This spirit of secularism is an outlook of life. It ensures a peaceful existence of all people, professing diverse religions or faiths.

Religion is the faith in spiritual presence—recognition of a higher unseen controlling power, an eternal principle. In fact, religion is a way of life and code of conduct. The origin of religion is in the society of primitive men. Natural phenomenon are the sources of ideas in religion. Religion was born in the insecure conditions of primitive men and it is not made by God.

Secularism is not antithesis of religious devoutness. Vivekananda and Mahatma Gandhi were the devout Hindus, but their entire life and teachings embody the essence of secularism. True religion does not hate those professing other faiths. There is one God; we call Him by different names.

The concept of secularism in India emerged in the context of religions' pluralism as against religions' authoritarianism in the West. Unlike Europe, secularism in India arose not in the process of conflict between state and church, but as an attempt to unite the followers of different religious faiths. The need of secularism arose in India and secularism was conceived in two related contexts—first, to encounter the challenge of communalism to national integrity and second, to provide a basis for nationalism or nationalist movement, which was shared by all Indians irrespective of their religions. Secularism in India arose in the context of communalism and not religion. It is not anti-religion in India.

Tukadoji envisages village as family and treats a judge as its core pillar. Whatever five judges speak with responsibility reveals the sign of village religion and in it, idealness of our village prevails. *Gram Sabha* and *Gram Panchayat* attribute democratic and republic spirits to village administration.

Whatever five judges speak, the sign of village religion;
In it idealness of our village in our eyes. ||98||
Our village one family, the core pillar, a judge;
Pressure of justice on all, this pinnacle of progress. ||99||
With justice people behaved in truth era though no government;
Its conversion *panchayat,* democracy, republic. ||100||
(Canto XXXIX, 'Earth Paradise')

In his conception, justice, irrespective of caste, race, creed, and religion direct society to the pinnacle of success. Village, the unit of society, operates in democratic spirit, delegating power to masses. Mass power is reformative and energy is intrinsic in all people.

Time this of mass strategy, energy intrinsic all in people;
Can bow down empire, the power of mass determination. ||14||
(Canto XI, 'Village Security')

When potential energy in masses becomes kinetic, it topples down mighty empire too.

There is urgency in today's globalised and interdependent world to understand and define the term multiculturalism as a way of life, a philosophy, and a global phenomenon. Multiculturalism is contemporary global reality and concerns with more than one culture in a geographical area, called as a society. Culture deals with language, beliefs, ethos, and geographical identities. In a multicultural society or a plural-ethnic society, cultural differences prevail due to variables. Though the study of 'multiculturalism' had received impetus in 1990's, multicultural trends existed in human society before that, and exists in the present society in various forms. Multiculturalism is multifaceted reality. To C.W. Watson, it has implicit meaning of openness to change, receptivity to difference, passion for equality, and ability to recognise familiar self in the strangeness of others.[32] U.S.A., Canada, and India have multicultural societies but they vary in nature.

Religious tolerance is the essence of Indian secularism. All religions/isms whether it is Hinduism, Islam, Christianity, Sikhism, and Buddhism preach tolerance, equality, kindness, and brotherhood. Therefore, all of them are secular. In Tukadoji's song which has been accepted as the University song of Rashtrasant Tukadoji Maharaj Nagpur University, he exhorts:

> Let there be brotherhood always in India,
> Render us blessing,
> Let all sects, paths be one,
> Let no differences be,
> Let live poor-rich with happiness unanimously,
> Be then he be Hindu or Christian or Muslim,
> Let contentment of freedom be pervaded in all,
> Render us blessing.[33]

Tukadoji's vision is secular and prays for unity in diversity. He expounds that all sects and paths are to be one, diminishing differences. There should not be cleavage between poor and rich, Have not and Have, and let approaches in Hinduism, Christianity, Islam, and various other religions avail freedom for welfare of society to think and act freely.

Economic Aspect

Gramgeeta is dedicated to villagers and Tukadoji urged:

> Let your labour receive dignity, all attention be converged on you;
> Let light of humanity be glittered in world by this mean.
>
> ('Dedication leaflet')

He insisted on dignity of Labour and humanity.

Hon'ble C.D. Deshmukh, Finance Minister, Government of India, answered in March 1956 while discussing on budget,

> Indispensable issues of significance of urban and rural progress, creation of socialistic society...we will discuss latter. Now government is focusing on rural improvement and investing money. The same work is carried by Tukadoji in the states of Madhya Pradesh and Hyderabad, and his efforts are appreciable. It is in the

> interest of nation to motivate and organise villagers to improve village. For that purpose he wrote *Gramgeeta* and it is to be read in every villages. It is to be reached in the different states by translating it because progress is inherent in it.[34]

How can democratic power be operative for village elevation? Which are the economic pointers for village reform? These issues are delineated in *Gramgeeta* and Tukadoji's economic thought are pragmatic from the standpoint of rural restructuring. His economic remedial measures, such as (1) more production, (2) village self-reliance, (3) abolishment of economic inequality, (4) equal distribution of wealth, and (5) eradication of unemployment are still applicable to the development plans of the government of India.

More Production

More production is indispensable for progress of a nation. Labour power and intellect are wasted and, thus, by utilising human resource, labour power, engrossingly, village can be made happy. Tukadoji deconstructs the conventional meaning of *Geeta*, interpreting it in a new light, imparting restructured meaning to labour, worship, and *yajna*.

> Today ample production, medium it of mass service;
> Whoever will struggle for it, experiences *Geeta*. ||18||
>
> To dig a land of hand-length, worship this better than others;
> Impact its more than hundred lecturers. ||20||
>
> Which makes food available to labourer, work, the best than *yajna;*
> Otherwise something else not to support by mentioning *Geeta*. ||21||
>
> All have to work, village's wealth to increase;
> Here poor-rich not to be seen for work. ||26||
>
> (Canto XVIII, 'Labour Wealth')

All have to work, irrespective of poor-rich, to increase village wealth. To increase production to elevate living level of people and to increase national income with more speed are the prime

Occurred this of poverty-richness, distanced labourers;
Here owner they became, who were money receiver. ||20||
(Canto XVII, 'Poverty-Richness')

Tukadoji satirises duel nature of so called religious person:

Exploited thousand lives to increase diseases in them;
Then opened charity dispensaries, treating oneself religious. ||24||

Looking at today's labour, no bread to him;
Works he day night; what religious owner is! ||25||
(Canto XVII, 'Poverty-Richness')

Many persons accumulated money but no utility of it for society and they are as burgers,

Reverse happens even though, continues this ballad;
Figure this of rich-poor to wipe out in time to come. ||55||
(Canto XXXVIII, 'Village Family')

Equal Distribution of Wealth

To eradicate economic inequality Tukadoji emphasises upon equal distribution of wealth. Why to create inequality?

Why this phase to arrive? some plan to search out;
Poor-rich both will live better. ||37||
(Canto XVII, 'Poverty-Richness')

In village, wealths of rich persons are village property and wealthy persons have to help others for social welfare.

Wealth, blood of poor, let rich be behaved understanding it;
Labour, treasure of village, so it to respect. ||54||
(Canto XVII, 'Poverty-Richness')

He urges rich persons and land owners to contribute for village prosperity.

Wealth to give by rich persons, land to give by land owner;
Labour to give by workers, by all means. ||80||
(Canto XXXVIII, 'Village Family')

All people have to contribute for village prosperity to maintain equality by bridging up cleavage between oppressor and oppressed, and have and have not.

Eradication of Unemployment

The crucial problem in underdeveloped and developing nations is unemployment. Developed nations practically attempt to create jobs and from the perspective of elimination of unemployment, economic planning plays significant role. The wasted human resource is a tragedy of unplanned economic planning.

> But, those who want to be officer to dominate others;
> Expects laxity without work, unemployed they remain. ||33||
>
> (Canto XVIII, 'Labour Wealth')

To Tukadoji, everyone has to perform work. In village, efforts are to be directed to eliminate obstacles in life by adjusting business and hobby to all men-women. In village industries, skilled jobs, such as production of bags, footwear from leather of dead animals, mattress, chairs, bucket, cot, carpet, soap, decorative of oxen, and colours are to be performed.

> Such skilled jobs to perform, cottage industries;
> Anywhere unemployment will not be seen growing. ||67|
>
> (Canto XVIII, 'Labour Wealth')

In rural economic operation, Tukadoji points at practical parameters, such as business committee, share of wealth from village's rich persons, small saving rural bank, and co-operative enterprises.

> In village, business committee to be for continuous progress;
> Will channelise rural economic life by taking rein. ||87||
>
> By acquiring share of wealth from village's rich persons;
> For welfare of all in day-night it to be utilised. ||88||
>
> Some are landlords, rural economic store they are;
> Their all work to be handed over to workers. ||89||

Or if rich persons not turned by strength of farmers, workers;
Drop drop to be accumulated of their small savings. ||90||

Out of it, collection of objects to create, useful storehouse for all;
Without doubt, shop of all items to run collectively. ||91||

(Canto XVIII)

In cooperative enterprises, ownership is to be of all. There is to be a grain storage in which shares of people are to involve. When time demands, grains are to be distributed from it and taxation is to be decided by all.

In village prevails competition, this will check it;
Village bank will paralyse business man, moneylender. ||96||

(Canto XVIII)

In cooperative enterprise, Tukadoji supports the idea of shares of people, small savings, and opening of village bank for rural finance. He relates remuneration for work and increase in production.

A person without work, his name to suggest to committee;
Village service officer will provide work to him. ||100||

His duty to provide work, out of deposited fund in village;
Remuneration to give to him for work useful. ||101||

Full labour charges to give for happy family life;
Likewise production to increase in village. ||102||

All will be happy, quench the thirst of life;
Village state will be fine, wealthy of finance. ||103||

(Canto XVIII, 'Labour Wealth')

Remuneration for work to labouers is to be given from village fund for their family welfare. This stance will increase production which will subsequently eliminate hunger, poverty, and unemployment to create village state *(gramrajya)* with economic prosperity.

Muhammad Yunus concerns with cooperative enterprises, village bank, and small saving groups, and delineated these issues in his book *Creating a World without Poverty*. He initiated the process of small savings at Jobra village in Bangladesh and his efforts culminated into the establishment of village bank in 1983. Money lenders were exploiting the poor people of Bangladesh and the load of debt on farm labourers compelled them to work in company with more capital to benefit capitalists. In the villages in Bangladesh, he had given financial assistance with less interest to poor women to make them self-reliant.[35]

Yunus had interwoven the network of village banks and the related activities. Eye hospital with nominal fee for poor persons; Rural Danone Composite Project, initiated in collaboration with multinational Danone in February 2006 for edible product Yogart, useful for disease resistant vitamin; and rural phone company to know information technology are the practical parameters. Rural bank is a social industry. As in Bangaladesh, rural bank is in ownership of poor women; on the same line, a massive company can be in ownership of poor persons.

His conception of welfare society can be viewed practically in his Nobel Prize for peace acceptance speech on 10th November, 2006, at Oslo in Norway,

> In my view, poor people are dwarf plant. When you sow the best seed of tall tree in a small container, you get the exact replica of tall tree. No wrong is with the seed you selected; the land selected for it is not fertile. No wrong is with poor people. Society had not given support to them for progress. To bring poor people out of poverty, the need is to create conducive surroundings. Once momentum is given to energy and creative capacity, poverty will end in short time. We have to come forward to provide proper opportunity to manifest energy and creative capacity in every person.[36]

He was against exploitation of poor by rich and his structure of rural life was based on decentralised progress and self-reliance. In the era of globalisation, production system is speedily turning urban centred and dependent on foreign capital and technology.

The situation to manufacture raw products in village and then supply it to city is surfacing up. As thus, situation is creating to manufacture raw materials in village and to depend on city for seeds, manure, pesticide, construction materials, textiles, and modern technology, and consequently they will lend to exploitation of villagers. To Srinivas Khandewale, the question is, whether people have to live dependent, dull, and oppressed life, and why to live it? To answer these questions, it is justifiable to see what central and state governments, political parties, social organisation, and religious institutions can do.[37] In this context, when the issue creeps up what rural people can do, it becomes indispensable to know what *Gramgeeta* has to point at and how can it be implemented.

> Awake! Awake rich!, Officers! Intellectuals!
> Literates! Sages! Call for revolution. ||114||
>
> Enlight every village; diminish differences completely;
> Light the lamp of village elevation, Tukadya says. ||115||
>
> (Canto XVII, 'Poverty-Richness')

Before Independence especially in British period, the overall economic condition of India was very weak as the Britishers were not interested in the economic prosperity of India. Right from the dawn of Independence, it has been the constant endeavour of the central and state governments to change the depressed outlook of the rural economy in India. In the light of this objective, a wide gamut of rural construction programmes were launched from time to time to ameliorate the economic, social, and cultural life of the rural masses. But, these programmes has succeeded in achieving the desired goals. The Government of India continued its chain of efforts and accordingly launched a new strategy of rural development, namely IRDP in the year 1978-79, which extended to the entire country with effect from 2nd October, 1980.

IRDP (Integrated Rural Development Programme) is a centrally sponsored scheme funded by both the central and the state governments. It is implemented by the DRDA (District Rural Development Agency) at district level, BDO (Block Development Officer) at the block level, and VLW (Village Level

Worker) at the village level. The entire programme runs under the Director of the DRDA at the district level. The DRDA is entrusted with implementation and coordination among the various departments.

Villagers are to be made conscious about the schemes, the availability of bank loan, and subsidy components. Identification of beneficiaries should be given priority and, as per the guidelines, should be made joint responsibility of *Gram Sabha* and the agencies related to the implementation of IRDP, such as VLW, BDO, DRDA, bank, concerned circle officer of the revenue department, members of village community, and gramsevaks who should take active part to bring together these agencies in the credit camp.

Educational Scenario

The real education enhances the dignity of human being and increases his self-respect. In education, quality is an enlightenment and awakening the hidden potential of an individual and hence, quality in education of an individual is long, continuous, and ceaseless odyssey. Education is visualised as an evolutionary as well as transformative force so that each individual is enable to evolve from material consciousness towards superior planes of intellectual and spiritual consciousness.

Macaulay's Educational Strategy

Lord Macaulay's British Education Policy was decisive in changing Indian Educational scenario, and the Policy's essence is mirrored in his speech, delivered in British Parliament on 2nd February, 1835:

> I have travelled across the length and breadth of India and I have not seen one person who is a beggar, who is a thief. Such wealth I have seen in this country, such high moral values, people of such calibre, that I do not think we would ever conquer this country, unless we break the very backbone of this nation, which is her spiritual and cultural heritage, and, therefore, I propose that we replace her old and ancient education system, her culture, for if the Indians think that all that is foreign and English is good and greater than their

> own, they will lose their self-esteem, their native self-culture, and they will become what we want them, a truly dominated nation.[38]

Macaulay's educational strategy was to break Indian spiritual and cultural heritage, to think all that is foreign and English is good; to lose self-esteem; and to root out native culture. As such, today's orientation towards native culture, searching of native roots in the fast blowing wind of globalisation, is of paramount importance.

Indian Approaches

Mahatma Jyotiba Fhule opened the first school for girls at Bhide Wada, Pune on 1st January, 1848. Savitribai Phule became the first women teacher of India, and her associate was Fatima. Vitthal Ramji Shinde, Rajarshi Shahu Maharaj, Karmveer Bhaurao Patil, and Maharshi Dhondo Keshav Karve were instrumental in providing access to education to masses. Rabindranath Tagore revived the ancient *Gurukul* system amidst nature with spirit of freedom in the form of Shantiniketan.

Vivekananda opined that education is manifestation of potential which is already present in man. To W.B. Yeats, education is not filling of pail but lighting of fire. Tukadoji also asserts that education is manifestation of infinite potential in self.

> As thus strength infinite being, manifests silently with study;
> No end to self power for anyone. ||7||
>
> (Canto XXXVI 'Art of Life')

Light is infused in us and a stone becomes a diamond by processing. As the musk in the naval of musk deer adorns the forehead of a king, inner knowledge when manifested reaches to a higher level. Besides knowledge, Tukadoji attributes importance to conscience, "one who accepts the road of progress, enlights conscience inside (37:17)".

Mahatma Gandhi stressed on all round development of an individual:

> Man is neither mere intellect, nor the gross animal body, nor the heart or soul alone. A proper and harmonious

> combination of all the three is required for the whole man and constitutes the true economics of education.[39]

To him, education is coordination of body, mind, and spirit, and basic education is physical, intellectual, and moral development of children through the medium of handicraft; adult education includes political education and literacy education; religious education means not only ethics but also the doctrines of various religions of the world with reverence and tolerance; and self-supporting education is industrial training and learning of skills. Education is necessary for new society of intellectuals. Multi-disciplines are to be taught in curriculum.

> Different educative modes to teach, though poor or rich;
> By this mode village to supply more wealth. ||107||
>
> (Canto XIX, 'Life Education')

In the *ashrama* system, knowledge of archery, Ayurveda, weaponry, painting, leather art, construction work, pottery, music, cookery, fine techniques of home management, horse test, and emerald test were taught to students. Diverse arts are to be taught to students. In his conception, an impetus is to be provided to handcrafts and cottage industries. Boys and girls have to be given practical teaching. Education is to enhance dignity of village and "Planning of our rural structure is to be taught". Potential is hidden and it is to be manifested in various forms.

> Many will be service-oriented, many skilled artists;
> Village they will enrich with industries, business. ||77||
>
> Many will create machines, many will be historian;
> Some will be skilled advisers in our village. ||78||
>
> Many will be judges, many creator of poetic world;
> Many will increase yields in farm by new researches. ||79||
>
> Many will be politicians, many philosophers;
> Many will bring laurels in sports for village. ||80||
>
> Many saint adviser; many brave, protector;
> Many export in commerce, servicemen, in every work. ||81||

In his eyes, the disciplines like engineering, medical science, agriculture, social sciences, sports education, commerce, management, fine arts, and literature play crucial role in reformation of human society. Research culture is to be developed to investigate truth and carry out research in various disciplines for welfare of village and society at large. Adult education has to play the role to literate people and make them conscious of their rights.

Rural Restructure

In his speech at Kishoreganj (now, in Bangladesh) in 1907, Aurobindo Ghose emphasised the importance of village committees and village institutions:

> ...Without education and enlightenment of masses and labour class from political perspective, new nation can't function well. Initiation is to be from villages to know about independence of masses. Consciousness of independence is to be created with the help of village committees in villages first and it is to be expanded to district, state, national levels. It is not possible to comprehend and consent the concept of national independence to people in villages at present. Utility and necessity of national independence will be understood after the experience of independence by village institutions. It is difficult to educate masses by imparting political education without establishment and operation of village committees.[40]

He emphasises upon the self-governance of village administration as the necessity of national and political independences.

> Village rules village state, no over indulgence of anyone;
> In village, we will live by all means. ||83||
>
> (Canto XIX, 'Life Education')

He advocates self-reliance of village and no excess interference of external forces. Education is not to be confined to elites but it is to percolate to masses, and new society of intellectuals will emerge of it.

> Father, shepherd, brings wooden sticks; uncle sells bengals, clothes;

> Another uncle, job holder, but he, security guard, an attendant. ||91||
>
> Staple food to eat, herd of cattle in company;
> Why not to appreciate, if he proceeds for study? ||92||

Education is not monopoly of any one but its doors are to be opened to those who deserve and long for it. In education, keeping aside differences of rich and poor, sense of equality is to prevail. In his essay published in *Hindustan,* New Delhi, on 2nd February, 1956, Tukadoji elucidated:

> With five year plan, the nation is marching forward. Along with this if we make learners in school laborious and entrepreneur, production in villages and cities can be increased by cleaning and beautifying them. I intend to implement the programme of village reform in school-colleges by limiting it to for some months or a year and to activate it besides regular curriculum. The examination results are to be based on the completion of constructive work, not only on written or oral answers based on bookish knowledge.[41]

Students learn agriculture from the teachers who themselves practice agricultural activities, and their curriculum is based on these practical agricultural activities. In such case, students learn fast and perform well when their results are declared. Likewise construction work, blacksmithy, carpentry, and *khadi* weaving are to be taught in villages to make them self-reliant.

Quality in Higher Education

Quality in higher education is of prime concern for the countries world over. It is quite clear that higher education present challenges to quality assurance.

> To be seen with quality, intellect, work;
> Though these kinds to be, sense of equality not to leave. ||71||
>
> Receives society education this, a fortunate day it is;
> Then no fear in future to fragment consciousness. ||72||
>
> (Canto XVII, 'Poverty-Richness')

In education, quality is an enlightenment and awakening the hidden potential of an individual, and hence, quality in education is long, continuous, and ceaseless odyssey. It is never an accident, it is to enhance and sustain for excellence. Education is to be life oriented. Right impression in life is the sole motto of education. If inclusive elevation is not possible by education system, it can't free man from psychic slavery.

Besides the core values, such as contributing to national development, fostering global competence among students, promoting the use of technology, and quest for excellence, the quality network of National Assessment and Accreditation Council, Bengaluru, is based on inculcating human value system among students.

> Although skill development is crucial to the success of students in the job market, skills are of less value in the absence of appropriate value systems. We have to shoulder the responsibility of inculcating the desirable value systems amongst the students. In a country like India, with cultural pluralities and diversities, it is essential that students imbibe the appropriate values commensurate with social, cultural, economic, and environmental realities, at the local, national, and universal levels... The seeds of values sown in the early stages of education, mostly aimed at cooperation and mutual understanding, have to be reiterated and re-emphasised at the higher educational institutions, through appropriate learning experiences and opportunities.[42]

NAAC stresses upon learning experiences and opportunities fused with values in education, envisaging social, cultural, economic, and environmental facets.

Gramgeeta insists on inculcating the core universal values like truth, righteousness, love for nation, dignity of labour, cleanliness, secular attitude, equality, discipline, cooperation, character, collectivity, justice, honesty, environmental conservation, politeness, and tolerance.

(1) Truth

Why to do this? Practice after searching truth;

One to drown, other to take to hell, this not to happen with selfishness. ||62||

(Canto XLI, 'Glory of Books')

(2) Love for Nation

Festivity people like, search for remedy in that way;
Awakening of national spirit dauntlessly, festival it to follow. ||92||

(Canto XXIII, 'Festival Celebration')

(3) Dignity of Labour

To dig a land of hand length, worship better than others;
Effect its, more than hundred lectures. ||20||

(Canto XVIII, 'Labour Wealth')

(4) Cleanliness

All to clean village for hygiene well;
Through dirt, manure, new glory will come up. ||73||

(Canto XII, 'Village Purification')

(5) Secular Attitude

No party, no sect, no caste, discrimination, opposition some;
With joy our village lives like single family. ||3||

(Canto XXXIX, 'Earth Paradise')

(6) Equality

All to turn to equality, oneness to implement practically;
Entire world to harmonise at supreme, thinks saint. ||75||

(Canto XXXII, 'Saint Nature')

(7) Discipline

Sitting arrangement by all, all to sit in row peacefully;
Increase it in the righteous emotion in all minds of prayer. ||54||

(Canto XXVII, 'Collective Prayer')

(8) Cooperation

Strong notion of cooperation, the focal formula of education;

No importance to education without cooperation. ||33||
(Canto XIX, 'Life Education')

(9) Collectivity

So to experience this knowledge, constructed the mean with vast mind;
The place of collective prayer for collectiveness. ||46||
(Canto XXVII, 'Collective Prayer')

(10) Justice

With justice people behaved in truth era, though no government;
Its conversion *panchayat,* democracy, republic. ||100||
(Canto XXXIX, 'Earth Paradise')

(11) Environmental Conservation

Company of plants, the essence in the sunlight;
Labour in pure air, an ambrosia to all. ||87||
(Canto XV, 'Improvement of Cow Race')

(12) Character

The prime base human conduct, this to maintain best;
To make village, well-equipped, the ideal picture of world. ||48||
(Canto I, 'Vision of God')

(13) Tolerance

Proceeds with conscience, lifts who is fallen;
Becomes victim for the welfare of others. ||62||
(Canto XXXVI, 'Art of Life')

(14) Politeness

Pity, forgiveness, peace, politeness, honesty everywhere;
Simple and affectionate nature, the gift of God. ||37||
(Canto VII, 'Strength of Behaviour')

It is essential that students imbibe the appropriate values commensurate with social, cultural, economic, and environmental realities, at the local, national, and universal levels.

The knowledgeable books will purify village and instill love, knowledge, truth, and joy.

For this village will be pure; love, knowledge, truth, joy;
Will be for all, such responsible books to be in village. ||122||

(Canto LX, 'The Study of Book')

Everyone has to know the nature of the world, duty, and the means for welfare of all.

Prayer educates humanity and inculcates the values of discipline, peace, maturity, and knowledge of conduct. The motto of prayer is to move the world in righteous direction. Co-ordinated text of prayer is not a steel boundary but scope is there for everyone to enter. We can take principle from anywhere but it shouldn't be one-sided. One has to be tolerant towards others. Such prayer is influential for peace and vastness requires for it. When hearts come nearer, intimacy will develop and in the world love, happiness, and peace will prevail. The conflicts among religions, sects, and nations cannot be resolved without love.

Every religion has its own principles of prayers and knowing unison pertaining to each, all have to merge in one and there is to be one prayer for the world.

One prayer of all world, one stance of all world;
Why not to bring unison in all world? ||94||

(Canto XXVIII, 'Prayer and World Religion')

Narrowness of mind creates hindrances in coming nearer to the unison of principles in all religions, which is to be taught; and it will cultivate respect for other religions.

Prayer, the school of humanities; the core feel of rural culture;
In the mould of prayer, ends conception of difference. ||96||
Companions we all are, thought such to increase;
On this rests the heavenliness of village. ||97||

(Canto XXVII, 'Collective Prayer')

Village being basic unit for development, prayer is to continue in village and so the lamp's flame of collectivity will light for all time.

Peace can be the world, how impossible it for village?
For ever unity by collective prayer, Tukadya says. ||100||

(Canto XXVII, 'Collective Prayer')

The remedy for world peace is coordination of all religions and collective prayer is the school of mass reformation. It is to retain human values, and will bring peace and unity in village and the world.

Stress on Science and Technology

Truth is hidden in the world which we see with our eyes. Science, religion, and literature explore truth in diverse modes. Science investigates truth in the world by experimental mean and applying logic, analysis, and objective stance. Truth in science is experimentally verified and relates to cause and effect relationship. It is objective truth, inferred, keeping aside caste, sect, language, hate, and pre-notion. Scientific approach comprises of components, such as fact, cause, effect, logic, and objectiveness. Truth in science is applied to technology, which operates in objective mode. But, individual or collective preferences channelise the operation of technology in positive or negative direction.

Religion attempts to know the truth in the world with the means of faith and experience. No doubt, a man is mighty and intellectually strong, but he realised from ancient time, century to century, that he had not created water on the earth, the sunlight, living beings, life force (spirit), systems in human body, and vastness of cosmos, and, thus, came to know his limitations. Man ventured to know, out of curiosity, creation of vast cosmos and nature and purpose of human life by means of faith and experience which have culminated into emergence of religion. Religion and science are the different means to find out truth in the world.

Science is paralytic without religion, and vice versa. Albert Einstein has exhorted, "Science without religion is lame, religion without science is blind."[43] He has profound faith in religion and its adherence to human values.

Vinoba Bhave expounded in his speech on 12th July, 1965 at Gurukunj:

> My assertion is that the power of science is to conjunct with spiritual knowledge and by combining two, village creation is to be. Today science has started devasting

> villages and spiritual knowledge is left behind, as native entity...this which is the power of science is to be applied in agriculture.[44]

He viewed that science and spiritual knowledge are to be amalgamated for national and global progress.

Religion, science, and literature are explorers of truth. Literature is not only form and structure but also content; and coherent amalgam of form and content, structure and meaning. Tukadoji's language, conversing with heart and intellect of a reader, is a mass language, which has clarity of scientific presentation, and though not clustered with images, has simplicity and fluidity. His diction has dialects from rural life, e.g., *fadi* (flatslab), *mot* (leather container), *sandor* (rope), *berdya* (nose rope), and *muskya* (mouth mask);

> Breaking stones created flat slab, sharpened it straight;
> Look beautiful all after fitting it house. ||38||
>
> Broom, mat, weaving strips, cots, doormat, leather container, rope;
> Made beautiful sowing pipe, plough in new style. ||39||
>
> Spinned separating cotton, weaved fine cloth, sweater;
> Made, nose-rope, mouth mask, rope net. ||40||
>
> (Canto XIII, 'Art of Village Creation')

and *kunpakati* (fence of thorns), *gawati shakar* (thatch), and *udwe-hude* (waste, dust particles).

> Thorns fence, grass weed possibly not to be in village;
> Waste, piles, dust particles not to be scattered. ||78||

Tukadoji's diction is crystal clear, familiar, and syntax, not complex. In the structure of couplet, there are arrangements of statements besides non-irrupted flow and, as thus, it has the fervour of rhetoric.

Rhetoric language is the indispensability of *Gramgeeta* because the positive change in mass psychology, taking into confidence the masses, is the pivotal motto of it. Narration is in the form of the conversation between narrator and audience, and has impact on readers. Usha Madhav Deshmukh has reflected in *Maitra*:

> Maharaj's *owi* (the couplet) doesn't wait for poetic and artistic but it manifests spontaneously with momentum, force with whatever chemical composition is created on the level of consciousness, as thus this poem is like direct words as Tukaram's. The objective of *owis* in *Gramgeeta* is to reach to people's mind and inspire them to work. So one in this poem, experiences momentum, force, buoyancy of words. This poem attempts to eliminate our inertia. Understanding, explanation and to structure the content in rhetoric style is the strength and limit of *owis* in *Gramgeeta*.[45]

The limit, rhetoric style, which Usha Madhav Deshmukh underlines, is also the strength of *Gramgeeta*. Because of rhetoric fervour—simple verbal mould with ease—narration transmits influentially to readers. 'Song of Myself' from Walt Whitman's *Leaves of Grass* has this limit too but Whitman and Tukadoji, both, are integrated and honest with their purport in their creative venture, with statement centered and rhetoric fervour.

Canto opens in the dialogue form between a narrator and listeners. Its texture has no softness of silk, no smoothness of native *khadi*, but has thickness. Structural construction of *Gramgeeta* has scientific precision and is divided into eights parts (Quintets), each part having five cantos. Canto XLI depicts significance, purpose, result, and practice of *Gramgeeta* and the role of readers. It is an accessory to the core of *Gramgeeta*. Structurally, each Canto has three components—consequence, reason, and remedy—and Canto XIII, 'Art of Village Creation' illustrates them.

Consequence:

> Where work, wealth enters; knowing this formula;
> Than city, our village to beautify. ||1||
>
> Forgot people this; misfortune due to laziness;
> Prevail misery, poverty everywhere in village. ||2||
>
> Arrived machines; paralysed industrial skills in village;
> For work, to city, skilled persons have gone. ||3||
>
> To city, intellect of village, prosperity of village have;
> Labour power, handicrafts too have gone. ||4||

Remained chiefly farming in village; continues it somehow;
At different end, the flow of special intellect, power, wealth. ||5||

Wander highly qualified, an energetic for employment;
How can village be elevated, if not industries, farming? ||6||

Reason:

Because raw materials at village, provide livelihood;
Situation deteriorated in village, no refining of raw materials. ||8||

At low rate, raw material; price, fourtimes when refined;
How can villagers be happy? Empty bellied, though producers. ||9||

Remedy:

Total self-reliance, the core mean of their happiness;
Not depending on city, all have to work. ||10||

Planning, the best intellectual skill, strength of power;
Self-reliance to enhance, shedding laziness of all. ||11||

Here and there love for self-reliance, some work at home;
Others to help with detachment, doing one's work. ||12||

At home, children to work; farming, work, business to do self;
Wife, children to be happy, labouring hard. ||13||

In hand, the mean for industry; reflection on the name of Rama;
Great is this religion of village people. ||14||

Each element of village, artist, serviceman to be;
Who decor ate village making one's home beautiful? ||15||

The structure is constructed by logically arranging the components, i.e., consequence, reason, and remedy. Tukadoji insists to link with truth and pure life, which infuses gravitational force to act. He urged "not to succumb to orthodoxy or dry intellect (LX:47)".

Rational View and Environmental Consciousness

In the name of deity, some kill living beings and, as thus, this practice is to be ceased improving people's sentiments. Some deceive people and teach delusionary opinion and penance, but one has to be aware of it.

> Then 'frowned goddess' some say; call some for an incantation;
> Deeming it due to outer cause, waves lamps. ||14||
> Treat it some, a black magic, an evil; controls some ghost;
> Kills patient without medicines, with nonsense. ||15||
> (Canto XIV, 'Village Hygiene')

Tukadoji hammers on superstitions, such as frowning of goddess and treating patient without medicines by a black magic and controlling of ghost.

As Gadge Baba was instrumental in cleanliness drive, Tukadoji too assigns importance to cleanliness to purify village. In villages, roads are dirty having protruded platforms, which cause difficulty for vehicles; there are sanitary openings on roads; and wells are not repaired and have polluted water. Char latrine to be made, and manure prepared out of waste leads to fertility of land. Cow-urine and cow dung increase soil fertility and consequently grain production.

> All to clean village for hygiene well;
> Through dirt, manure, new glory will come up. ||73||
> (Canto XII, 'Village Purification')

To keep hygiene well, health home is to be run in village for welfare of all beings. Naturopathic means are to be available for treatment.

> Plants, creepers, nodules, roots to use for medicines;
> By naturopathic means they are to provide. ||110||
> (Canto XIII, 'Art of Village Creation')

Understanding the role of photosynthesis and sunlight as an energy source, Tukadoji writes,

> Sunlight produces roots, vegetables, fruits;
> Nutrients they all are for hygiene. ||106||
>
> (Canto XIV, 'Village Hygiene')

He relates nature, sunlight, labour in pure air, and hygiene in his words:

> Company of plants, the essence in the sunlight;
> Labour in pure air, an ambrosia to all. ||87||
>
> (Canto XV, 'Improvement of Cow Race')

These lines remind of Tukaram's line, "Tree creepers, our relatives, forest dwellers". Environment is complimentary to living beings, and environmental conservation inclusive natural resources is need of time for survival of human beings, plants, and animals. Ramification of industries in the process of globalisation causes the emission of green-house gases and poses threat to nature and consequently to human existence.

Freedom of Action and Conscience

Physical exercise, *yoga-asana*, expels inertia and pours sportiveness in body. Besides blood circulation, it develops mental ability. For a well built bull and more milk yielding cow, an ideal ox, a green pasture, and ample fodder are to be in village to facilitate fertilisation process. To Tukadoji, result is an outcome of an action—"But no fruits of *rui* to coconut tree; reap as one sows (35:24)."

> Sowed chilly, sugarcane in farm; fruits pungent, sweets in hands;
> What is role of water here? Fruits form as sow. ||61||
>
> (Canto XXXIV, 'Fatalism')

Pleasure and pain are fruits of action. A man is an outcome of his thought and action.

> Freedom to act, mega power, this in man's hand;
> Architect of our fortune, we are. ||27||
>
> (Canto XXXV, 'Effort Influence')

Birth is a play of will and in the world, there is an amalgam of many wills. Freedom to act is mega power in the hands of man, and responsibility of human action lies on the shoulder of a man.

> Grafting differently, flowers blossom variantly;
> Can this happen ever with inactiveness? ||106||
>
> (Canto XXXV, 'Effort Influence')

As a man grafts on a plant differently, myriad flowers will blossom.

"Struggle for existence" and "survival of fittest" are important Darwin's prepositions for the existence of living being. In today's world, one has to make fit to compete.

> But this regulation, not humane; decorate it to beast-birds;
> Oviparous, viviparous, microbes, plants, on this way. ||51||
> Proceeded human being on that way, caused chaos in the world;
> 'Might is right', this verdict, not to call art of life. ||52||
> Which animals did survive in the world without collective tendency?
> Live and let live beings, people, this real art of life. ||53||
>
> (Canto XXXVI, 'Art of Life')

Man has conscience which differentiates human beings from other beings. Aggression is not the rule in human life but the real art of life is "to live and let live". *Gramgeeta* propounds the role of ethical values besides rational exploration in human life. Struggle for existence is inevitable to survive and compete. One should not rely on fate but on human efforts. Human efforts and research are transformative forces to search human life, the world, and space.

> Fascination of youth in other nations, relentless new research much;
> Spell of it to experience by educated village youth. ||56||
>
> (Canto XVIII, 'Labour Wealth')

In educated village youth, research attitude and zeal to investigate are to be developed, as in youth in progressed and progressive nations. Research in various disciplines made it possible to scale new heights in exploration in space, climbing high mountain, invention of nuclear weapons, electrical and electronic devices, and controlling happenings in the world.

Tukadoji doesn't disdain progress in science and technology which has brought human comfort but he points at utilising scientific and technological measures with conscience for welfare of society.

> Flew to the Mars, climbed Himalaya's peak completely;
> Searched fire-rockets, nuclear-rockets, massive hydrogen too. ||112||
>
> Listen from crore miles, singing, lecture of each other;
> Bringing within reach, the world made home to inhabit. ||113||
>
> (Canto XXXV, 'Effort Influence')

His scientific precision in structure construction, attack on superstitious practices, measures for hygiene, environmental conservation, pragmatic attempts, and research attitude constitute scientific approach.

Sri Gurudeo Seva Mandal

On 25th March, 1935, Raosaheb Thakur and his mother Gangabai Thakur donated four acres of land at Mozari for Tukadoji's humanitarian and social welfare work, where Sri Gurudeo Dharma Sevashram was opened. *Aarti Mandal*, first at Sangvi-Mohadi, was founded in November 1936 and subsequently at other places, centers were active as the means for rural unity. Besides self reliance of villages Tukadoji infused national spirit in masses at Chimur-Ashti in Chandrapur district of Maharashtra and in its vicinity in 1942, which resulted into revolt against the British dominance and oppression. On 15th April, 1943, the first issue of *Sri Gurudeo*, monthly magazine, was published to propagate his mission of rural development, national development, and global development, under editorship of A.W. Nawade, Sudam Sawarkar, and the management of J.D. Nikam and Pandurang Sabnis, from Saraswati Printer; and the function was inaugurated at the hands of Polegaonkar Maharaj. At the time of inauguration Dr. Shivajirao Pathvardhan, Veer Wamanrao Joshi, Nanasaheb Bamangaonkar, Hirlekar, and Londhe were present. Thakurbag at Mozari was named as Gurukunj in March 1945. In September 1945, *Sri Gurudeo Mahila Mandal,* the woman wing of the missionary programme, was inaugurated, and it was directed by Radhadevi Goenka, Prabhatai Deshmukh, Vimala Thakar, and Venutai Wankhade. Its Central Office was at Asra and its network was ramified and the camps were organised to educate women. Vimala Thakar was also active in the Land Donation Movement of Vinoba Bhave. From 1960s to 1980s, she taught meditation in thirty-five countries. Her conspicuous publications are *Life is to be Related, Blossoms of Friendship, Totality in Essence, Nijmegan University Talks, Talks in Ceylon and California, Banaras University Talks, Five Talks Given At Claremont, California*, and others. Her works have been translated in Dutch, French, German, Spanish, and Portuguese languages.

Tukadoji met with Mahatma Gandhi at Ganpatrao Tikekar's house at Nagpur on 30th March, 1936. He stayed at Sevagram from 14th July, 1936 to 13th August, 1936 and involved in daily programmes at *Ashrama*. Here, he came in contact with Mirabehn, Sarhadda Gandhi, Dr. Rajendra Prasad, Pandit Jawaharlal Nehru, Acharya Kripalani, Mahadevbhai Desai, Manu Gandhi, and Amrit Kunwar.

Conception and Practice

Tukadoji succinctly said to welcome *Sri Gurudeo Seva Mandal* with the intention to converge the attention on "the principle based reformative plan of new era" besides the elevation of villages; and involving oneself in its philosophy of convincing the people.

His direction to *Sri Gurudeo Seva Mandal* was definite which he implemented practically in the concrete form.

> ...We have encourage to create collective spirit among people and to erect the sign of their righteous work; pre-decided it is but it is redetermined—its rejuvenation is initiated. Difference is that, what I saw, to attribute importance to their grades and groups of cults, keeping

> aside the basic philosophical vision, to me, being felt as an appropriate, I am planning to assign it new utilitarian nature.[46]

Wandering in India and abroad he unfurled the flag of *Sri Gurudeo Seva Mandal,* whose focal objectives are spiritual development, village development, social development, national development, and global development, to harmonise relationship between man and man, and strive for world peace. To Tukadoji *Sevamandal* is not only the service center of *Ramdhaoon* and mass prayer but it also includes culture and organisation besides other issues beneficial for life. He reiterated that prayer doesn't deviate man from work but it infuses beauty, sanctity, and enthusiasm in it, and from the standpoint of life, prayer is to be conjuncted with entrepreneurship.

Tukadoji links World Religion and *Sri Gurudeo Seva Mandal* and highlights:

> By emphasising upon sublime principles of all religions in the world, to direct towards the art, to live together, to the people of all religions, and to tell about the road of happiness and peace is the crux of World Religion what we understand and it is the mission of *Seva Mandal*.[47]

He links the *Mandal* and the people of the different religions, giving a clarion call to "come from any religion; come from any sect" and to be conscious for love for the world. P.Y. Deshpande—philosopher and editor of *Bhavitavya*—reiterated that the social work of *Sri Gurudeo Seva Mandal* is the new mould of traditions of saints and progressive in nature.

> I contend that Saint Tukadoji Maharaj and the work of *Gurudeo Seva Mandal* is progressive because he is enabling common villagers to break the shackles of tradition against progress. He changed the opinions of lacs of people to eradicate untouchability among masses. He is igniting the flame of duty by hammering on inactiveness and stressing the significance of utterance of name.[48]

P.Y. Deshpande alleges that *Gurudeo Seva Mandal* being the new mould of traditions of saints, breaks the limitations of traditions, and crosses the barriers towards progress. Acharya Pralhad Keshav Atre deciphered in the issue of *Sri Gurudeo*, February 1965, "Gurukunj is not *ashrama*. It is not penance place, it is not temple for *bhajan*, worship, prayer, but as what Maharaj asserted, this is massive, pious experiment to create new man for new India." [49]

Sri Gurudeo Seva Mandal runs Residential School, Sri Gurudeo Industry, Sri Gurudeo Ayurved Hospital, Sri Gurudeo Exercise Temple, Sri Gurudeo Library, and Sri Gurudeo Publications, besides the women wing to render service to masses, and its odyssey is from self elevation to mass elevation. Vimala Thakar, the leading personality at women wing, said, "Enlight ourselves. This is the base of service and this is pinnacle of service".

Gurukunj Mozari, the experimental center of *Sri Gurudeo Seva Mandal,* was visited thrice by the then President of India, Hon'ble Dr. Rajendra Prasad—on 12th February, 1949 for Gandhi Memorial Function; on 25th April, 1954, the next day after the foundation ceremony for *Sri Gurudeo Sevashram* at Nagpur; and in 1961—and the then Vice President of India, Hon'ble Dr. Sarvepalli Radhakrishnan visited on 29th January, 1958 for inauguration of a Training Centre. Hon'ble Indira Gandhi visited the center on 19th March, 1956 and the then President of India, Hon'ble Pratibha Patil visited on 6th January, 2010, on the occasion of Tukadoji's Birth Centenary Celebration.

Tukadoji understood the gravity of consequences of his endeavour, *Sri Gurudeo Seva Mandal* but material orientation in employees was increasing and service oriented, selfless, unattached and spiritual servicemen were on decline. Material oriented tendencies and service oriented tendencies can't live together. Tukadoji had decided to create an independent platform for the propagation of practical philosophy of *Sri Gurudeo Seva Mandal* for the workers who were service oriented, selfless, and living spiritual life. Tukadoji made it clear about *Seva Mandal*, "It is not institute, but an attitude". He deciphered the mission of the service venture in *Sri Gurudeo*, Issue 6, 1945:

> *Seva Mandal* in not created to perform what is unnecessary; it has to accept all directions logically

> whatever have emerged for the development of human society, though they are ours or of other but its core purport is human welfare by accepting the qualities whatever are indispensible for inclusive progress of human society.[50]

Sudamdada Sawarkar, Shyamraodada Mokdam, and Tukaramdada Gitacharya dedicated missionaries were instrumental to bring Tukadoji's proposed ideas into practice. Sudamdada and Shyamraodada were involved in the organisational work of propagation and Tukaramdada in the establishment of *Gram Sabha* for village creation. To implement his thought, he freed his dedicated serviceman, *Karmayogi* Tukaramdada Gitacharya who was at the apex position for nine years at Mozari. On the suggestion of Tukadoji, Balasaheb Desai, the Home Minister of Maharashtra, became the Apex Officer of *Sri Gurudeo Seva Mandal* for administration and practical measures.

Tukaramdada practiced silence and penance for twelve-years to boost up spiritual power at Adyal-Tekadi in the district of Chandrapur, Maharashtra. The different phases of *Gramgeeta's* practical and self-power came into practice through the penance of Dada. Adyal-Tekadi is embodiment of its practical aspect. The focal objective of this experiment is to create self-reliant, self-respected, and self-regulated society based on the dignity of labour and curbing social injustice, malpractices, fall of character, and material obsession to infuse in spiritual strength to society. Keeping pace with objectives, the experiments like organic farming, organic manure, weaving, preparation of mat and tooth powder, and domestication of cows are in practice, and the programmes like Master Diploma in Panchagavya Therapy, Diploma in Naturopathy and Yoga Science (D.N.Y.S.), Certificate Course in Yoga and Naturopathy (C.C.Y.S.), and Certificate Course in Diet and Nutrition (C.D.N.) run by Naturopathy Centre; training for village security and operation of *Gram Sabha*; vocational courses in carpentry and construction work; basic knowledge of electric fitting, plumbing, winding, welding, cutting, grinding, and screen printing, are implemented. Products are manufactured in industries with self-reliancy. Gramgeeta Global University runs *Gramgeeta* oriented Life Education College which conducts the courses relating to practical knowledge, physical exercise, music, hygiene, and industries with self-reliance.

The villages like Chorati, Lakhapur, Bothali near Brahmapuri in district Chandrapur; Amgaon in district Bhandara; and Sirsoli in Ashti tehsil of Wardha district are the practical examples of his theoretical conception. Nearly seven hundred fifty acres of forest is governed by villagers of Lakhapur as per resolution by *Gram Sabha* (village assembly). Besides self-reliance of villages, Tukadoji infused national spirit in the minds of people at Chimur-Ashti in 1942, which resulted into revolt against Britishers in 1942. In Sirsoli, the famous village in 1942 freedom movement, cooperative society and public grain store are opened for the benefit of villagers.

Tukaramdada (the staunch propagator of Tukadoji's mission), Shyamraodada Mokadam, Vimala Thakar, Anna Hazare (reformer of village, advocator of human rights, and crusader against corruption), Dr. Brahmananda Sharma (activist of tribal and masses), and Lakshmandada Narkhede were instrumental to bring Tukadoji's utopian vision into practice. Anna Hazare's native village Ralegaon Siddhi in Parner taluka, in the district of Ahmednagar, which he reformed, is living embodiment of *Gramgeeta's* utopian vision. Popatrao Pawar, *sarpanch* of Hiware Bazar, the village in Ahmednagar district, has turned barren land in the village to fertile land by raising the level of water, and made the village an ideal experimentation by practicing in masses de-addiction drive, literary programme, cleanliness, village industries, and opening educational institution for rural students. Devaji Topha is a pivotal force in strengthening the tribal village, Lekha-Mendha in Gadchiroli district, which became the first village to be granted community forest rights and has used the opportunity to the fullest and sold bamboos worth twenty lacs in 2016 by seeking the resolution in village *Gram Sabha*. Now, no villager is in debt. Patoda-Gangapur, the village in Aurangabad district, was transformed as the ideal village by Bhaskarrao Pere Patil by providing toilets in every home, closed drainage system, CCTV surveillance, hot water to every home, and sensor operation in *Gram Panchayat*. At Rajgad in the district Chandrapur, Chandu Patil Marakwar closed his liquor shops and then ventured to mould his village ideal by insistence on unopposed election, no contract of village development to outsider, planning by *Gram Sabha*, and no corruption. Bhaskarrao Dighe actively participated in the drive, "Restrict soil, restrict water" and in the span of one and half months, with the collective efforts of villagers, excavated 12 lakes by working day and night; and Umatha, the village in Narkhed taluka of Nagpur district, was honoured with the award of forty-five lacs rupees by Maharashtra Government. Maharashtra Government has implemented Village Cleanliness Drive and an ideal village plan for rural development.

Tukadoji's utopian vision is reflected in Canto LXI, 'Glory of Books', of *Gramgeeta* in condensed form where he wishes for welfare of the world.

> Differentiation–isms will end, love pure will prevail in village;
> Joy will be everywhere in all people with all intent. ||135||
>
> Devil, savage in human beings will cease to light divinity;
> Pure principle will vitalise in life, new, in all. ||136||
>
> Help of nature time to time; bloom-blossom trees, creepers;
> Rivers, lake will fill with water not leaving one's limit. ||137||
>
> Health will be ornament of all; poverty, lacuna, ignorance will end;
> No one will be miserable, downtrodden; no wicked, evil elements. ||138||
>
> Social structure of equality; peace for beings, human beings;
> New inspiration of progress to elevate home. ||139||
>
> The bondage of exploitation or administration will end;
> No aggression of rival, village being self-sufficient. ||140||
>
> Slave will be trifold troubles; enmity, sins will cease;
> Village being heavenly, peace will be in the world. ||141||
>
> Immortal in heaven wish this; this in the minds of saint, sages;

When such habitation in village, why to go to forest? ||142||

With self-realisation; assemblance of saint, righteous persons;

Glory will be imparted to such village with freedom of life. ||143||

With their message religion, moral; service, devotion in their company;

With their influence peace, power will awake all time. ||144||

Such resultant fruitful of *Gramgeeta,* in which fulfillment of saint's;

Spoke God in mind, blessed speech. ||145||

Stands on the brick of the world, *Vitthal*, All Mighty;
Extension of His grace, Tukadya says, *Gramgeeta.* ||146||

(Canto LXI, 'Glory of Books')

Tukadoji's focus is inclusive and expands from village, human society, and nation to the world. Differences will cease and love and joy will prevail everywhere. Evil in human being, poverty will end and none will be miserable and downtrodden. Nature will blossom and bear fruits. The chains of exploitation and administration will end and there will be no aggression. Village will be self-reliant and social structure will be based on equality, peace, and freedom. With self-realisation, glory will prevail to enlighten village and the world. Such is fruitful resultant of *Gramgeeta*, in which saint's determination of society based on freedom, equality, fraternity, justice, love, peace, and harmony is fulfilled. Tukadoji's utopian vision in *Gramgeeta* keeps pace with welfare vision in *Jnaeshwari.*

How many the soul of the universe be pleased with this sacrifice of words and in his satisfaction bestow his favour on me. ||1772||

Many the wickedness of sinners cease, may their desire for good deeds increase and may all beings live in harmony with each other. ||1773||

> May the darkness of sin disappear, may this universe see the rise of the sun of righteousness and may the desires of all creatures be satisfied. ||1774||
>
> May all men meet ceaselessly with the company of the saints devoted to the Supreme, who shower down blessings on them. ||1775||
>
> Saints who are walking gardens full of trees of desire, living villages of stones of desire and speaking words like oceans of nector. ||1776||
>
> Moons without blemish and suns without heat; may they be the friends of all. ||1777||
>
> May all men be filled with joy in all words, forever worshipping Brahma. ||1778||
>
> May all those in this word to whom this book is their very life be blessed with success in this world and the next. ||1779||[51]

Jnaneshwar in *Pasaydana* urges for ceasing of the wickedness and prevalence of good deeds and harmony. He prays for disappearance of the darkness of sin and the rise of the sun of righteousness. Let all may be in the company of the saints to shower down blessings on human beings. Let they be the friends of all men. Let all men be filled with joy, and be blessed with success in this world and beyond. Both *Gramgeeta* and *Jnaneshwari* long for elimination of evil and restoration of good—human society pulsating with harmony and joy.

It provides the alternative realities to the model based on Gandhian approach. Tukadoji never called himself a disciple of Gandhi nor considered Gandhi as his devotee. He was with Gandhi but on him (Tukadoji) none's right.[52] He reflected that freedom will be attained, "Not by revolt nor by peace. But at the time, freedom will be when peace seekers will revolt."[53] *Gramgeeta's* exemplar is the alternative mode of Gandhian ideology, and stresses on strengthening *Gram Sabha* to which political power is attributed, collective prayer for integration and enlightenment of masses, and his militant tone, not succumbing to the extremes of non-violence, in the resistance to hegemonic power and knowledge.

It imbibes the counter discourse of social stratification, woman subjugation, communal forces, greed, rift between have and have not, Macaulay's strategy of education, dwindling of human values, superstitions, aggression against nature, and stresses on equality, unity in diversity, tolerance, self-reliance of villages, village industries, empowering of *Gram Sabha,* equal distribution of wealth, cooperative enterprises, self-esteem, native culture, skills orientation, collective prayer, scientific temper, cleanliness, hygiene, environmental consciousness, conservation of natural resources, and freedom of action and conscience.

The utopian world, the welfare society, which *Gramgeeta* creates, is the projected world based on consensus reality, which deals with 'absence', 'invisible', in the present world. Though, it appears to be 'other world', it has close links with the real world which disseminates the practicability of *Gramgeeta* on spiritual, ethical, social, political, economic, educational, and scientific counts.

References

1. T.E. Hulme, (1972), 'Romanticism and Classicism' quoted in David Lodge, ed., *Twentieth Century Criticism*, New Delhi: Longman, p. 103.
2. Sigmond Freud, (1974), *Complete Psychological Works of Sigmond Freud*, London: Hogarth Press, Vol. 5, p. 566.
3. *Ibid.*, vol. 12, p. 224.
4. Rosemary Jackson, (1981), *Fantasy: The Literature of Subversion*, London: Methuen, p. 3-4.
5. *Ibid.*, p. 10.
6. Harold Bloom, (1981), *Agon: Toward a Theory of Revisionism,* New York and Oxford: Oxford University Press, p. 206.
7. J.R.R. Tolkein, (1966), 'On Fairy-Stories', *Tree and Leaf*, New York: Ballantine, p. 44.
8. *Ibid.*, p. 20.
9. Thomas D. Clareson, (1971), 'The Other Side of Realism', (ed.), *SF: The Other Side of Realism: Essays on Modern Fantasy and Science*, Bowling Green University, Popular Press, p. 23.
10. John H. Timmerman, (1983), *The Other Worlds: The Fantasy Genre*, Bowling Green University, Popular Press, p. 49-50.

11. Ann Swinfen, (1984), *In Defence of Fantasy: A Study of Genre in England and American Literature Since 1945*, London: Routledge & Kagan Paul, p. 10.
12. *Ibid.*, p. 92-93.
13. Kathlyn Hume, (1984), *Fantasy and Mimesis: Responses to Reality in Western Literature*, New York: Methuen, p. 20.
14. *Ibid.*, p. 21.
15. Northrop Frye, (1965), '*Varieties of Literary Utopia' Daedalus,* Vol. 94, Win – Spri, p. 332.
16. Martin Buber, (1949), *Paths in Utopia*, (tr.), R.F.C. Hull, London: Routledge and Kagan Paul, p. 5.
17. Thomas More, (1982), 'Introduction', *Utopia*, Everyman's Library, Dutton: New York, rpt. p. ii.
18. *Op. cit*, p. 330.
19. David Riesman, (1947), 'Some Observations on Community Plans and Utopia', *The Yale Law Journal*, December, p. 173.
20. Fiehrik F. Infield, (1956), *Utopia and Experiment*, London: Atlantic Press, p. 5.
21. Report of Technical Meeting, (1945), on Co-operatives in Asia and the Far East FAO of the United Nations, December, p. 49.
22. Joseph W. Eaton and Saul M. Katz, (1945), *Research Guide on Co-operative Group Farming*, New York: H.W. Wilson, p. 20.
23. *Harijan*, March 1935, p. 93.
24. Tukadoji, *Voice of Saint Tukadoji*, Vol. I, No. I, July 20, 1997, Adyal - Tekdi, p. 2.
25. Tukadoji (2023), *Gramgeeta,* (tr.), Ratnakar D. Bhelkar, Canto I, 'Gramgeeta Perspectives', Couplet, 49, p. 6, New Delhi: Atlantic Publishers and Distributors (P) Ltd. (Subsequent quotations are indicated by Canto and Couplet numbers in parentheses).
26. B.R. Ambedkar, (2004), *Annihilation of Caste*, Nagpur: Samata Prakashan, p. 34.
27. Quoted from Tukadoji's Speech in *Voice of Saint Tukdoji*, Vol. III, No. 1, July 20, 1999, p. 2.
28. *Sri Gurudeo*, Dec. 1950, p. 20.
29. Simone de Beauvoir, (1972), *The Second Sex*, (tr.), H.M. Parshley, London: Penguin, p. 173.
30. *Sri Gurudeo*, Dec. 1950, pp. 6-7.

31. M.K. Gandhi, (2001), *India of My Dream*, Ahmedabad: Navjivan Publishing House, Eight Print, p. 50.
32. C.W. Watson, (2002), *Multiculturalism*, New Delhi: Viva Books Ltd., p. 110.
33. Tukadoji, (2004), *Collective Patriotic Songs*, (tr.), Ratnakar D. Bhelkar, Gurukunj Ashram: Shri Gurudeo Publication, p. 10.
34. C. D. Deshmukh, 'Discussion in the Budget Session', Govt. of India, March 1956.
35. Mohammad Yunus, Karl Weber, (2009), (tr.), in Marathi by Govind Godbole, *Garibimukta Vishwachi Nirmiti*, Aurangabad, Saket Publication, p. 51.
36. Mohammed Yunus, 'Nobel Prize for Peace Acceptance Speech', Nov. 10, 2006, Oslo.
37. Srinivas Khandewale, (2009), *Gramin Sanktachya Sandarbhat*, (ed.), Akshaykumar Kale, *Rashtrasant Tukdoji Maharaj: Vyakti Ani Wandamaya*, Visa Books, Nagpur p. 86.
38. Lord Macaulay, 'The Speech on British Education Policy', British Parliament, Feb. 2, 1835.
39. *Op. cit*, p. 186.
40. *Sri Gurudeo*, Dec.-Jan. 1961-62, pp. 13-14.
41. *Sri Gurudeo*, August 1963, p. 7.
42. Manual for Self-Study Report, National Assessment and Accreditation Council, Banglore, June 2013, pp. 4-5.
43. Einstein, Albert (2009), *Ideas and Opinions,* New Delhi: Rupa Co., p. 46.
44. *Sri Gurudeo,* July 12, 1965, p. 7.
45. Deshmukh, Usha Madhav (2010) *Maitra,* Nagpur: Maya Publication, p. 24.
46. *Sri Gurudeo*, Issue 6, 1945, p. 10-11.
47. *Sri Gurudeo*, Issue 7, 1947, p. 24.
48. *Sri Gurudeo*, Issue 4, 1947, p. 7-10.
49. *Sri Gurudeo*, February 1965, p. 10.
50. *Op. cit,* p. 10.
51. Jnaneshwar, (1969), *Jnaneshwari*, (tr.) V.G. Pradhan, Pradhari, London: Green Allen & Unwin Ltd., pp. 349-50.
52. *Sri Gurudeo*, October 1968, p. 19.
53. *Sri Gurudeo*, August 1959, p. 3.

Chapter 4

Mass, Culture and Society

Mass, Culture and Society

Mass, culture, and society are conjectured together, and have impact on each other. Mass is downtrodden, ignored, deprived, and on large scale illiterate. It is seen in myriad mass community, inclusive of diverse elements of culture, e.g., African mass community with different components of culture and Indian mass community with various facets of culture. In positive stance, 'mass' points at peripheral, workers, exploited, volatile, dynamic, revolutionary, excluded from privileged, elites, and displaced from the center. Carl Sandburg, an American poet, termed it as "teeming, seething mass". Karl Marx has especially focused on economically exploited mass, in the parlance of capitalists. Exploitation pertains not only to economical but also to race, class, caste, and gender. 'Mass' is pure man, beyond race differences, class discrimination, caste differentiation, workers, suppressed, wretched, subaltern, and expelled from main stream.

Culture is a system of learned behaviour shared by and transmitted among the members of a group. Since birth, man begins to learn the rules and regulations, customs and traditions, etiquettes and manners, values and norms, and folkways. The behavioural manifestations, such as singing, dancing, writing, painting, and talking are transmitted to him by someone after adopting them from the historical past. Through traditions only these patterns are persisted in the society. Culture is transmissive and distinctive through whole way of our life. It is a collective way to approach to our social life.

Perspectives on Culture

Matthew Arnold, in *Culture and Anarchy*, is primarily concerned with the individual and the 'perfection' at which he should aim.

> The pursuit of perfection, then, is the pursuit of sweetness and light. He who works for sweetness, works in the end for light also; he who works for light works in the end for sweetness also. But, he who works for sweetness and light united, works to make reason and the will of God prevail. He who works for machinery, he who works for hatred, works only for confusion. Culture looks beyond machinery, culture hates hatred; culture has but one great passion, the passion for sweetness and light.[1]

He deciphers that the men of culture are the true apostles of equality and have a passion for diffusing—"for carrying from one end of society to the other, the best knowledge, the best ideas of their time; to humanize it, to make efficient outside the clique of cultivated and learned, yet still remaining the best knowledge and thought of time, and a true source, therefore of sweetness and light." (70)

The term culture has different associations according to whether we have in mind the development of an individual, of a group or class, or of a whole society. T.S. Eliot contends in *Notes Towards the Definition of Culture*:

> ...the culture of the individual is dependent upon the culture of a group or class, and that the culture of the group or class is dependent upon the culture of the whole society to which that group or class belongs. Therefore it is the culture of the society that is fundamental, and it is the meaning of the term 'culture' in relation to the whole society that should be examined first.[2]

He means that the culture of the individual cannot be isolated from that of a group, and that the culture of the group cannot be abstracted from that of the whole society; and that our notion of 'perfection' must take all three senses of 'culture' into account at once. He relates religion and culture, and views "any religion, while it lasts, and on its own level, gives an apparent meaning to life, provides the framework for a culture, and protects the mass of humanity from boredom and despair".[3] What we call the culture and what we call the religion of people are, at the bottom, different aspects of the same thing. To Eliot, culture is "essentially, the incarnation (so to speak) of the religion of people."[4]

Raymond Williams has criticised Eliot's theory of culture chiefly for its ignoring 'the economic factor'.[5] He complains that Eliot has not been able to understand "the tendency of function to turn into property" and, thus, make "the view of class narrow and misleading."[6] In an industrialised society, like the one obtaining in modern times, it becomes misleading to equate class and function. Because some vested interests of inherited and accumulated property and money, as in the earlier civilisation, would vitiate the modern culture. As he writes, in Eliot's concept of culture, "the insistence, in principle, is on wholeness; the practice, in effect, is fragmentary."[7] The economic factor is certainly subdued in Eliot's scheme of things, and his main emphasis is on the spiritual and moral aspects of culture. But, that doesn't mean that Eliot is not aware of this factor. He has noticed, however briefly, the degradation of humanity on economic grounds, due to the perversions of modern social system, as in *The Waste Land* and *The Idea of a Christian Society*.

To Raymond Williams, culture doesn't operate only on the level of thought level but it is a material transaction also. The term '*cultural materialism*' emerges from it. In each period, besides dominant thought system, oppositional, alternative value system and transaction exist in society; they are residual or emergent. In cultural studies, to search dominant and other alternative thought systems are important.

In any period, varied texts and discourses are created but the relations between text and culture are not straight and simple, as in them, myriad tensions are hidden and new historicism takes into cognisance these strains to operate criticism on poly-level and make it polyphonic.

In traditional historicism, the stress is on continuity, coherence, and single direction of history. Here though history is changeable, static form is provided to tradition in long period. Secondly, it is assumed that history is continuous and coherent narrative of progress. From the perspective of Michel Foucault, the concept of history is to be deemed as discontinuous and incoherent, rather a focus is to be at point where the continuity in history writing is ruptured. History is not a continuous and coherent process; it is discontinuous and incoherent process. The assumption is that the relationship between past and present is not organised and continuous; it is discordant, discontinuous, and ruptured inside. History changes in the context of new knowledge and let it is to be changed.[8] So, in any period, oppositional discourses are created and in each discourse, there is organised conceptual and value based framework and so it provides outlet to innate variation and poly-direction in history. Culture is made of various sign systems, and sign system, medium system, and thought system provide meaning to social happening or production. In literary works, many sounds are transformed and in them some sounds keep pace with tradition based, orthodox, existent power relations and conserve them; some other denounce them and intend to bring changes in power relations. Counter of these oppositional sounds means sometimes to repress them and consequently to repress the tensions created due to differences in classes, races, *varnas,* and genders.

New historicism challenged the concept of the traditions of great literary works and literary cannon, and accepted the existent counter currents against tradition. New historic stance is basically post structuralist stance and aims at tensions prevalent in literary creations as any new historicism takes text into cognisance and opposes monophonic. Mikhail Bakhtin's conception of polyphonic discourse as well as Jacques Derrida's principle of deconstruction of text mean to read how counteracting and intersecting elements of meaning exist and how they struggle. From the perspective of cultural studies, in America, the critical writings by Fredric Jameson and Gerald Graff are important and in Britain, Stuart Hall and Richard Hoggart founded Centre for Contemporary Cultural Studies (CCCS) to provide momentum to cultural criticism.

In *The Political Unconscious: Narrative as a Socially Symbolic Act* (1981), Fredric Jameson's basic contention is that in reading any text, time context or historical illustration is indispensable, and he begins his book with the proclamation, "Always historicize". The nature of literary texts is fundamentally symbolic and in them the political and economical meanings are hidden, meaning in literary texts, political and economical subtexts exist.[9] Sigmund Freud's conception of unconscious mind is individual oriented and Fredric Jameson had attributed social and political dimensions to it.

In *Professing Literature: An Institutional History* (1987), Gerald Graff exhorted that literature is not to be dissociated from social reality, ethics, and cultural values.[10] Literature is created in society and it doesn't exist in isolation, cut off from society and has links with culture. Conflicts in society are important to comprehend reality. If literature is to assign social, cultural, and ethical essence, the priority is to be given to the conception of conflict in intellectual approaches if it operates as the mean of teaching.[11]

In *The Uses of Literacy* (1957), Richard Hoggart enumerated two projects relating to the labour class culture. The first project explores the relations of the language, values, and family system of British working class with the institutes, such as sports and pubs made by working class. The second project is to investigate the decline of British working class culture due to American popular culture.[12] The subtitle of this book is *Aspects of Working Class Life with Special Reference to Publications and Entertainments*. Hoggart's stance is that the culture of working class is simple and sometimes seems powerful but it is native and that culture has provided motivation to live positive life to bigger class.

Stuart Hall, the active participant in New-Marxist movement, 'New Left', and editor of *New Left Review,* in his essays 'Cultural Studies: Two Paradigms' (1980) and 'Each Culture Studies and its Theoretical Legacies' has alleged that the concept of culture can't be established by simple and easy definition; it will be always problematic because it is operated with diverse intentions. Social group has culture, conception, approach, art, social signification, and value system. Cultural studies point at transmission of political, economical, social, artistic, family based, technological contexts, and investigation of cultural nuances of social groups, such as women, working class, youth, minority, downtrodden and weak, and post-colonial society. Its core objective is to nourish multiculturalism, massism, intersecting monoculturalism, elite-centrism, Eurocentrism, and male-centrism. In the ensuing analysis and interpretation, endeavours are directed to explore the nature of mass culture and society in diverse manifestations in *Gramgeeta*.

Culture, says Edward Said, means two things in particular:

> First of all, it means all those practices, like the arts of description, communication, and representation, that have relative autonomy from the economic, political, and social realms and that often exist in aesthetic forms, one of whose principal aims is pleasure. Second, and almost imperceptibly, culture is a concept that includes refining and elevating elements, each society's reservoir of the best that has been known and thought, as Mathew Arnold put it in the 1860's.[13]

The difference between the two concepts of culture is the same as the difference between the actual and the ideal. The first is a descriptive term and the second is a normative term. As J.B. Paranjape has aptly pointed out "the marginalised segments of society who seem to occupy the peripheral status exert pressure, causing displacement of established centres".[14] Here he envisages the dialectic between marginal and established, peripheral and center, outsider and insider, and how 'other' exerts pressure and resists dominance to reach to center by displacement. Culture evolves through a continuous process of centering and decentering. He contends that "the new centers are to be found by coming in terms with the 'others' who are different from us, and not wiping them out."[15]

V.S. Khandekar, the first *Jnanpeeth* awardee in Marathi, has pointed at Tukadoji's significant and unique role in Indian social revolution:

> Faith in religion was the conspicuous quality in Indian culture. But that faith has not taken the cognisance of changing scenario and consequently its vitality was paralysed. Disguising this the material reformers in British regime neglected faith. But faith being the base of social life in rural area, its negligence was destructive to nation's progress. These reformers couldn't bring their intellectualism to masses. Tukadoji diagnosed a lacuna in Indian social revaluation and directed the avenue to progress, which is acceptable and assimilable to rural public. From this perspective his place in modern reformers is significant as well as specific.[16]

Besides philosophical import, *Gramgeeta* is oriented towards masses and Tukadoji intends to awake and enlighten masses with the help of mass communicative means, mass language, mass psyche, and mass culture.

Mass culture from this standpoint has reference to the culture of masses, i.e., the vast general population of nation. Mass culture in India is still by and large the one that prevails in our villages where over 77 percent of our people live. Folk media continues to provide the main source of entertainment, and also of instruction and education in religious, social, economic, and political matters. Mass culture is an engrossed term which is inclusive of masses. It doesn't and can't remain static in our society, primarily because it follows the needs of the people rather than fashioning them. Physical, verbal, and psychological developments engrossedly are the objectives of our tales, *kirtan, bhajan,* festival, pilgrimage, worship, celebration, and discourse.

Mass welfare and mass elevation, being the mission of saints, they understood the crux of mass culture and comprehended its potential. They adopted the means of mass media to communicate with masses on wider scale. Mass literature, with oral tradition and writings, being the medium of their lives, they spiritualised and socialized mass literature, as distinguished from elite literature.

Tradition and Saint Literature

Saints were outcaste by elites. Elites didn't accept in the initial phase Saints' deity *Vitthal*; didn't accept *Geeta* which exposed the core of knowledge in *Sruti,* and opposed orthodox practices. They didn't admit Marathi, the medium of communication used by saints and its status. Moreover, they didn't anticipate conduct, thought, and utterance of saints. In any movement of mass elevation and reformation, saints who were outcaste by elites, born in masses or developed kinship with masses, and pained by the sorrows of masses, are to be subject of honour. They are to be deemed as sources of new motifs, inspiration for implementing influentially the essence in tradition, in new context. Before medieval saint movement, Buddha and Mahavira provided impetus to rebellion principles in pre-tradition and interpreted other powerful aspects in tradition, keeping pace with their attitude and tendencies, practicised in their works. Their resistance to dominance by the use of Pali, Prakrit defying stratification in society, non-violence had paved space for counter culture. Saint elevates masses with them from the earthly level to transcendental level. "Whatever beings meet, they are divine" is the result of saint's devotion. Saint is a person who treats deprived and distressed ones as his own. To help others is good but to pain others is a sin. Saints with compassion, "Drowning these people, not tolerable to see" express their emotions and thoughts through mass media.

Saints who are discarded, are mass oriented. Though saints' vision is transcendental, they observed human sorrows with sympathy. Their insistence was to percolate their experience, thought up to the grass root level, and with this intent they accepted media which were familiar to masses and popular. The rebel of saints to express in native languages is seen from the beginning of saint movement. Saints and masses are linked together from the beginning because they communicated in native languages and gave call to all to participate in the movement of enlightenment. Saints' thoughts are not book oriented, but based on genuineness of experience, and masses received assurance for self-elevation and as thus, mass literature encompasses saint literature.

R.C. Dhere has exemplified that in the perceptive world of Jnanadev and Tukaram, *Vitthal* is not hyper imagination, means fantasy, and merely myth but mega reality. From earthly atheistic point of view, whatever is myth is mega reality for saints.[17]

> He, the king among men, incarnate special mine;
> To whom all masses render service. ||
>
> (*Jnaneshwari,* 110-219)

Saint's *Vitthal* is popular in familiar form of Srikrishna in Andhra, Maharashtra, and Karnataka, and develops kinship variously with saints. He is lover, friend, guide, and all. Saints described deity in different forms. To them, the motherly love of *Vitthal* is as important as His kingship. He is accepted as Supreme Lord, and masses and kings accepted His Lordship of God, Supreme power, with faith, not only in Devotional Literature but in inscriptions during the Jnanadev time and its post time witnessed it. *Vitthal* is Vishnu and Krishna; and Saints' faith is that He lives with two hands on waist in Pandharpur. He was saviour of Pandav and destroyer of Kaurav; offspring of Devaki and death-knell for Kansa.

The conception of God's power is prevalent in the area of mass religion. Mass God and God for village security are power holders in the communicative field of masses. Today, at the time of fast changing social-religious environment, we find faith, behaviour, ritual, and signs which witness the power of people's gods and gods for village security. People live with the bliss of them, and in spite of it, they are of people, developing intimacy with people, easily accessible, and mass oriented. Saints' God is Supreme King as well as companion of masses. In real sense, He is 'the King of people', put forthing ideal before people, enlightening them, enriching self, observing good and evil in material world, and providing the parameters of sublime human values.

Saint's Hero Archetype

The concept of hero in folk culture and Saint's concept of hero have polar distance. The former is self-violent and the later is self-elevative. Their difference is in nature and kind. Though both move beyond corporal attachment, from the standpoint of social repercussion, heroicness perceived by saint is creative for the world welfare. Saint's stance of 'hero' is to be understood in the light of archetypal approach. 'Hero archetype' is encompassed in ancient epics and the treasury of folk tales in the world. As *'sadguru'* represents 'saviour archetype', spiritual hero who crosses barriers to attain freedom represents 'hero archetype'.

Saint's life is based on conscience and the nature of conscience is like fire. To hypocrite, it is scorching, and to devotee, it is like a tree for shade, giving relief. The reformative resultants of Jnaneshwar's *Guru* System are Chokhamela and Tukaram. Chokhamela was an untouchable, *shudra*, living outside of village, performing leather work according to traditional village system. It was a hell of pain. Jnaneshwar, the sufferer of dominant system, opened the self-followed road to salvation for untouchables, deprived masses, peripheral, and marginal. It was understood by Gora Kumbhar, Narahari Sonar, Savata Mali as well as Chokhoba who writes,

> Sugarcane crooked, but juice not crooked |
> How are misled by outer colour? ||
> River crooked, but water not crooked |
> How are misled by outer colour? ||
> Chokha crooked, but intent not crooked |
> How are misled by outer colour? ||

He reiterated not to lure by external colour and glare. He accepted *Guru's* initiation from Namdev. Society was reluctant to accept him but in the company of saint and from the message of *sadguru,* he experienced,

> Who is profane? who is polluted?
> Different from both, *Vitthal*, mine. ||

Chokhamela and his family were isolated and his descendants were also not free from the clutches of untouchability.

> Made our caste downtrodden;
> Don't you realise Lord? ||

"Don't you understand Lord, why you lowered down us?", the question posed by Karmamela was unanswered. Banka also experienced the stings of caste discrimination.

Tukaram was *vaishya, mahajan* in rural system but he was *shudra*. He had nausea of ego, tradition, emotionless conduct of elite, and satirises it in the lines, "Born in *Shudra* race, as thus freed from ego", and "Better, *Kunbi* became, otherwise would have died with ego". He warned that though the right of vedic study was not given to them, it didn't mean that the readers of vedas understood them.

> Vishnu enthused world, the religion of *vaishavites* |
> Illusion of discrimination, not good omen ||

This realisation is manifested in the verses from Chokhamela to Tukaram, and has origin in transforming the right of *Guru's* initiation. Being influenced by the compassionate work of Jnaneshwar, saint Ekanath extended his work by seeking the shelter of *Bhagwat:*

> Let they be downtrodden, advising them divine knowledge
> Uddhava, no stigma to be, this my true speech||
> Without greed, with grace, advises downtrodden, *Sadguru*
> One who elevates wretched, no blot to his advise ||
>
> (Eknath's *Bhagwat*, 560, 563)

Guru cult is accommodative for *shudra* as well as women. Prior to this, Buddhists and Jains kept open the doors of *Guru's* initiation for women. Saint had given simplified initiation of devotion to masses inclusive of males and females instead of the initiation which was directing to forest and mountain. The crux of reformative work of *Guru* system is that it opened the road to those, who were expelled; who were at periphery; and who were deprived and marginalised, for higher goal in life, keeping aside hindrances. Besides the initiation by *Guru,* the utterance of Name (*Nam*) also rendered freedom for masses to seek sublime knowledge.

Mass Communication

Modes of communication play crucial role in enlightening masses, and modes of communication and culture develop together. Indeed, communication is an expression of a community's culture, and culture in its turn embodies a community's communication.

Communication and culture are inextricably tied to each other; we cannot understand one without understanding the other; nor can we speak of one without understanding other; and nor can we speak of one without referring to one other. Communication, language, culture, society, civilization, and their Indian equivalents may have meanings of their own, but they are intimately linked to each other, and have evolved together, though the pace of evolution might differ from community to community. Moreover, changes and development in one influence the others.

Bhajan is a traditional mode of communication in which song is sung with musical instrument/instruments. Tukadoji practised *bhajan* to educate masses by playing on *khanjiri*. He heard *khanjiri* in childhood from Hanuvatibuwa at Yawali, which mesmerised masses. *Gaulani, bharud, kirtan, tamaṣha, bhajan,* and *gondhal* are traditional modes of mass communication and have origin in folk culture. *Khanjiri* is treated as the younger sister of the *damaru* of Shiva, and was born during the time of Macchindranath and Gorakhnath, the ancient Indian sages. Ms. F. Kazard, a delegate from America for World's Parliament of Religions in 1955 at Shimizu, Japan, revealed the impact of Tukadoji's *bhajan* and *khanjiri*:

> Though language not known, with crystal clear smile, loving nature, innate knowledge, and melodious, *khanjiri,* this great being not only regaled Japanese but also the delegates of differnt nations. New eyes are given to my heart.[18]

The tradition of *bhajan* is stretched back to Meera, Nanak, Chaitanya Mahaprabhu, and Kabir. Meera left royal glory and engrossed herself in love for Krishna by singing *bhajan* with devotion. Chaitanya Mahaprabhu performed *bhajan* and *kirtan,* suffused with love for Krishna in Bengal, and Kabir and Guru Nanak sang *bhajan* in India and abroad.

Nanak's disciple Mardana too was a good singer, who accompanied him constantly on tours. Mardana was a Muslim who sang *kirtan*. The other companion, Bala was a Hindu *jat* and had accompanied Nanak on a few of his tours. Music for Nanak (as for Kabir and others), was the purest mode of devotion. Once he settled at Kartarpur as a farmer, *satsang* became a regular activity. The works of Nanak and the other saints' *bani* were complied in the *Granth Sahib*, which includes the six *Sikh* poets and thirty-one non-Sikh mystic poets. The *bani,* regarded as the word of the *Guru,* was sung by *Ragis* who only sang from the *guru bani*, based on the *ragas* in which it had been composed.

The Sikh tradition gave rise to four kinds of religious singing. The first is the traditional *kirtan* sung by the *Ragis*, which is the expression of *bhakti,* a quest for the *nirajan,* the eternal being. The music is meditative, invocative, and uplifting. The second variety is that sung by the descendants of Mardana who have preserved the tradition set by Mardana, through the centuries. They are known as *Rhababis*—practicising Muslims who sing *kirtan*. The third type of religious singing was by the *Dhadis*—the bards from the time of the sixth Guru Hargobind Singh, in the seventeenth century; they would sing standing upright. The fourth type is that of the two and a half-hour long morning prayer, "Asa-di-var" which was borrowed from the folklore of Rajasthan.

Bhajan

"Wealth, elevated all, my lovely *bhajan*."

Eknath has practiced the poetic forms of *bharud* with humorous as well as satirical import, and *gaulan* with romantic and spiritual fervour. Gadgebaba performed *kirtan* with dialects to discourse with thousands of audiences. In Maharashtra, *tamasha*, narrative presentation on stage with song, dance, and music, is performing folk art, made popular by *shahir,* a core performer. It is 'carnival' where performers experience freedom to express with the help of humour, satire, and mockery. *Pendya,* comic character, recalls Fool in Shakespeare's comedies. *Gramgeeta* elucidates the significance and impact of folk form, *bhajan,* on masses.

On 1st January, 1954, Tukadoji performed *bhajan* at Rashtrapati Bhavan, New Delhi, in the presence of Dr. Rajendra Prasad and Guljarilal Nanda. On 23rd October, 1954, The World Religious Congress at Shimizu, Japan, was opened with Tukadoji's *bhajan*, "O Lord of Cosmos, give me cosmic consciousness."

In Canto XXX of *Gramgeeta,* 'Influence of *Bhajan*', an audience asked how sanctity can be there if *bhajan* is the means of propagation? Tukadoji views that religion means trust and beautiful, and encompasses the thought of all aspects of life. *Bhajan* and *kirtan* have enlightening power to change life. To make the masses understand Prakrit, saints and sages penned *bhajan* with trust in devotion. Some narrated metaphors in Vedanta, some with renunciation, and some in humorous vein. Some constructed *bhajan, bharud,* multi-role play, *gaulani,* and *gondhal* in the folk forms. Saints performed *bhajan* to end evil tendency, to implement dutifulness, and to retain healthy state of society.

Singing and dancing in many modes for infusing devotion in song, they enlightened and made masses wise. Tukaram, Namdeo, Sheikh Muhammad, Jnandeo, Chaitanya Prabhu, Nanakdeo, Jana, Meera, Muktabai, Kabir, Tulsidas, Ramananda, Surdas, Dadu, Brahmanand, Narsi, Deonath, Parmanand, and many composed *abhang* and performed *bhajan* to elevate masses. As thus, Tukadoji insists on not to leave *bhajan* mode, and learn conscience in *bhajan.* One is to be conscious where *bhajan* is to be performed and what to communicate and to whom. He discerns:

> *Bhajan* to perform who realises this all;
> Innocent people all to be made wise. ||27||
> Ritualistic society has become, principle pure to tell there;
> Social work to be elaborated whatever time demands. ||28||
> Viewing occasion message to be given, not to leave principles truthful;
> Truth to tell with sweetness envisaging time. ||29||
> Understanding this created saints books, songs, *bhajan;*
> Likewise all to be interpreted today newly.[19] ||30||
>
> (Canto XXX, '*Bhajan* Influence')

The poet is confident that *bhajan* will find solution to the problems of our village by coordinating all sects and maintaining harmony among all castes. Some sectarians perform *bhajan* but blow their own trumpets and quarrel for beds in necklace. Some avoid singing *bhajan* of other saints, deeming that their *bhajan* is for them only. The mystery of *bhajan* is that though Hiranyakashipu had disgust for name, he had a pull towards the *bhajan* of Narada. Tukaram's *abhang* has emotional warmth, satirical tone, and communicative power. He warns and occasionally convinces with the abusive words.

In speech, social approach, religious approach, politics, public issue, and scientific approach may seem dry but use of *khanjiri* and *mrudunga* makes the people passionate to listen bhajan. In village, *bhajan* is to enlight old, young, women, girls, and all righteous people.

Shepherd, farm-labourer, shopkeeper, tailor, carpenter, smith, and 'the subaltern' sing *bhajan* in their own languages to express their innate voices, and oral performances are continued from generation to generation. *Gramgeeta* takes the cognisance of 'the subaltern' whose voice was suppressed. 'The subaltern' is a term used by Antonio Gramsci to indicate groups in society subject to the control of ruling classes. The subaltern classes traditionally include peasants, workers, and others to whom access was denied to control power. Gramsci, interested in politics and the state, focuses on their historiography. Gayatri Chakravorty Spivak links the notion of the subaltern to that of Indian women, such as Rani Gulari and Bhuvaneswari Bhandari, who were silenced, marginalised, and disenfranchised economically and socially. We can expand the range of the term to those who are silenced, marginalised, and deprived of. Spivak in her famous essay 'Can the Subaltern Speak?' (1988), asks:

> Whether post colonial studies can help to give a voice to suppressed people...the construction of the subaltern group by other groups essentialised the people so defined, who were silenced by the elite who defined them, and so should they try to speak, they could never escape using the language which itself constructed them as secondary, subordinate.[20]

She points out that anyone who has achieved the literacy and sophistication to produce writing which is defined widely by others, is almost certainly not themselves, as subordinated or sub-altern in position and so disqualified from speaking for the people they are supposed to represent.

> Friends! now this to leave from core of being;
> Righteous speech of any saints to utter with love. ||45||
>
> *Bhajan*, not comprehensible, not to say without strength;
> Repercussion reverse of it occurs in society. ||46||
>
> Enlightenment of village, heart, work by *bhajan* to be;
> Orientation towards righteous work by all to tell people. ||47||
>
> Performer of *bhajan* lazy, what he will tell people?
> Make fun of oneself, not to practice this by anyone. ||48||
>
> Work to perform with understanding; no step without thought;
> Leads thought to salvation, witness rich of great ones. ||49||
>
> (Canto XXX, '*Bhajan* Influence')

What to do of the *bhajan's* performance which keeps aside conscience? To counteract the means which provide harm to society, the voices of saints' thoughts are to be heard. Self-elevation by study is to be done and excessiveness to be omitted. He points at:

> Tunes to be set modern to attract towards words;
> But will show, in present, saints spoke the same. ||57||
>
> Let many kinds of *bhajan*, of thoughts in past, future;
> But springs out saints' poetry sublime with impact. ||58||
>
> In *bhajan* of saints, not worship of God, anecdote from life too;
> Occasionally convinced with abusive words too. ||60||

Saints' sublime poetry is to be interpreted in the light of the present context and past, and present and future are to be linked. In *bhajan*, saints not only worship God but also deal with the anecdote from life.

Veena and *chiplya* turned into beggars' hands, and penance of saints seems to be vanished behind it but this is to be changed again to infuse people with *sanskar*. The mean of *bhajan* is to be improved in the light of the contemporary scenario and Tukadoji treats *bhajan* as a medium to educate masses.

> Love for all, in it emergence of service;
> Increases honour of character after *sanskar* of *bhajan*. ||96||
>
> Continuity of *bhajan* tradition, spring of righteous attitude to people;
> No remedy pious of people education than this. ||97||
>
> So urged villagers! Youth! Old people!
> All to sing loving songs, such propagation to be. ||98||

He insists that *bhajan* tradition is to be continued to spring righteous attitude to retain folk culture and mass culture for the enlightenment of masses.

Funeral *Sanskar*

"Real pind to lift by us; life to adore by work."

In Canto XXII, 'Funeral *Sanskar*', the poet focuses on ritualistic practices of funeral and doesn't intend to exaggerate those practices. As river merges into sea leaving all differences, after death, spirit also becomes one with timeless reality, breaks bondages of attachment, and turns to self-nature. The cycle of changes in nature keeps pace the changes in human life, birth, growth, adolescence, youth, old age, and death. The poet sees no cause to weep and cry because our's is same course.

> Attains what one observes, why to weep?
> Something substantial to be done for fame. ||21||
>
> Whatever left to be done, to honour his name;
> Honorable to become in one's family, proud for elders. ||22||
>
> (Canto XXII, 'Funeral *Sanskar*')

One has to perform concrete work for honour and fame. Not considering caste and creed, when someone demises, he is to be carried by all. Death is to be treated as good and cooperation is to be sought for funeral procession with *dindi*, rhythmic verbal rendering. Custom, to the poet, is not to be evil, ugly, and nauseatic.

At graveyard, arrangement is to be for *sanskarmandap* for all. Tukadoji poses ironical situation between *shastra* and fact:

> Need of new cloth though suggested by *shastra;*
> Not known to *shastra* how we run our home. ||32||
> No meal without butter; who follows this dictum?
> Why to stress *shastra* for butter to massage corpse? ||33||
> Death in one's home; no grain to eat at home;
> For what aloofness to maintain by him? ||34||
> Starvation for poor if no work in a day;
> Tell you, how can he be on fast for ten days? ||35||
> So work finished after burning, bath at home after return;
> Death place to make holy; completion of funeral *sanskar.* ||36||
>
> (Canto XXII)

He doesn't exaggerate the procedure of funeral *sanskar* but stresses on practical reality and simplicity. Emotions are to be controlled with conscience, and prayer on the thirteenth day is to be performed amid joy of *bhajan* experienced by the people. Living beings experience fruit of self-deed and attain joy and bliss due to good fame, not because of offspring. If one has more money, better to utilise it for the welfare of village, such as in making well, school, hostel and road. To understand this, the best education is important. Fame is "heaven indeed" and defame is "hellish zone".

> In work heaven-hell; appreciation futile of blind faith in book;
> People misplaced in illusionary fiction of selfishness. ||64||

He vehemently criticises the attainment of heaven after death only when the *'pind'* (rice ball) is picked up by a crow, and the entanglement of the spirit of dead if it doesn't happen. Keeping aside selfishness and blind faith, the poet attributes significance to work and the gravity of work only creates heaven or hell. Milton in *Paradise Lost* views:

A mind not to be changed by place or time.
The mind is its own place, and in itself
Can make a Heaven of Hell, a Hell of Heaven.

Paradise Lost, Book I (253-255)

Mind itself creates "a Heaven of Hell and a Hell of Heaven" and has transformative nature. It was the devilish serpent who instigated Eve to disobey the command of God. It was *satan*, the garb of serpent, whose trickery roused by jealousy and revengefulness, deceived Eve, the mother of mankind. On account of his pride, he had been expelled from Heaven in the company of the multitude of rebellious angels with whose help he believed he could rise to the same status as God. He started unholy war in Heaven and waged a battle in vain attempt to seize the throne of God. The Almighty God thereupon flung him and his companions from the heavenly sky to the innumerable depth of Hell. The overthrown Archangel said that the mind can operate supremely over circumstances. Mind has power to derive happiness from the worst of conditions, and it has capacity to feel miserable in the best of the conditions. Milton exhorts that Heaven or Hell lies in individual, and are states of mind in relation to work which deals with action and action with stimulus and response of mind. Consequently, work or action links with mind which has capacity to perform good or evil action which creates Heaven or Hell, accordingly. Milton and Tukadoji both allege that mind's perspective creates outer world.

People believed that if a corpse is buried at Maghar, his soul goes to Hell. Reacting to such prevalent notion, Kabir suggested his disciple to take his body after his demise to Maghar. He insisted that Heaven or Hell are not outside but here only and they are imaginatively created by men. Kabir says,

"वहाँ न दोजख, बहिस्त मुकामा। यहाँ ही राम, यही रहमाना।।"

Selected devotee Kabir, the resident of Kashi Maghar for *samadhi;*
Door to hell, people call it, turned into holy land. ||87||

As Kabir, Tukadoji attacked orthodox superstition. It is believed, if a crow takes away *pind* (rice ball), symbolic food offered to soul of a dead, soul goes to heaven otherwise entangles somewhere.

> After death spirit wanders, goes to heaven after giving *pind;*
> Otherwise falls in hell, meaningless such words are. ||67||

Tukadoji assigns importance to work and the best work has positive repercussions and elevates the life. Real *pind* is to be lifted by us by adoring life by work. He asks, what gain one has by giving *pind* to crow? Why to folly by spending lavishly on *shradha*? Instead of it, the glorious qualities are to be remembered with trust. Whosoever is demised of disease, help is to be given to village hospital. Tukadoji asks,

> At Kashi one attains salvation, increases illusion in people;
> Do insects emancipate when they die in the water of Ganges? ||86||

Salvation is internal purification and not the washing of corporeal frame. One has to be determined not to touch liquor, opium, and *bhang,* and he should cooperate to perform righteous service. How can *pandya* elevate society when he is addicted and misbehaved?

> So blind orthodoxy not to nourish by anyone;
> Village to treat Ganges; everything to offer to her? ||102||

One purifies oneself by searching lake, river, or well for bathing. Why to search for pilgrimage outer when it is inside? Not succumbing to greed for corpse, which is to be merged with five elements by *agnisanskar.* The best tribute to a dead person is to create a place where people can seek education and a memorial to be dedicated to villagers. Motive is to be right order to strengthen village state.

> Through death or birth celebration, not merely adoration;
> By saving, village glory to increase, Tukadya says. ||117||

Village is a temple and it is to be worshipped to set society in order.

Pilgrim Place

"Honour of truth in the celebrations of all sects."

In man's life, holy water, place, and temple have seminal significance from the ancient time. Man's life is influenced by the binaries of profane/polluted and sanctity of unholy/holy. Our social psyche had travelled through the conflict of sacred and profane—this water sacred, that profane; this place sacred, that profane; this object sacred, that profane. Man's life is basically profane and for changing it, we have to long for sacred life—this urge is relentlessly existing in social psyche. The longing to transform profane into sacred had resulted into the planning of holy water, pilgrim place, temple, penance, and rituals. Mircea Eliade has practically deciphered that when we come in contact with sacred, our unholiness ceases and we become sacred—this honest trust is the cause of the world of sacred.[21]

Tradition has accepted the importance of holy water from the ancient time. Water is life giving and a cause for the creation of animals and human beings. So, it is deemed as the form of mother. It washes away dirt and makes one feel fresh. Water being the mother principle, immersing in water and then emerging is as new birth. The traditional supposition is that a dip in holy water brings changes in life. The connotations of the end of former birth and the birth of new divine life are in legends and folk tales with reference to water. At present we look at holy water as a means to purify life.

Man's mind is engrossed and influenced by Nature's aggressive-tender, creative-destructive, savior-killer, and pleasant-painful aspects. When a man understands his limit of power before the mighty strength of Nature, his mind ventures to know—How to control the Nature's forms? How to avoid terrible and destructive sorrows? How to relate Nature's power with man?

The concept of *yagnya* has undergone a lot of changes. It is a ritual to sacrifice animal for welfare of village, tribe, and fertility of woman and land. Now, the term *yagnya* is interpreted as small and larger sacrifices to protect life nourishing values and boost up all constructive actions.

Saints had applied this approach to holy water, pilgrim place, and temple. Desire fulfilled actions are *yagnya* oriented actions, and non-vedic actions are actions, such as the construction of well, lake, steps on the bank of river, *ghat*, temple, and charity home. When vedic actions were denied to masses except Brahmins, non-vedic actions received momentum. From Kushan–Gupta period to the attack by Islam, the motivation was reached to the pinnacle that many carved temples were constructed during that period. Architecture, sculpture, dance, and music were progressed, centring temple. Entire rural life was regulated by the centre.

Traditional education was linked with temple because school, legend, and discourses were in practice within the shelter of temple. Envisaging the relations among festivals, celebration, pilgrimage, and fair, temple system had profound impact on traditional life of the people.

But, the constructive approach to holy water, pilgrim place, and temple had received a setback. Temples, enriched by royal patronage, turned into the means of social oppression and started exploiting devotees and each other too. Saints understood the significance of pilgrim place as the place to be away from the humiliating experience of untouchability. As thus, saints hadn't disrupted the concept of holy water and pilgrim place; denied sanctity of temple, anticipating traditional concepts of dignity, they infused sublimity in these concepts.

The most respected leader of the movement of *veerashaiva,* Basaveshwara, born at Bagewadi in Karnataka in 1106 A.D., before Jnaneshwar, attacked vehemently outer rituals, in *vachanas*. The idea of an egalitarian and casteless society of the *vachana* movement still draws the attention of historians, literary scholars, sociologists, anthropologists, and creative writers towards the events of that time. He observed festivities and celebrations, controlled by servicemen appointed by kings and donations of land and money, and to express his restlessness, he calls his deity, Kudalasangamadeva,

> The wealthy build
> Temples of Shiva

Lord
What can I do
A poor man
My legs are the column
And body itself a temple
My head the golden crest
Listen o lord kudalsangama
Things fixed shall end
The moving shall stay.[22]

(P. 114)

Jnaneshwar too satirises external action without inner purification. It is like giving a bath to donkey in holy water.

As death adorned, donkey bathed in holy water;
As bitter milk covered with jaggary. ||468||[23]

(*Translated*)

Jnaneshwar and other saints reiterated the strength to change life in righteous company and saints' stance is that righteous company is real pilgrim place with reformative potential. Jnaneshwar, his guru, his companions, and saints in post-Jnaneshwar period had deemed body as abode of God, Pandhari. Tukaram experiences the presence of Vitthal in self.

See in our body, ten doors, this *Pandhari;*
Brahma on brick, reality to search inside. ||

Ekanath too affirms Tukaram's stance and alleged that his Pandharpur is here only; why to go away? Vitthal is infused here, not at distance. He asks why to wander to meet with Vitthal?

Body, this Pandhari, spirit, this Vitthal;
Resides only Pandurang. ||

Though Pandhari on broad level is town on the bank of Chandrabhaga, and on the level of experience, body is Pandhari. When Eknath views that body is Pandhari and spirit is Vitthal, the two concepts of pilgrim place and temple are merged in his verdict. He visualised Pandhari in body, people, and nature, and became *warkari,* traveller to pilgrim place.

Saints lived, spoke, and wrote with magnetic pull to experience divinity in the temple of life. Saints' earnest longing was to make visible and concrete forms beneficial for inner purification, complimentary to enlighten life. But, saints satirised when the core objective of holy water, pilgrim place, and temple was kept aside. They felt indispensable need to expose the fake religion, which was mushrooming around holy water, pilgrim place, and temple, and on other side, they ventured to elevate mass psyche taking into cognisance of mass signs of faiths, living among masses to protect mass institutions.

From the standpoint of common men, ideals are always at height. The distance exists between ideal and fact, and it is feasible to bridge gap by applying practical means. Society's eyes are to be oriented towards ideals to bring them into practice by their awakening. Tukadoji points at awakening of masses:

> Enlight village to village, diminish differences completely;
> Light the lamp of village elevation, Tukdya says. ||115||
>
> (Canto XVII, 'Poverty-Richness')

Saints struggle for men of flesh and blood; simple and innocent devotee against hypocrite, rich, operating monopoly of religion; orientation towards cosmic divinity; and being honest to pure inner motives against decorative means. They have to experience unity in the relations of being, world, and supreme. They need temples to install motivation for divinity in life. Temple is a symbol and saints' efforts are to know the principle behind it.

Symbol is to point at core principle, and to recall that principle. But, when the potential of symbol declines and fades away and when symbols become mere formalities, the purpose of creation of symbol ceases and then opportunists, hypocrites, and selfish people eclipse social life. *Warkari* cult is not closed sect in conventional sense. Jnaneshwar and Namdev initiated the *nath* cult; Eknath was disciple of *Datta* cult; and Tukaram received the message in dream, from the sage of Chaitanya cult. Though they were vaishnavites, they never disdained shaivites. Non-dualistic devotion is the live principle of saint's penance and proclaimed with experience, "with attribute, without attribute, one Govind". Though they sang the importance of pilgrim place,

Pandhari and deity, Vitthal, they never detracted from "Body, this Pandhari, spirit, this Vitthal". They never off sighted the approach to devotion, "whenever beings see deem them gods." They also warned that mark, cap, and necklace didn't achieve the principle of Vaishnavism and being *mohant* of *math* didn't experience depth of *guru*. They were conscious of purification of tradition. Saints' stance to accept the essence of truth in tradition and bring time suited changes is of invaluable significance. They experimented to elevate masses by being conscious of limitations of masses and speaking in their dialects. They had a great respect for folk and mass cultures, and attempted to elevate them with enlarged compassion for masses. They consciously endeavoured to coordiante tradition and folk and mass cultures on the base of human religion, searching for the essence and potential in urban tradition.

Saints were pilgrims to realise self on the road pointing towards to know beyond, as well as, the leaders of the movement with the spirit of mass elevation. The humanistic vision of life longing for happiness of human being and freedom, dialogue between man and nature, love and compassion, and inner elevation is spiritual vision of life. Material oriented can't deny love, compassion, dignity of knowledge infused with compassion, and knowledge infused compassion; its relation is indispensably with spiritual thirst.

> One who call poor, wretched, ours;
>
> He to know as sage; there God to realise. ||

To Tukaram, sage embraces oppressed and deprived, where God prevails, and this life oriented humanistic vision is acceptable in perpetual time.

Great souls and epoch makers, living with flesh and blood, accept limitations of their time and when we substract those time related limitations and focus on their speech and action, with conscience, in any time slot and life context, their uncommon motivation provides immense strength to us. Saint and saint literature are imperishable treasure for those who have this conscience. In his introductory speech at Saints' Meet, he deciphered:

> Religion is in practice for nourishment and progress; so how can it be aloof from social sense and national spirit? What is the output if society doesn't receive directions from great person, and pilgrim place is not only to offer bael leaf, to ring bell and read script throught a day but it is the place which creates right system in society.[24]

Gramgeeta, in Canto XXIV, 'Pilgrim Assembly', approaches village as a pilgrim place, and insists on unification of sects. An audience queried how to search for remedial measures for differences in village. In village, sects are different; religions are different; celebrations are in different temples; some are worshippers of idols; some are opponents of image worship; and they don't care whether village turns desolate.Tukadoji answers the queries viewing the panorama of village. People celebrate but implement wrong conduct providing impetus to superstition. He observes the waste of ample money and sowing of evil customs and deeds to increase cleavages in people. It is pragmatic to celebrate anniversary of a saint as holy day at public place, unitedly. Not keeping aloof, cooperation which is the crux of an organisation is to be sought. Saints are to be admired, not telling miracles, and influence of the best conduct on society is to be communicated. Tukadoji refers to eminent saints, thinkers, and reformers, whose biographies are to be placed before masses to channelise, and their birth anniversaries are to be celebrated.

> Saint Jnaneshwar, Tukaram, Namdev, Sawata, Chokha unparalleled;
>
> Eknath, Damaji, Bhagsatottam to narrate to people. ||24||
>
> Sajan Kasai, Ravidas cobbler, Sena, Santaji, Gora potter;
>
> Krishnadayarnav, Vaman, Sridhar, Saint poets too. ||25||
>
> Ramdas, Tulsidas, Keshavdas, Kabirdas;
>
> Sundardas, Vishnudas, Surdas etc. ||26||
>
> Shankarcharya, Ramanujacharya, Madhawacharya, Vallabhacharya;
>
> Radhaswami, Basawarcharya, Raman Maharshi, Sri Chakradhar. ||27||

Shahadatta, Goraknath, Govindnath, Dayalnath;
Narsi Mehta, Ramtirtha, Sri Samarth Adkoji. ||28||

Great soul Mansoor, Muhammad, Kawaram, Sheikh Farid;
Zaratustra and Gautam Buddha, Vivekananda influential. ||29||

Guru Govindshingh, Nanakdeo, Chaitanya, Gaurangdeo;
Ramkrishna Paramhansdeo, Jain Mahavir Swami. ||30||

Great Soul Yeshu, Tolstoy, Marx, Socrates dauntless
Great Soul Gandhi, Rajmohan Roy, Dayanand, knowledge seeker ||31||

Devotee Meerabai, Muktabai, Kanhopatra, Janabai
Rangnaiki, Bahinabai, Anni Bessant, Nivedita ||32||

Their monumental contribution to society and the vast vision to nourish humanity are to be communicated to masses. Though saints differ in bodies, their motto is to unify the differences and to bridge cleavages.

Convincing this with study, unity of various sects will be;
In all means, abolishment of superstitious practices. ||37||

People have to search for avenue leading to real knowledge, not turning to unreliable stories and practicing evil custom. At pilgrim place, celebration of saints is to be organised with sense of unity and their philosophic discourses are to be around to learn core principles, which are the hallmarks of pilgrim place. If people don't receive any direction at pilgrim place, what gain is to people running after there? Pilgrimage is to inspire thoughts and on its occasion, conference of different sects is to be organised. All sects have to unite for constructive work of all, not insisting on sterile issue. Pilgrim places are the centers of culture and enlightenment in India. From these pious places, the currents of thought and action are to be flown to make powerful nation. In the Editorial of *Sri Gurudeo,* in January 1966, Tukadoji deciphered:

> Pilgrim place is the means of knowledge and inclusive development. But this motive is vanishing. To fulfill lacuna, Gurukunj, the pilgrim place is created. To keep pace with time, this space is created to rebright the importance of pilgrim place. From this perspective this is to be created by beautifully orchestrating religion and cultural vision with national tendencies to achieve the pious objective of nation, the world and to continue inflow of spiritual awareness in masses.[25]

He doesn't idealise only pilgrim place and warns not to leave family in turmoil and succumb to ritual by *pandya*.

> Why to go *Kumbhamela,* starving kid at village?
>
> God, in village less, at pilgrim place different, not this. ||53||

Village's public place is to be treated as pilgrim place.

> Village, pilgrim place beautiful, where such saints, servicemen reside;
>
> Receive people inspiration to turn village into paradise. ||57||

At village's public place as pilgrim place, body, mind, and wealth of magnanimous persons are to be involved. By service of such worthy treasurer to pilgrim place, village will gain upliftment. Tukadoji makes aware of village cleanliness without which disease will not cease. In village pilgrimage many evils operate and to curb them village pilgrim committee has to organise assembly, celebration, and fair, and organisation for village upliftment is to be infused with national spirit. Fine road and pure, clean, and hygienic water are to be maintained. Entertainment is to continue but not permitting addiction, and attention is to focus on performing arts like music and behavioural art of humanity. In pilgrimage celebration, unity of all, how to walk on road? how to sit? how to speak? and how to behave at home and community? are to be taught. Swami Dayananda Saraswati worked tirelessly for improvement in pilgrim places and Gadgebaba, who worked in masses and for masses practiced the practical measures for village purity. Pilgrimage means 'come closer' and it is to instill on people' minds. The programmes for mass education like exhibitions, competitions, and conference for all sects are to be organised. In the *Granth Sahib*, the compositions of various saints, such as Kabir, Namdev, Gurunanak, and Sheikh Farid have been collected, and Mahipati wrote the biographies of saints to reveal unity in diversity. Continuing such celebration, the earth is to be deemed as *Pandhari* where male and female will be pleasant. In the Editorial of *Sri Gurudeo*, in April 1955, Tukadoji viewed:

> If emotion with seriousness is coupled with freshness, man progresses with ease and for this pilgrim place, pilgrim, convention, temples, celebration, and festival are implanted in the lives of nation and individual. We have to learn to utilise those beautiful practices from the perspective of principle.[26]

He asserts that if in pilgrimage no such operations take place, no salvation to life is possible in life.

Festive Celebration

Festivity people like, search for remedy in that way.

In Canto XXIII, *Gramgeeta* encompasses Indian festivals which are performed on mass level and have ancient traditions; and reveals the nature and purpose of festivals. Having a heritage of ancient culture, Indian culture is enriched with myth, legend, and rituals. Celebration of festival is an essential fabric of Indian culture. The constructive programs are to be implemented to seek inspiration by masses from festival. Instead of creating glamour, human power is to be operated for service and for the festival, assembly, rituals, and conference; or remembrance of great persons are to be practiced.[27]

Though there are various cultural trends, some festivals, such as *Diwali*, *Ramanavami*, *Gokulashtami*, *Ashadi*, *Rakshabandhan*, *Pola*, *Dasara*, *Bhaubij*, and Ganesh Festival are celebrated on mass scale. An audience asked the purpose of festive celebration. Custom and tradition of India were scrupulously planned with a motto to regulate society. Some festivals are domestic and some are to be celebrated at public place. Money is to be saved to celebrate festival with cooperative spirit. On occasion of festival, meal is to be taken together to nourish brotherhood.

The mass performances, such as *katha, kirtan,* and *dindya* are to be followed to channelise society, and religion is to practice with thought. Tukadoji mentions various mass festivals in *Gramgeeta*:

> Datta, *Ramanavami*, Hanuman birth anniversary, *Gokulashtami*;
>
> *Shivratri*, *Ashadi*, *Kshrushipanchai*, to practice with varied work. ||28||
>
> *Vatsavitri*, festival Sharada, *rakshabandhan*, *sankrantparva*;
>
> Worship of Gouri, festival of women to celebrate collectively. ||29||
>
> Day of industry, get together, progress of strength, day of prayer;
>
> Day of mind progress to *Geetajayanti*, penta-celebration necessary. ||30||

Competition, village purification programme, and speeches are to be arranged in festival celebration. In *Pola*, the festival of oxen, a pair of oxen are arranged in row and their bodies are to be decked up with the coloured body cover and chain of cowries; and horns are painted or gelatin paper is used to stick, beautified by small mirror design. Those who excels in service is to be felicitated and prizes are to be given by villagers. The pair of oxen visits homes in village and gifts given are taken by caretaker. Tukadoji attacks the practice of playing cards on day after *Pola* and suggests to arrange wrestling instead of it and give prizes to persons who are stout and agile. In village, the worship of Laxmi is to be at single place, in massive *pandal* and meal is to be given to all. The motto of *Bhaubij*, the festival of the bond of love between brother an sister, is to boost up brotherhood and sisterhood, which is on decline in society. The worship of the cow mother is a significant aspect in Indian mass culture. Cow with more milk and bull with qualities are to be honoured to instill the significance of cattle on people's minds.

On the onset of new year, *gudhi,* inverted brass pot covered with new cloth on long stick, is erected on the top of house. Cow dung manure is to be preserved by digging land and used in farm for more yield. In *Diwali,* houses are cleaned and cow-dung mixed with water is sprinkled on front yard. On the pretext of *Diwali,* cleanliness and holiness are to be learnt, and lighting of the lamps is done at homes.

Holi is the festival of colours, ancient sign of village cleanliness and in it, people also worship fire.

> First public worship of fire, in it burning of evil tendency;
> Then ash to take at garbage place; bath to take collectively. ||77||
>
> Such joy of village service, imparts fragrance to others;
> To create pleasantness, plan for entertainment. ||78||
>
> At places, singing, music play; smearing of colours, powder;
> To keep mind pleasant, the plan for *Holi* festival. ||79||

The plan for *Holi* festival is to burn evil tendencies, and entertain with singing, music, and smearing of colours and powder. But, in the course of time, the way of celebrating *Holi* has deteriorated and people have taken it as a occasion to abuse each other or settle their enmity. On *Holi,* people wander and some throw waste in drainage; trouble to people; steal wood and dump items from home in fire—these practices are to be stopped for village improvement.

The mythical links associated with *Holi* are that on that day Prahlada, the son of Hiranyakashipu, was tortured by Holika but being the devotee of god, Vishnu, he didn't experience sorrow; and Lord Shiva burnt Kam, demon, with his third eye with anger and army retaliated Kam making loud sounds. Tukadoji also refers to Krishna who played *Holi* with colour in Vrindavan and Mathura.

Various festivals, such as Village Purification Day, Mother Day, Children Day, Labour Day, Humanity Day, Independence Day, and other festivals are to be celebrated for healthy village psyche.

> Festivals celebration for progress, some festivals for unity;
> All to conduct it collectively with cooperation. ||88||

The core purport of festival celebration is for progress, unity, and to provide impetus to collective spirit.

Lokmanya Tilak, the reformer with national spirit, initiated Ganesh Festival for national unity in pre-independence period. Tukadoji points at installation of single idol of Ganesh in village for collective spirit.

> Single Ganesh of village, programmes for all;
> National attitude it will nourish, this intention to be. ||90||
> The best festival, festive day, fulfilled with national tendency;
> This is to practice massively, addressed saints in society. ||91||

Festivals in all religions have to honour man and the main crux of festivity is to infuse collective spirit, not to discriminate rich and poor, to channelise misdirected, and to lift people who have fallen down. Tukadoji warns not to enter selfishness in festivity.

> Service pure this to enlighten inner lamp;
> Question of belly fulfillment not to enter in festivity. ||105||

Festival in real sense has righteous motive and if it is not, it calls for trouble. To avoid it, village is to be organised and functional.

> No unemployment in village, no extravagantly spending;
> Whatever motivates in right direction by festival to perform. ||110||
> Righteous motive, festival it, otherwise call for trouble;
> To avert it village to organise and functional. ||111||

Every culture is enriched with festival mode and provides identity to culture. *Diwali, Dasara, Id, Christmas, Onam, Pongal,* and *Kali Puja* are celebrated on mass scale. Irrespective of specific festival, the kernel of festival celebration is to nourish traditional mass cultural fervour and create enthusiasm in work, peace, unity, and harmony.

An Idol Worship

Cosmic it to make, this only motto of worship.

An audience asked the question, "Why to support idol when Lord, vast, engrossing, perfect?" in Canto XXVI, 'An Idol Worhip'. An idol is created by man and any idol doesn't ask for worship or ritual. In one of his *bhajan*, Tukadoji exhorts that one doesn't need to encounter the Lord when trust is not inside. The idols of the Lord, made of wood, clay, and gold, have fear of fire, water, and a robber, respectively.

Trust not inside, but urge to know Lord;
In this mode Lord will not meet;
Vegetable in market He is not. ||
The Lord of clay has fear of water;
The Lord of gold, silver has fear of a robber;
The Lord of wood has fear of fire. ||1||

Divineness of the Lord, place to place;
No experience without melting of ego;
Listen this speech, Tukadya says. ||4||[28]

Pandharpur, 24.06.1958

Though any sign of religion, man has created idols. The pertinent questions are, "Where is godliness there? Why to worship it?" ||26:311||. He discerns that to create love for an idol and make it cosmic is the only motto of worship. The planning of the image worship is to make mind reflective and develop fascination for the road to comprehend the abstract conception of Lord. It is to increase the quality of duty and nourish holy attitude. Tree, animal, and bird are deemed as virtues, concretised in Idol worship to realise truth to a man:

To make *bhakri* of clay to prepare the best *bhakri* in practice;
As showed idol worship a road to an abstract Lord. ||83||

At core Lord is inside, its devotional principle outside;
Prevails no distinction when realisation with conscience. ||84||

The righteous knowledge to do the righteous work;
Mode of idol worship over of a seeker. ||85||

(Canto XXVI, 'An Idol Worship')

Idol worship is a means, not an end to attain the phase of cosmic realisation. It is practical and a step to develop cosmic consciousness to know real and not to succumb to appearance. It is an ascending process to climb step by step.

> Melted corporeal ego as realised Lord consequently;
> Merged salt in sea water; uniform sea has become. ||94||
> After this next step, climb up adhering to tendency;
> As experience being becoming cosmic inside. ||95||
> Says, manifests self in all; becomes cosmic in cosmos;
> Begins to perform all work for inner reality. ||96||
> Nothing left without me; permeates in atoms, molecules;
> Perfect *yogi* when experiences this. ||97||
> Saw in beginning idol in temple; then in beings, masses;
> Manifestation of self in all forms, when perfection. ||98||
> To realise treasure of joy, installed Lord for idol-worship;
> To see invisible-visible vision in our Principle. ||99||
>
> (Canto XXVI, 'An Idol Worship')

In cosmic consciousness, corporeal ego melts as salt merges in sea water and a devotee becomes vast as sea. One experiences the existence of spirit, inner energy, inner reality, and realises manifestation of self. Prevalence of one principle in all forms is *yogic* experience in which energy permeates in atoms and molecules. Idol and temple are basically images and these images have myriad connotations and, as thus, they become symbols. The symbolic significance of an idol in temple expands to people's lives and the symbol enriches by social dimension. He doesn't anticipate the approach to discriminate images as higher or lower, which leads to hatred. Better not to stick to an image but to ascend stepwise to know the Supreme.

Tukadoji spiritualises and socialises the concepts of an idol and a temple, which are mass oriented. To him, "people are Lords (1:63)"; villages are temples, and the worship is to render service relentlessly to masses.

> All people, our lords; all villages, our temples;
>
> To render service relentlessly, worship, ours. ||104||

Honest work, chanting of Lord's *nam*, and unified love for all beings are our religion.

Transcendental not greater than this when deeply determined;

Or the essence this transcendental of those who experienced. ||106||

His conception of transcendental is not ethereal and not alienated from human society and masses. Here and beyond, material and non-material, visible and invisible, virtual and eternal, and human life and transcendental are conjucted together.

Incarnation

Incarnations all, human forms but work with power.

Good and evil exist in the world, which represent godly and demonic attitudes. God-incarnation destroys evil to free people from sorrow and those who had done it, turned into legend. Some believe in different incarnations but our adherence to devotion it is, and consequently steps of service of incarnation will come to know.

Some worship Mhasoba and Khandoba; some treat Ram-Krishna as incarnation of Vishnu; some trust in incarnations of Mahavir, Buddha, Dutta, and Muhammad; and some are in tradition of Guru Nanak.

God is self-power, wears never corporeal form;

Elevation of man in realisation of Him. ||48||

(Canto XXXIII, 'Incarnation Work')

Man's elevation is in knowing self-power and inner energy. Someone has asked Tukadoji, "To whom do you deem incarnation?" He exhorted in *Sri Gurudeo,* in June, 1955, "I deem everyone who is manifested on the earth is incarnation. But, some incarnations are restricted to belly feeding, some are of their families, and some are of village, state, and nations."[29] All incarnations are human beings and their objectives are freedom of life.

Incarnation, all human forms but work with power;

Supposition their life liberation, remains it for ever. ||57||

Bring with them *sanskar* of many births;

To elevate material beings incarnation shows road. ||58||

(Canto XXXIII, 'Incarnation Work')

In incarnation, individual self is elevated to cosmic level and, thus, incarnation is evolution of self as superman.

> So incarnation is progressivism, manifests as power operates;
> Self-sufficient with cosmicness, deem we incarnation. ||63||
>
> (Canto XXXIII, 'Incarnation Work')

Aurobindo believes in the idea of superman, i.e., evolution of individual self. The tenet of incarnation is to eliminate evil and protection of good by enlightening human religion. He satirises the decorum of the festivity to honour saints but to deviate from the spirit of service. It is the sign of feeble mind to wait for incarnation of God to relieve from a burden.

> God will incarnate, so to wait to relieve;
> Entered this feeble thought more in the people's mind. ||91||
>
> Oh! now this all to forget, what saint told to be done;
> What pious work is than improvement of man by man. ||92||
>
> (Canto XXXIII, 'Incarnation Work')

So, he urges to realise human essence and accept the signs of the principle of incarnation to become serviceman. One who keeps aside selfish motto and trusts in welfare of the world, is oriented towards the work of incarnation; and so, Tukadoji directs to render service to village and then expand to the world.

> Service devotion to God; in performing work, power of nation;
> Leads to liberation; enters luminance of incarnation inside. ||100||
>
> (Canto XXXIII, 'Incarnation Work')

Service is devotion to nation and God. In it, there is essence of deliverance. Luminance of living is infused in it for welfare.

Guru

Guru, pure knowledge principle of experienced.

Nanak is the first major poet of Panjabi literature. The *bhakti* and the *sant* traditions had already influenced the practice of *satsang* (community singing of elevating mystic hymns), among Indian public. Nanak added to this the practice of *langar* where all used to sit together and eat food cooked in a common kitchen. Another unique concept that he introduced was that of *daswandh* (das meaning the number of ten, and *daswandh* meaning the tenth portion). According to the *daswandh* principal, every ideal human being was obliged to regularly use one-tenth of his earnings for the benefit of his society.

Saints deviated from the traditional set of initiation, and attributed significance to utterance of *nam*. *Upanayana* is a necessary initiation to be born newly and to become an element of society. To A.M. Hocart, "Initiation ceremonies throughout the world are usually an introduction to adult life and occur at, or about puberty."[30]

In India, initiation is known as the twice-born, a title which expresses the whole theory of initiation—it is a ceremony of rebirth. To Mircea Eliade,

> The term initiation in the most general sense denotes a body of rites and oral teachings whose purpose is to produce a radical modification of the religious and social status of the person to be initiated. In philosophical terms, initiation is equivalent to an ontological mutation of the existential condition. The novice emerges from this ordeal a totally different being: he has become "another".[31]

One, who is not initiated is deemed as *shudra*. *Vedic* rights and *sanskar* were denied to *Vaishya* besides *shudra* and women of all *varnas*. *Kshatriya* were also pushed to *shudra* terrain. Consequently, the right of twice-born was confined nearly to *brahmins*. After *Upanayana*, a ceremony of twice-born, an individual was permissible in the *ashram* of *guru* for vedic studies. Such condition, necessary for the right to knowledge, is also found in the tribal initiation of primitive tribes.

> The (initiated) young man learns not only the behavior patterns, techniques, and institutions of adults, but

> also the myths and the sacred traditions of the tribe, the names of the gods, and the history of their works; above all, he learns the mythical relations between the tribe and supernatural beings as those relations were established at the beginning of time.[32]

Initiation for twice born keeps pace with social initiation of tribals. Traditional conception of sanctity had denied touch to profane, and to get unsanctified by the touch of polluted. It creates the citadel of rituals synchronizing it, operates for selfishness, keeps profane and polluted in service, and strives to treat polluted as undignified, humiliated, and oppressed. For saints, the birth of sanctity is not in external ritual practices but in righteous conduct through purification of heart and mind. Saint's sanctity is not self contented but it sanctifies others and is not polluted by touch of profane. Saint finds profane whenever evil and wickedness pervade. Saint's elevated and sublime conception of sanctity is different from traditional conception.

Only some places sanctified; some water sanctified; some plants sanctified; some birds sanctified; some time sanctified; some directions sanctified; some persons sanctified; and some objects sanctified, such traditional selection of 'sanctified' is not in saints' conception of sanctity. It is a traditional conception that a man gets salvation if he dies in Kashi but goes to hell if dies in Maghar. To prove the vanity in this assumption, Kabir intends to die at Maghar. He doesn't need pilgrim place and says that there are sixty-eight pilgrim places in the body.

Initiation was denied to Jnaneshwar and so he accepted initiation by *Guru*. His parents were outcaste and, therefore, he was socially treated as undignified, *shudra*, to whom initiation for twice-born was denied. It was a painful event in the lives of parents and offsprings.

Those, who were deprived of the right of initiation, were polluted. This presumption leads to treat the touch of polluted as fearsome. The origin of untouchability is in depravity for initiation. Property is not the base for *varna* system. Sanctity on the basis of birth is the base for it. Persons, sanctified by birth and rich with property, became higher and those, polluted by birth and poor, turned lower. *Varna* system is descend of stratum. It is not descend of property but of sanctity. The origin of *varna* system is not in the sacrifice of any person or class or hypocrisy but in the collective conception of sanctity. If a man has to free from adverse effects of the conception of sanctity, the traditional conceptions of sanctity are to be kept aside, and it means the acceptance of humanity.

Saints had accepted the cult of guru and guru cult is related to primitive assumption of sanctity. D.K. Bedekar, while linking traditional conception of sanctity with guru cult, has viewed that tree worship, idol worship as well as hero worship emerge from the worship of power. King was deemed to be the part of Vishnu. The same is recurring in the hero worship in diverse ways. In guru cult, hero worship is dominant. Treating *guru* as the centre of power, a disciple longs for blessing and sacrifices everything.[33] Saints are acceptor of *guru* cult and elevated primitive conception of sanctity to new faith.

So, the idol of Vitthal was placed before masses which triggered of unity among all sects enlightening love and knowledge in Maharashtra. In Bengal, Chaitanya Prabhu, infused new life to Krishna tales and propagated them among masses, eliminating *tamas* devotional custom. Saints changed the modes of devotion taking into cognisance the turbulent period.

Tulsidas and Ramdas directed towards an archer Ram. Depending upon nation and time, a centre for organisation is to be selected and the mode to be selected, keeping pace with the present. For this Tukadoji selected Gurudeo, Supreme Guide, who is for welfare of all and not confined to any sect and party, and a witness for all nations. In all religions, Hindu, Islam, Christianity, etc., respect is for Gurudeo.

> Be it in Vedic or other, respect for Gurudeo in all sects;
> Devotion to Gurudeo immense in Islam, Christianity.
> ||33||
>
> (Canto XXVII, 'Collective Prayer')

Sect propagator and *guru* are different, and dualism exists there. Independent and experienced *guru* is different, who relies on knowledge.

> *Guru*, not of bones, flesh; *Guru*, not caste-sect;
> *Guru*, pure knowledge principle of experienced one. ||35||
> One who receives this knowledge, cosmic his mind becomes;
> Cease sect-party-religion; all merge there. ||36||
> (Canto XXVII, 'Collective Prayer')

To Tukadoji, *guru* is pure knowledge, principle of experienced one, and with the experience of knowledge, his mind becomes cosmic—"less knowledgeable being moulded cosmic" (XXXI: 97). Tukaram too has cosmic experience and he becomes vast expanse of the sky—"became Tuka as that of the sky".

Guru is a companion and supporter of humanity, and is not alien to any language. He creates right emotion, guards deprived and sorrowful, and eliminates evil roads by body, speech, and mind. He is supreme who has encompassed everything and so deeming God prayed *Gurudeo*. The great persons are different but they became *guru* dissolving subjectivity, religious sect in the nature of *guru*.

> His worship not be *tilak*, his temple vast;
> Limit to vastness but *Guru* indefinite than it. ||42||
> (Canto XXVII, 'Collective Prayer')

Tukadoji's cosmic vision is to experience *guru* in infinite.

How can there be hate-chaos when we understand knowledge of Him? And to know this, the medium is structured with open mind for mass prayer to unify masses. In mass prayer, mass God is to be conceptualised as per faith and then to experience in work and visualise a cosmic level, *Gurudeo*.

Nam

Conscience there to be; single mindedness to be in nam, chant.

Saint literature is infused with significance of *guru* as well as significance of *nam* (name). Significance of *guru* and significance of *nam* are two uncommon characteristics of Saint literature. All practitioners believe that the journey with the means of *nam*, directed by *guru*, leads safely to the abode of salvation. Saints had provided an opportunity for new birth to deprived masses and women, by *guru* initiation, which was denied by traditional society. They provided the means of chanting name of divine/ God to masses who were deprived of reading and utterance of *Vedic* chanting. Though saints' ultimate motto was salvation, they opened the road for self-elevation, not differentiating, and made possible the means to boost up self-confidence. Saints attempted to shape the psyche of masses who were deprived of sanctity (twice born) and knowledge, and lift them with self-confidence.

Saints hadn't anticipated the differentiation to utter *vedic* chanting and, as thus, they searched out an influential alternative of chanting *nam* to emerge out of the complex of denial of *Vedic* practice.

> For twice born, here spell of *Nam*, for hym;
> Utterance it profane, realises principle. ||
>
> (*Jnaneshwari* 16: 103)

Tukaram writes, "*Nam*, non-differentiating, solvates all". Savata Mali pleads, "With strength of *Nam,* not to fear entirely, on the forehead of turbulent time, hammering will be".

Saints had not only given the alternative of chanting of *nam* to *vedic* chanting but also instilled the specific significance of chanting on the psyche of masses, and reasons are: (1) *Vedic* right is for twice-born only but right to chant *nam* is to the lowest born also. (2) If utterances of *Vedic* chanting are not pure, it is sinful act and deterioration begins but an utterance of *nam* purges a man. The saints' proposed importance of *nam* is worthy from the standpoint of salvation as well as social dimension. Sinful Ajamil and wretched Pingla were elevated by the utterance of *nam*.

Jnaneshwar calls 'Mauli' (Mother) to 'Shruti' 'नाही श्रुतीपरौती माऊली जगी' (No mother in the world as *Shruti*), (*Jnaneshwari*, 16: 459). This *Sruti* means the speech of *Upanishad*, the part of Veda. The end of Veda is acceptable to *Bhakti* tradition. The free reflection of this part of '*Shruti*' inspired Buddha. Though the protectors of Veda ventured to hide knowledge part, it was already reached to masses. Out of three parts of *Shruti*—ritual part, penance part, and knowledge part—saints denied ritual part and accepted knowledge part, simplifying penance practices.

J.G. Frazer, J. Abbott, and R.P. Masani studied faith related to *nam* (names) of primitives and masses, and inferred that in the psyche of masses, no differentiation is between a name and a person. R.P. Masani exhorted:

> Although there was no objective resemblance between a name and the person bearing the name, the association of the two, in one's mind, engendered the belief that there was an intimate connection between them.... The nature of the name, its power, and influence, as conceived by it, led to the connection that the name of a man out of existence.[34]

It gave rise to quaint customs rooted in the fear and horror of evil spirits and sorcerers ready to cast their spells on persons through their names, to do harm to them and even to wipe them out of existence.

The faith on union between a name and a person is primitive. *Bhakti* cult emerged from folk tradition and mass oriented legends. It attributed uncommon importance to *nam* in practice. *Guru* gives divine birth through initiation and *nam* facilitates a visit of name bearer. *Guru* and *nam* have unified significance.

In Canto XXVI, 'An Idol Worship', Tukadoji deciphers that *nam* is the verbal idol of the Lord. Many persons chant *nam* and move chain and beads, not knowing the motto of utterance of *nam*.

> Conscience to be; single-mindedness to be in *nam*, chant;
> Then in life place of happiness one attains. ||49||
>
> On tongue reflection on *nam*, in hand social work;
> But maintains character, devotee real is. ||50||
>
> (Canto XXVI, 'An Idol Worship')

Chanting of *nam* is power to face catastrophe and fruitful it is when *purushartha*, action to perform duty, operates. Though, no chanting, to him, better it is to live, not making other's life sorrowful. The utterance of *nam* is associated with progression and meditation, and Tukadoji focuses on certain image and then social service for right work. Chanting of *nam* without virtues doesn't lead to self-elevation. The utterance of *nam* is to end ignorance, illusion, and root of sorrow.

> World to save, saving oneself; it to infuse with power, tact;
> People to awaken with *nam*, pointer of saint. ||72||
> (Canto XXVI, 'An Idol Worship')

Saints point at utterance of *nam* to save oneself and to awaken masses and enlighten their psyche.

Collective Prayer

The place of mass prayer for collectiveness.

Canto XXVII, 'Collective Prayer' and Canto XXVIII, 'Prayer and World Religion' deal with nature of prayer, necessity of mass prayer, and its operational mode. Prayer is initiated to move the world in righteous direction. Coordinated text of prayer is not steel boundary but scope is there for everyone to enter. We can take principle from anywhere but it shouldn't be one-sided. One has to be tolerant towards others. Such prayer is influential for peace and for peace vastness requires. When hearts come nearer, intimacy will develop and in the world with love, happiness and peace will prevail. The conflicts among religions, sects, and nations can't be resolved without love. In every religion, the principles of prayers are based on knowing unison in purity, all have to merege in one, and there is to be one prayer for the welfare of the world.

> One prayer for the world; one stance of the world;
> Why not to bring unison in the world? ||94||
> (Canto XXVIII, 'Prayer and World Religion')

Narrowness of mind creates hindrance in coming nearer to each other. Unison of principles in all religions is to be taught to masses, which will cultivate respect for other religions. Tukadoji emphasised upon the indispensability of mass prayer in *Sri Gurudeo*, July 1955:

> The first door to merge attitude in world is Mass Prayer... but the necessity of Mass Prayer is to enlighten mass consciousness. This is the school to mould emotion vast by reflection. Introspection is the most important for

> social workers. Easy it is to point out other's mistakes but difficult it is to point out one's. Essential it is for social workers to be blameless. Introspection is must for turning an attitude inward. Vastness of heart, vast vision is the significant at the second place without this cosmic consciousness is baseless.[35]

Mass prayer is for world peace and happiness, and to know unity in diversity.

> Without the germination of the theoretical philosophy among masses;
> Not possible for ever to eradicate hate for sects. ||106||
> Feasible it is to germinate this principle by collective prayer;
> As thus, effort to be for this work in village to village. ||107||
>
> (Canto XXVIII, 'Prayer and World Religion')

The sense of equity for all religions and coordination among religions will honour the earth with heavenly bliss. Mass prayer is coordination of all religions, remedy for world peace, and the school for mass improvement. The question is how to select one among many temples and gods for mass prayer? When sects were conflicting among themselves, the problem was before saints also in the past.

For prayer, the places like temple or square are to be searched where women, men, and children can sit in evening with righteous intent. First serviceman has to clean ground for prayer. Then, all people should be called for prayer and they should sit in a row. Purity and cleanliness are to be in surrounding and all to stop conversation. In front, platform is to be erected and covered with beautiful cloth of *khadi* produced in the village. On it, a large sized round cushion is to be placed for sitting. On one side, rapporteur, singer, and speaker and on another worshipper and reader are to sit. Devotees are in rows and security person at backside to maintain discipline. A worshipper lights lamp and *dhoop*. All have to pray in harmony and then the chanting of the name of *Gurudeo* to dispel differences and illusions. At the end, rapporteur informs to deliver a speech on 'Collective Prayer'.

We all are one, then why to see differences?
All to be cooperated as family. ||67||

Right conduct deeming man, are component of world family;
To infuse energy prayer to be before powerful. ||68||

All saints are same; all gods, came motto;
Listening all messages, knows one principle in all. ||69||

As thus all to cooperate as possible by one;
Family to be make heavenly at our level. ||70||

(Canto XXVII, 'Collective Prayer')

P.B. Shelley, in the 'Adonais', the elegy penned after the demise of John Keats, reflects about perpetual, immortal, principle of spirit, which is inseparable facet of beings on the earth, and others like shadows change and vanish.

The One remains, the many change and pass;
Heaven's light forever shines, Earth's shadows fly;
Life, like a dome of many-coloured glass,
Stains the white radiance of Elernity,

('Adonais', LII, lines 460-463)

"The One" is here unifying principle which unite the diversities and other, transient, succumbs to time and perishes.

In mass prayer, one nourishes a sense of oneness among all and then walls of differences created by man collapse. After speech, *shantipath* is to recite and then all have to stand to utter the name of *Gurudeo*. Tukadoji's reflection on religion is mass oriented.

God ours resides in society; works all for society;
Encompasses all on the seat of prayer. ||79||

Meets One in public work; as prayed we;
Infused trust pouring spirit in prayer this. ||80||

(Canto XXVII, 'Collective Prayer')

He links God for unity, harmony, and society. He is not away, but meets by mass elevation work.

Knowledge-perceived and cosmic presence, *Gurudeo* is the experience of these fundamental principles in the prayer. Prayer is structured to know the basic forms and the depth of all religions. Veda and Upanishad prayed, "सर्व भूतें हितैरत:" (Let welfare be of all beings). Jesus Christ prayed for peace; Muhammad prayed to unify Islam and organize masses; Zarathustra taught purity; Mahavira taught patience; and Buddha taught non-violence. Saints performed *kirtan* chanting names. The singing of *bhajan* is also a form of mass prayer which organises people and enlightens them. Mass prayer is for human elevation and world peace:

> Prayer, the school of humanities; the core feel of rural culture;
> In the mould of prayer, ends conception of difference. ||96||
>
> 'Companions we all are', thought such to increase;
> On this rests heavenliness of village. ||97||
>
> At the end of prayer, sermon to give to know culture to all;
> Tradition this to continue in village ours. ||98||
>
> Prayer this to sustain in village, then survival of rural culture;
> All time the lamp's flame of collectivity will light. ||99||
>
> Peace can be in the world, how impossible it for village?
> For ever, unity by collective prayer, Tukadya says. ||100|||
>
> (Canto XXVII, 'Collective Prayer')

Collective prayer is to retain human values as it will bring peace and unity in village, state, nation, and the world. It is the process to purify inner and outer.

Wedded Life

Female, male, two wheels, complementary to each other really.

Guru Nanak proclaimed the dignity and identity of women, and promoted the values of their status as mother and man's partner in life. He writes:

> From woman, man is born;
> within woman, man is conceived;

to woman, he is engaged and married.
Woman becomes his friend;
through her, the future generations come.
When his woman dies, he seeks another woman;
to the woman he is bound.
So why call her bad?
From her, kings are born.
From woman, woman is born;
without woman there would be no one at all.
("Asa-di-var", GS 1563)

Wedding is an important aspect of family system in human society. *Gramgeeta* in Canto XXI, 'Wedding Life' envisages the various angles related to wedding, *purushartha*, responsibility, inter-caste marriage, child marriage, widow marriage, dowry, vail system, astrological suppositions, *sanskar*, and man-woman relationship, and satirises evil, mass practices; and provides suggestive measures to improve the prevalent situation.

Male and female, the two elements of society, operate the cycle of world. When the two wheels, male and female, become complimentary to each other, village becomes an ideal. To Tukadoji, wedding life is for *purushartha* which includes *artha, kam, dharma,* and *moksha* in Indian context. Of these, the first two which respectively mean 'wealth' and 'pleasure', are purely worldly values. The other two may be described as spiritual. But, increasing ignorance and greed disrupt society. He asserts that freedom of thought is to be given to both, boy and girl. With the consent of both, wedding is to be arranged to live family in harmony. If wedding is deemed only for sensual pleasure, family runs with blindness and they live on animal level. Animal instinct of dog gives birth to puppies and once they are born, they are left over. It is not with human beings, they have to live with responsibility.

If marriageable youth intends to marry in different castes, with thought, consent is to be given. With the sense of conscience, marriage is to be performed. Some parents arrange marriage of their children at the age of three years or some time at the age of three months. When they grow up, they are not known to each other and fight as snake and mongoose. Sometime some girls turn widow at the childhood, which causes a big trouble for them. Raja Ram Mohan Roy initiated the window marriage.

> Such evil customs whatever are to be discarded;
> Again new creation of social rules ought to be. ||44||
>
> (Canto XXI, 'Wedded Life')

Widow who intends to marry has to speak with elders and with kind heart, marriage is to be arranged treating it a nature of life.

Tukadoji vehemently attacks dowry system. Some arrange marriage and take dowry matching their desires without considering match or mismatch of the boys and girls. A person takes money whether boy or girl is to be disdained and the incorrect insistence will be crumbled.

In some community, veil on face as custom creeps up trouble after marriage. Tukadoji humorously mentions that pertaining to veil system, wise turns fool too; bridegroom comes to know something after wedding, and husband if misplaced in crowd falls prey to miscreants.

> Such strange customs to demolish in society;
> No single person to stigmatise for it. ||66||
>
> (Canto XXI, 'Wedded Life')

He highlights paradoxical situation in an astrological observation:

> Bargaining with an astrologer manipulates numerical;
> Telling alternative name increases unreality seriously. ||77||
>
> Observe planets in the sky, here in nature different insistence;
> Revulsion which rises in life, not seen by them. ||78||
>
> Says, the best of bride, bridegroom, matched thirty-six numerical;
> Here rivalry or polarity full, spoils life. ||79||
>
> (Canto XXI, 'Wedded Life')

He doesn't favour exuberant expense in marriage and unworthy rituals. He poses the question, which God has told to celebrate marriage with debt; why to make mimicry of richness?

If hindrances are many, insistence is not to be on specific date for wedding, and such tendency, custom oriented, is not to be nourished. Fresh air, water, and season are the apt factors for wedding and other indifferences are to be treated as meaningless. Not much massive expense is to be for *pandal* and for wedding, the spot in nature of temple may be choosen. Well planning saves time, money, and labour. Keeping aside caste and wealth-illusion, supreme importance is to be given to virtues. Meeting place is to be beautified and suitable people to be invited. Bride and bridegroom are to be in front and they are to be introduced with the guests. Mass cultural and ceremonial proceedings are to be in wedding and they are to be treated as religious *sanskar*, wedding *sanskar,* which means in Indian context holistic practice to instill worthy impressions on mind in order to regulate human society.

> Introduction of bride, bridegroom; determination for good work;
> Holy work to be performed by uttering *manglashtaka.* ||92||
>
> In *manglashtaka* motto of wedding; proper advise by a person virtuous;
> Not to indulge fragment of decorum, unholy in it. ||93||
>
> Meeting to be with honour; not to smoke;
> Wedding, religious *sanskar* remembering fire goddess. ||94||
>
> Blessing of elders to receive, to behave with love for all;
> Occasion of marriage to perform with pleasant talk. ||95||
>
> Rural *khadi* for bride, bridegroom, old or new simple;
> With such attire auspicious rice granules to fall on both heads. ||96||
>
> (Canto XXI, 'Wedded Life')

Gramgeeta takes into cognisance mass cultural practices as *manglashtaka,* religious *sanskar*—worship of fire goddess and wearing of rural *khadi* to attribute traditional and religious fervour and impetus to cottage industry. To Tukadoji, the significance of marriage as *sanskar* is great, and beautiful social temple is to be constructed with its sound base.

> Female-male, two wheels, complimentary to each other really;
> with heavenly joy village will flourish, Tukadya says. ||103||

Male and female are not isolated islands. They are not polar opposite to each other. On the contrary, being the two wheels of a chariot, they are complimentary to each other. Following this tradition, Tukadoji affirms that village will flourish with joy.

Effort Influence

No avenue without action; to God, duty elevates man.

Tukadoji exhorts to leave feeble pessimism which views that man is a puppet in the hand of unseen power which is irrational and blind. In the very title of his magnum opus, *The World as Will and Idea*, Schopenhauer made the fundamental principle of his philosophy clear. He neither begins nor ends with God, with the isolated consciousness or its experiences and concepts, but with the man. Man's relationship to the world is, it is true, illuminated philosophically and epistemologically from the outset, but his knowledge is seen in conjunction with his physical being, his needs, and his involvement in the endless mechanism of life and its relationships. Schopenhauer sees his involvement as vulnerability, as suffering, and with this as its starting point—this too is a breach with the European tradition—his entire doctrine is pessimistic. Pessimism is here not to be understood primarily as hopelessness regarding the future, but as a negative and critical attitude of rejection towards the world and life in general. Schopenhauer agrees with Kant's view that man experiences and knows the world only within his own idea of it. That is to say, the world is conditioned by the subject's mode of knowledge.

> However, there was for him, in contrast to Kant, something on whom these ideas are based and which is thus independent of all experience and knowledge, which Schopenhauer called the "Will". The Will is not a goal or an intention but a kind of all pervading force of nature. As a "thing in itself", the Will is the basis of

> reality in its entirely, but it always appears in individual phenomenon of the will, which are manifestations of this one Will.[36]

To Schopenhauer, all pervading force of nature is not benevolent but crushes man under its iron heel. In *Gramgeeta,* Tukadoji attributes core significance to human action which is responsible for consequences. Right work is to perform to prevail glory in a village. Feeble despair is to be kept aside and efforts are to be continued to rise up fortune. One may be wealthy but may not be fortunate. Fortune lies in happiness and contentment, and not in superfluous things. He has the contention that human action has potential to change fortune:

> Fortune fruitful by work; heavenly happiness by work;
> Everything happens of human beings by work. ||41||
>
> Fortune sleeps when man inactive; walks ahead when active;
> With determination efforts turn into fortune. ||42||
>
> (Canto XXXIV)

We have to be effort oriented and with strong desire righteous fortune is to blossom. Result is outcome of our action and reap as we sow.

> Threw we stone above, fell it on forehead by mistake;
> How does gravitation operate from our side? ||60||
>
> Sowed chilly-sugar-cane in farm; fruits pungent, sweet in hands;
> What is role of water here? Fruits form as sow. ||61||
>
> (Canto XXXIV)

Every human action has its own effect, and a man has freedom of action. He assigns more importance to desire and its *sanskar*.

> Action freely by an individual; experience of its return other;
> Fruit of action performed; output of desire only. ||74||
>
> (Canto XXXIV)

Power of desire is responsible for whatever happens. Action requires as per desire and then output is possible onward. *Sanskar* of desire and *sanskar* of duty are accumulations from time before and their preservation is conspicuous whatever a man performs. The wheel of human life, the play of desire-effect, moves with birth-death and pleasure-pain.

Death is really a dream and a place for resting of the body or changing of the body, but it is not a solution to sin or good done in the life. Tukadoji relates desire and change of body after death.

> As change of cloth to pull new over body;
> Being to deem in death; changes body desire. ||89||
>
> (Canto XXXIV)

These lines keep parallel with what *Geeta* says:

> वासांसि जीर्णानि यथा विहाय नवनि गृहणाति नरोऽपराणि।
> तथा शरीराणि विहाय जीर्णान्यन्यानि संयाति नवनि देही।।22।।
>
> (*Geeta*, Canto 2, *Sankhyayoga*)

Geeta alleges that when body decays, spirit releases and enters into a new body. Spirit, in the form of energy, cannot be destroyed but exists in another form, which is the law of conservation of energy in science.

Fortune becomes virtual when focus is diverted from efforts. Saints advice to the world to improve action.

> No avenue without action; to God, duty elevates man;
> Be firm-minded, effort oriented, Tukadya says. ||102||
>
> (Canto XXXIV)

Man has to be firm on human action, and duty with sterneous efforts elevates man. His emphasis on human action has kinship with Ramdas's insistence on human efforts, not on fatalism. He stresses on qualities, virtues in man, and on achieved status, and not on an ascribed status based on birth.

Human Nature

Freedom to act, mega power this, in man's hand.

Deciphering his approach to human nature Tukadoji asserts:

> ... In whom, society is important than an individual this consciousness is man. In whom, national spirit pervades is man...in brief, my crux is that I long for

> the world based on virtues, not on castes. Virtues are to be human conduct but it will not only suffice, in it knowledge of inclusive nature is to illumined with readyness for duty.[37]

To him, human being is valuable and he doesn't discriminate human beings on the tenet of the colour of skin and externalities but attributes significance to virtues.

In Canto XXXV, 'Effort Influence', he exhorts that non-conscience, cruelty, and ego lead a man to death road.

> Birth, the play of will, in the world assembly of wills;
> Struggle indispensable there; pleasure, pain, fruits of action. ||16||
>
> (Canto XXXV, 'Effort Influence')

We are driven away by wrong will and company, and blame fate. We consider the effects of planet as good omen or evil omen. Some attempt to dilute the influence of planets on human life by reading script and tying threads, but doesn't strive to wipe out illusion.

> Effects of planets on the world, but they all occasionally;
> The store of our good, evil work, fructify time to time. ||22||
>
> Whatever we sow, spout in respective seasons;
> What time has done? Helped to initiate. ||23||
>
> (Canto XXXV, 'Effort Influence')

Whatever we sow, remain dormant for some period and sprout in respective seasons into sapling. Envisaging the choice, freedom of action to relation man, he creates consciousness about human power.

> Freedom to act, mega power this in man's hand;
> Architect of our fortune, we are. ||27||
>
> (Canto XXXV, 'Effort Influence')

Man has innate potential and it is his duty to manifest potential into work. Man has massive power of freedom to act and, thus, he is an architect of his fortune. Vivekananda expounded at the Parliament of the World's Religions, Chicago, in 1893, to shake off delusion:

> Come up, O lions, and shake off the delusion that you are sheep. You are souls immortal, spirits free, blessed and eternal; ye are not matter, ye are not bodies; matter is your servant, not you the servant of matter.[38]

He doesn't treat man as feeble, but deem as energetic with spirit, living force and perpetual. Man has to manifest spirit inside to control nature. He exemplifies that his vision has four propositions:

> Each soul is potentially divine. The goal is to manifest this divinity by controlling nature, external and internal. Do this either by work, or worship, or psychic control, or philosophy—by one, or more, or all of these—and be free. This is the whole of religion. Doctrines, or dogmas, or rituals, or books, or temples, or forms, are but secondary details.[39]

Man controls external nature through his knowledge and application of physical sciences, politics, and economics. This lifts his life from the primitive to the civilised level. But, this control of external nature alone can't help him to handle and resolve the tensions of his civilised state which overwhelm him and threaten to destroy him and his civilisation. Albert Einstein has observed that 'Science can denature plutonium, but it can't denature evil in the heart of man'. Envisaging the insufficiency of the external approach, the visionaries explored the internal nature of man and discovered the infinite and immortal dimension behind the finite man, beyond darkness and delusion of ignorance. I reflect on finite and infinite in human life in the prose lyric 'Chakrabalicah Pravas' (Odyssey of Wheel's Victim):

> ... the motion of the sun, the motion of the moon can't be changed. The revolution of the earth, man can't change. To face situation in vicinity, change in self and others, are in man's ambit. One who is capable, fit to struggle, will survive. Reliability of Charles Darwin's theory in *Origin of Species* (1859) is still there, after one hundred and fifty years in the post-Darwinian time. In the history of living world the giagantic dinosaures existed but in the flow of time perished. The greatness, deepness we

> experience of Tukaram's line, "Flood destroys trees, moss survives there". Indispensible to retain existence is struggle, persistence and consistence. Turbulent flow of water demolishes trees but moss retains. True it is what Nobel Lauret William Faulkner said, "...I decline to accept the end of man". Man is immortal because man has self-consciousness, energy, which are able to experience and create compassion, sacrifice, tolerence.[40]

'Struggle for existence' and 'survival of fittest', these Darwin's principles man experiences in struggle. Human values, persistence, consistence, compassion, sacrifice, and tolerance are valuable in human struggle. Upanishads, Tukaram, Vivekananda, Faulkner, and Tukadoji emphasise upon inner energy. In human struggle, man can be defeated; entire success can't be his share. In spite of it, odyssey of visionaries, may be of scientist, artist, saint, and thinker from the stance of human elevation, on individual as well as collective level, takes human culture and civilization forward. Man's energy to struggle can't be devastated. Ernest Hemingway in his novel, *The Old Man and the Sea,* writes, "But man is not made for defeat. A man can be destroyed but not defeated".[41]

To Jean-Paul Sartre, freedom of human action is of paramount significance in human existence. His stance is quoted in *The Story of Philosophy: From Antiquity to the Present.*

> He was the guiding intellectual force of philosophical existentialism, which is distinguished, by its radical rejection of all meanings that are on offer. It calls on every individual to decide on a life and to take responsibility for that decision, without having any criteria for determining which decision is the right one and which is the wrong one. Man in the nature of his being is not fixed as something specific as is a stone or a hammer but has to give himself his own being by acting in the world.[42]

To Sartre, man is free to act and responsibility to decision lies on an individual. His action in the world gives the colour of his own being. Succumbing to the lure of destiny, an individual immerses deep and deep, becoming a puppet in the hands of destiny. But, it is a false notion because an individual has freedom to work. One is one's friend and one's foe too.

> But, this false notion, freedom of action an individual has;
> Elevates with efforts, one's foe, a friend one is. ||36||
> (Canto XXXV, 'Effort-Influence')

In Canto VI, 'The *Yoga* of Self-Control' of *Bhagavadgeeta*, Krishna says to Arjuna to take right decision in dilemma:

> उदरेदात्मनात्मानं नात्मानमवासदयेत।
> आत्मैव ह्यामनो बन्धुरात्मैव रिपुरात्मन।।5।।[43]

(*Srimad Bhagavadgeeta,* Canto 6, *'The Yoga of Self-Control'*)

(One should lift oneself by one's own efforts and should not degrade oneself; for one's own self is one's friend and one's own self is one's enemy.)

People appear differently because their efforts are in various direction and the impressions on their minds, *sanskar,* are diverse. They are conversions of will-*sanskar* and duty-*sanskar*. The first, determination is there and then confirmation which turns into righteous work. Some *sanskar* are of parents and they accumulate providing impetus to good fruit. Effort inclusive ideal is an apex of all *sanskar*. Different works have different fruits. The best fruit of singing is not food but more than it; but how can one know it without a taste of it?

> Friends! Effort oriented to be; not to accept mightiness of fate;
> With enthusiasm one to glitter by work on the earth. ||85||
> (Canto XXXV, 'Effort-Influence')

Enthusiasm with work is decisive to make human existence meaningful.

Surdas was a visitor to harlot place but he became pure because of his efforts and attempts to sanctify the earth by *bhajan*. A farmer knows "with effort a seed to sow, then fruit of an ear of corn" (XXXV: 94). A tree is manifestation of a seed and entire tree is in latent form in a seed.

The core is effort only; fate too fruit of efforts;
Who can say, fruit, root are without tree? ||98||

Effort and fate are related and fate is too fruit of effort.

Grafting differently, flowers blossom variantly;
Can this happen ever with inactiveness? ||106||

As it human life, efforts need to elevate;
Untimely death, grim danger, averts by research. ||107||

(Canto XXXV, 'Effort-Influence')

Man is potentially divine and precise action can create an alternative world.

As thus tell, do effort; infuse thought power in effort;
Learn, teach, propagate all efforts village to village. ||109||

(Canto XXXV, 'Effort-Influence')

The nations which had acted on these lines, reached to the pinnacle of glory. The stature of life increased as they thought and acted.

Turned fatalist feeble; pragmatic more spirited;
Travelled ahead searching into space. ||111||

Flew to the Mars, climbed Himalaya's peak completely;
Search fire-rockets, nuclear-rockets, massive, Hydrogen too. ||112||

(Canto XXXV, 'Effort-Influence')

Man listens from crore of miles away, singing and speeches of each other, and makes the world inhabitant by controlling it. Efforts have reached to possible level but space still is left for efforts.

Becomes village ideal by efforts, happy native nation by efforts;
Become the motto of world peace successful by efforts. ||116||

(Canto XXXV, 'Effort-Influence')

Not only village but entire humanity will be elevated by efforts; and *Gramgeeta* stresses the pragmatic approach, linking mass, culture, and society.

Discarding evil in tradition, accepting traditional means as *bhajan* and prayer, attacking on superstition and irresponsible action, and relying on human efforts, Tukadoji enlightened masses, exploring new reality in the form of reformation to face challenges in life. It is discourse on indigenous oral tradition, musical instrument, sacred and profane, native festivities, virtual and eternal, human life and transcendental, evolution of self, *Guru*—the knowledge principle, chanting of *nam,* collective prayer, gender equality, and counter discourse on dominance of language for communication selfishness, blind faith, superstitions, orthodox and hegemonic customs and rituals, and deprivation of masses. The counteracting lines exemplify how cultural hegemony operates to strengthen the apparatus of cultural politics, and *Gramgeeta* resists dominance, deprivation, and expulsion, and anticipates tradition to the extent which is benevolent to human society but also deviates from traditional orthodox, authoritarian conceptions, and practices to encounter reality, in new historical sense.

In post-modernism, art and culture operate on two levels—(a) they revolt against the manifestation of art in which artistic forms are regulated by elite modernity, and (b) the difference between high or upper culture and mass culture, harboured by elite modernity, is collapsed in creativity of art.

Peripheral, marginal, oppressed, subalterns, wretched

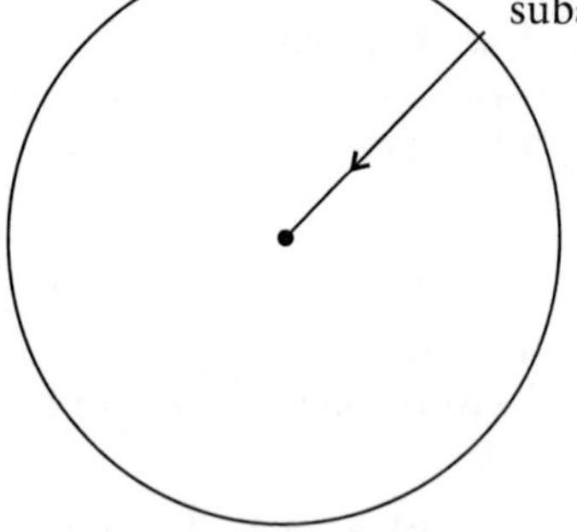

Post-modern approach to *Gramgeeta*
(Deconstruction)

From the perspective of post-modernism, *Gramgeeta* has located peripheral, marginal, oppressed, subalterns, and wretched who were at periphery to the center of the text, and deconstructs in Derridan sense via the binary opposites of past and present, by dislocating the center and bringing the masses at the center, and 'others' are placed 'within' in it. It has subaltern voices which were unheard and suppressed, and is polyphonic and inclusive of multidisciplinary in the text. It explores the myriad nuances of reality as religious, spiritual, social, and philosophical between mass culture and society. Native spirit is enthused in *Gramgeeta*, and besides retaining identity, it has national, global, and cosmic ramifications.

References

1. Matthew, Arnold (1966), *Culture and Anarchy*, Cambridge: University Printing House, p. 69.
2. T.S. Eliot, (1948), *Note Towards the Definition of Culture*, London: Faber and Faber Limited, p. 21.
3. *Ibid*,, p. 54.
4. *Ibid*,, p. 28.
5. Williams, Raymond, (1958), *Culture and Society*, London: Chatto and Windus p. 236.
6. *Ibid*,, p. 236.
7. *Ibid*,, p. 236.
8. Michael, Facault, (1972), *The Archeology of Knowledge*. (tr.), Alan Sheridan-Smith, New York: Harper and Row, pp. 4-5.
9. Fredrick, Jameson (1981), *The Political Unconsciousness: Narrative as a Socially Symbolic Act,* Ithaca: Cornell University Press, p. 120.
10. Gerald, Graff (1987), *Professing Literature: A Institutional History,* Chicago: Chicago University Press, p. 90.
11. *Ibid*., p. 148.
12. Hoggart, Richard, (1957), *The Uses of Literacy,* London: Penguin Books Ltd., p. 89.
13. Edward Said, (1993), *Culture and Imperialism*, London: Chatto and Windus, p. xiii.
14. J.B. Paranjape, (2000), 'Role and Place of Culture in the Twenty – First Century', *Journal of Nagpur University English Teachers' Organisation*, Vol. I, No. I, p. 92.
15. *Ibid*., p. 92.

16. *Sri Gurudeo,* April, 1950, p. 6.
17. R.C. Dhere, (2005), *Sant, Jan Ani Abhijan*, Pune: Padmagandha Prakashan, p. 70.
18. F. Kazard, *Sri Gurudeo,* Nov. 1955, p. 26.
19. Tukadoji (2023), *Gramgeeta* (tr.), Ratnakar D. Bhelkar, Canto XXX, 'Bhajan Influence,' New Delhi: Atlantic Publishers and Distributors (P) Ltd., p. 270.
20. Gayatri Chakravorty Spivak, (1988), 'Can the Subaltern Speak?' (ed.), C. Nelson and L. Grossberg, *Marxism and Interpretation of Culture,* London: Macmillan, p. 147.
21. Mircea Eliade, (1959), *Cosmos and History*, New York: Harper and Row, p. 5-36.
22. O.L. Nagbhushana Swami, (ed.), (2007), *The Sign: Vachanas of 12th Century*, O.L. Nagbhushan Swami, Laxmi Chandrasekhar, Vijaya Guttal, (tr.), Kannada University, Hampi: Center for Translations, p. 114.
23. *Jnaneshwar* (2007), *Jnaneshwari*, Canto 13 (ed.) Jnaneshwar Maharaj Trust, Pune: Maharashtra Government Press, 367-368.
24. *Sri Gurudeo,* April 1950, p. 6.
25. *Sri Gurudeo,* Jan. 1966, pp. 12-13.
26. *Sri Gurudeo,* April 1955, p. 6.
27. *Sri Gurudeo*, 'Editorial', June 1955, p. 8.
28. Tukadoji, Audio CD, Fountain Music Company, Pune, July 2010.
29. *Sri Gurudeo*, June 1955, p. 8.
30. A.B. Hocart, (1927), *Kingship*, London, p. 135.
31. Mircea Eliade, (1969), *The Quest: History and Meaning in Religion.* Chicago: Chicago University Press, p. 112.
32. *Ibid*, p. 113.
33. D.K. Bedekar, (1987), *Dharmachintan*, Mumbai: Lokwangdmay Gruha, p. 138-139.
34. R.P. Masani, (1966), *Folk Culture Reflected in Names*, Bombay, p. 7.
35. *Sri Gurudeo*, July 1955, pp. 4-5.
36. Quoted from Christophy Delius, Matthias Gatzemeier, Deniz Sertean, Kathleen Wunscher, (2000), *The Story of Philosophy:*

From Antiquity to the Present, Cologne: Konemann Verlagsgesellschoft mbh, p. 88.

37. *Sri Gurudeo*, 1947, Issue 6, p. 7.
38. Vivekananda, (1962), *Chicago Address.* Kolkata: Advaita Ashrama, pp. 34-35.
39. *Ibid.*, p. 10-11.
40. Ratnakar Bhelkar, (2011), *Chakrabalicha Pravas (Odyssey of Wheel's Victim)*, Pune: Snehavardhana Publication, pp. 25-26.
41. Earnest Hemingway (2000), *The Old Man and the Sea*, New Delhi: UBS Publisers and Distributor Ltd., p. 71.
42. *Op.cit*, p. 102.
43. *Srimad Bhagvadgeeta*. Trans, Gorakpur: Geeta Press, p. 103.

In Retrospect

Nuancing with knowledge and spiritual facet of Upanishads, *Gramgeeta* resonates with Alighieri Dante's *Divine Comedy* in its consciousness of political and social realities. Deconstructing *Bhagvadgeeta, Gramgeeta* discourses with masses to emerge from dilemmatic realities to combat injustice and resist oppression, dominance, and orthodoxy.

Contextualising vedic tradition, post-vedic tradition, and Upanishads, the exploration stresses the traditions of *nirguna bhakti* of Kabir and Nanak and Indian devotional poetry, locating *Gramgeeta* in the literary, historical, and cultural framework. Retaining indigenous roots, the text has nationalistic spirit, mirrored in the poetries of Sarojini Naidu, Rabindranath Tagore, and Aurobindo, and reflective temper and spiritual realisation, infused in the poetries of Vivekananda, Tagore, and Aurobindo. Being the post-colonial text, *Gramgeeta* imbibes the post-colonial dynamics; projects myriad realities; and encompasses multi-disciplines, trajectories of tradition, and reality.

Humanitarian vision of religion is embedded and it is the counter discourse of traditional conception of orthodox religion, fanatism, sectarianism, aggressive nationalism, immoderate individualism, selfish motives, the notion of sacred, and profane to fragment and superstitious rituals, and dominance to refrain from religious texts. It resists social stratification, cultural hegemony, and convergence on dignity of labour; accepts the conception of *guru* and the practice of *nam*, which open doors to excluded; and asserts that religion, at core, nourishes constructive human values. Collective prayer is a pragmatic mode to bring together all from various religions.

The parlance of *Gurudeo*, in the text, who is to be perceived as per one's perception, is in the tradition of *nirguna bhakti,* and is operable without discrimination, fragmentation, and stratification to infuse the spirit of freedom, unity, equality, and justice in society which cleavages on the tenets of language, race, caste, cult, sect, and religion. The vision, which permeates in it, is cosmic and expansive; focuses on life on the earth; and transcends towards cosmic. The synergy in the approaches to religion has been accepted by Tukadoji and Vivekananda as both stress on understanding, coordination, assimilation, tolerance, cooperation, peace, and love, which attribute to cosmic dimension.

The utopian world, the welfare society, which *Gramgeeta* creates with fantasy mode, is the projected world based on consensus reality, which deals with 'absence', 'invisible' in the present world. Though, it is created and transformed, the alternative world has close links with the real world which exemplifies its practicability on social, spiritual, ethical, political, economic, educational, and scientific counts. It provides alternative realities to the model based on Gandhian ideology, emphasising on empowering of *Gram Sabha,* collective prayer, and militant voice against dominance. The utopian vision, here, keeps pace with the welfare vision in *Jnaneshwari* and both texts promulgate the ideas of elimination of evil and restoration of good in human society, pulsating with harmony and joy.

The pragmatic stance, linking mass, culture, and society is conspicuous in *Gramgeeta,* which is the discourse of language for mass communication, indigenous oral tradition, musical instruments, sacred and profane, native festivities, virtual and eternal, human life and transcendental, evolution of self, principle of *Guru* knowledge, chanting of *nam*, collective prayer, gender equity, and the counter discourse of dominance of language, selfishness, blind faith, orthodox and authoritative customs and rituals, and deprivation of masses. The intersecting lines exemplify how cultural hegemony operates to strengthen the apparatus of cultural politics, and resists dominance, deprivation, and expulsion.

In nutshell, the critique disseminates the discourse of tradition, history, literary texts, religion, philosophy, mass culture, society, political governance, economy, education, science, technology, and environment, and posits the counter discourse of cultural hegemony, cultural politics, mono-centredness, dwindling of ethical values, social fragmentation, fundamentalist forces, aggressive nationalism, economic rift, discord with environment, orthodox rituals, and fatalism.

It has displaced marginal, oppressed, and wretched, who were at periphery, to the center of the text, and as thus, the post-colonial discourse deconstructs in Derridean sense, dislocating the center and locating masses at the center, and 'others' are placed within, to assert balance. It has subaltern voices which were unheard and suppressed, and though, enthused with indigenous spirit and mass cultural voices, it triggers national, global, and cosmic ramifications.

Comparative cultural criticism endeavours to fill void by coordinating cults and sects and nourishing democratic values, freedom, equality, unity and justice, tolerance, collective prayer; and not by emphasising the monocentric image and rendering vent to individual perspectives to bridge plurities. It intersects traditional, literary, religious, cultural, and historical hegemony by conjuncting ruptures and dissociation; and as a consequence, the post-colonial discourse nurtures the process of defragmentation with the components of coordination and conjuncture, which attribute the new dimension to it.

Being anchored in multi-disciplines and multi-realities, the post-colonial discourse becomes polyphonic. Envisaging historical and cultural realities, the critique offers the map diagnosing symptoms and deconstructing tradition; furnishes reformative measures; and renders pragmatic cure for ailments. The post-colonial discourse, here, celebrates coordination of nuances of unity in diverse cultures, familiarity of self in multi-cultures, and conjuncture to fill ruptures and void to integrate multivariant realities in the expanse of historical and cultural contexts, keeping pace with tradition, and whenever requires, deviating from it to counter, for evolution of individual, society, and culture.

Select Bibliography

Primary Sources

मराठी

तुकडोजी, (1970), अरूणोदय भजनावली, गुरूकुंज आश्रम: श्री गुरूदेव प्रकाशन।

तुकडोजी, (1988), ग्रामगीता, अड्याळ-टेकडो: आत्मानुसंधान केंद्र।

तुकडोजी, (1988), गीताप्रसाद, गुरूकुंज आश्रम: श्री गुरूदेव प्रकाशन।

तुकडोजी, (1991), राष्ट्रसंतांची अभंगगाथा, नागपुर: ग्रामगीता प्रकाशन समिति।

तुकडोजी, (1995), लोकशाहीचे पोवाडे, गुरूकुंज आश्रम: श्री गुरूदेव प्रकाशन।

तुकडोजी, (1995), आनंदामृत, गुरूकुंज आश्रम: श्री गुरूदेव प्रकाशन।

तुकडोजी, (1995), नवमावृत्ति (1988), अड्याळ-टेकडी: श्री गुरूदेव आत्मानुसंधान।

तुकडोजी, (1996), अनुभव सागर, गुरूकुंज-आश्रम: श्रीगुरूदेव प्रकाशन।

तुकडोजी, (1996), स्फुर्तितरंग, गुरूकुंज आश्रम: श्री गुरूदेव प्रकाशन।

तुकडोजी, (1997), जीवन जागृति, गुरूकुंज आश्रम: श्री गुरूदेव प्रकाशन।

तुकडोजी, (1997), विवेक माधुरी भजनावली, गुरूकुंज आश्रम: श्री गुरूदेव प्रकाशन।

तुकडोजी, (1997), प्रचार मार्गदर्शिका, गुरूकुंज आश्रम: श्री गुरूदेव प्रकाशन।

तुकडोजी, (1997), क्रांतिविणो भजनावली, गुरूकुंज आश्रम: श्री गुरूदेव प्रकाशन।

तुकडोजी, (2000), समाज संजीवनी, गुरूकुंज आश्रम: श्री गुरूदेव प्रकाशन।

तुकडोजी, (2000), दिव्यदर्शन भजनावली, गुरूकुंज आश्रम: श्री गुरूदेव प्रकाशन।

तुकडोजी, (2008), विश्वशांतियोग, गुरूकुंज आश्रम: श्री गुरूदेव प्रकाशन।

तुकडोजी, (2009), सामुदायिक प्रार्थनादीप, गुरूकुंज आश्रम: श्री गुरूदेव प्रकाशन।

हिन्दी

तुकडोजी, (1968), अनुभवप्रकाश, भाग-1, गुरूकुंज आश्रम: श्री गुरूदेव प्रकाशन।

तुकडोजी, (1968), अनुभवप्रकाश, भाग-2, गुरूकुंज आश्रम: श्री गुरूदेव प्रकाशन।

तुकडोजी, (1971), विवेक सरिता, गुरूकुंज आश्रम: श्री गुरूदेव प्रकाशन।

तुकडोजी, (1995), अनुभवप्रसाद, गुरूकुंज आश्रम: श्री गुरूदेव प्रकाशन।

तुकडोजी, (1996), लहर की बरखा, भाग-3, गुरूकुंज आश्रम: श्री गुरूदेव प्रकाशन।

तुकडोजी, (1196), ज्ञानदीप भजनावली, गुरूकुंज आश्रम: श्री गुरूदेव प्रकाशन।

तुकडोजी, (1996), राष्ट्रनौका, गुरूकुंज आश्रम: श्री गुरूदेव प्रकाशन।

तुकडोजी, (1998), लहर की बरखा, भाग-1, गुरूकुंज आश्रम: श्री गुरूदेव प्रकाशन।

तुकडोजी, (1998), जीवन-ज्योति, गुरूकुंज आश्रम: श्री गुरूदेव प्रकाशन।

तुकडोजी, (1198), क्रांतिदिप, गुरूकुंज आश्रम: श्री गुरूदेव प्रकाशन।

तुकडोजी, (1998), गांधी गीतांजली, गुरूकुंज आश्रम: श्री गुरूदेव प्रकाशन।

तुकडोजी, (1999), लहर की बरखा, भाग-2, गुरूकुंज आश्रम: श्री गुरूदेव प्रकाशन।

तुकडोजी, (1999), भजनकुन्ज, गुरूकुंज आश्रम: श्री गुरूदेव प्रकाशन।

तुकडोजी, (2000), ज्ञान-कुन्ज, गुरूकुंज आश्रम: श्री गुरूदेव प्रकाशन।

तुकडोजी, (2001), भारत साधु समाज की सेवा साधना, गुरूकुंज आश्रम: श्री गुरूदेव प्रकाशन।

तुकडोजी, (2002), श्री ग्रामगीता, सुदाम सावरकर, (अनु.), नागपुर: आशा प्रकाशन।

तुकडोजी, (2002), मेरी जपान यात्रा, गुरूकुंज आश्रम: श्री गुरूदेव प्रकाशन।

तुकडोजी, (2001), भक्ति सुधा भजनावली, गुरूकुंज आश्रम: श्री गुरूदेव प्रकाशन।

तुकडोजी, (2003), सद्विचार-प्रवाह, गुरूकुंज आश्रम: श्री गुरूदेव प्रकाशन।

तुकडोजी, (2005), मेरी जीवन यात्रा, गुरूकुंज आश्रम: श्री गुरूदेव प्रकाशन।

संस्कृत

तुकडोजी, (1984), ग्रामगीतामृतम, श्रीधर भास्कर वर्णेकर, (अनु.), अड्याळ: अध्यात्मकेंद्र, भू-वैकुंठ।

Secondary Sources

English

Abbott Justin E, and Narhar R. Godbole, (2007), *Stories of Indian Saints*, New Delhi: Motilal Banarasidass Publishers.

Adoratsky V., (1980), *Dialectical Materialism*, Calcutta: National Book Agency.

After, Emily, (2006), *The Translation Zone: A New Comparative Literature*, Princenton University Press.

Ahmad, Aijaz, (1992), *In Theory: Classes, Nations, Literatures*, New York: Verso.

Ahuja M.L., (2006), *Eminent Indians: Saint and Sages*, Rupa Co., New Delhi, 2006.

Ajwani, L.H. (1994), *History of Sindhi Literature*, New Delhi: Sahitya Academy.

Ambedkar B.R., (2004), *Annihilation of Caste*, Nagpur: Samata Prakashan.

Ambedkar, Babasaheb, (1989), On Economics, *Dr. Babasaheb Ambedkar Writings and Speeches* Vol. 6, Bombay: Education Department, Govt. of Maharashtra.

Ambedkar, Babasaheb, (1993), Unpublished Writings, *Dr. Babasaheb Ambedkar: Writings and Speeches*, Vol. 12 Unpublished Writings, Bombay: Education Department, Govt. of Maharashtra.

Ambedkar, Babasaheb, (1995), *Dr. Babasaheb Ambedkar: Writings and Speeches,* Vol. 14, Dr. Ambedkar and the Hindu Code Bill. Bombay: Education Department, Govt. of Maharashtra.

Ambedkar, Babasaheb, (1992), *The Buddha and His Dhamma, Dr. Babasaheb Ambedkar, Writing and Speeches,* Vol. XI, Bombay: Education Department, Govt. of Maharashtra.

Anand Balwant Singh, (1997), *Baba Farid,* New Delhi: Sahitya Academy.

Apter, T.E. (1982), *Fantasy Literature: An Approach to Reality,* The Macmillan Press Ltd.

Arnold, Matthew (1966), *Culture and Anarchy,* London: The Syndics of the Cambridge University Press.

Bahirat B.P., (1984), *The Philosophy of Jnanadeva,* New Delhi: Motilal Banarasidass Publishers.

Bakhtin, Mikhail (1981), *The Dialogic Imagination: Four Essays,* Michael Holquist, Aust in (ed.), Caryl Emerson and Michael Holoquist, (trans.), TX: University of Texas Press.

Bakhtin, Mikhail (1963/1984), Problems of Dostoevsky's Poetics, (Ed. & trans, Caryl Emerson), Minnneopolis: University of Minnesota Press.

Bahari, Bankey, (2005), *The Story of Mira Bai*, Gorakhpur, Gita Press.

Banamati S., (1990), *Lights of Sadguru Kabir Saheb,* Baroda: Kabir Jnana Ashram.

Bande, Usha (2012), *Culture, Nature and Literature*, Jaipur: Rawat Publications.

Barry Peter. (2010), *Beginning Theory,* New Delhi: Viva Books Private Limited.

Barthes, Roland (1970) *S/Z* , (Trans.), Richard Miller, Berkeley, CA: University of California Press, 1976.

Becker, George. (1980), *Realism in Modern Literature,* New York: Fredrick-Unger Publishing Co.

Bennigton, Geoffery (With Jacques Derrida), (1991), *Jacques Derridu,* Paris: Seuil, (Trans), Geoffery Bennigton, Chicago, IL: Chicago University Press, 1993.

Bhaba, Homi, (1984), *The Location of Culture*, London: Routeledge.

Bhaba, Homi, 'Forward to Frantz Fanon', (1986), *Black Skin and White Mask,* Trans., Charl's Lam Markmann, London: Pluto.

Bhaba, Homi, (1990), *National and Narration*, London and New York: Routledge.

Bhattacharya, Asutosh, (2007), *Folklore of Bengal,* New Delhi: National Book Trust.

Bhelkar, Ratnakar D., (2019*), Indian Literature: Translated Texts, Indianness and Beyond,* New Delhi: Atlantic Publishers and Distributors Pvt. Ltd.

Blackmore, Susan, (2005), *Consciousness: A Very Short Introduction,* New York: Oxford University Press, Inc.

Bleich, David, (1984), *Utopia: The Psychology of a Cultural Fantasy,* Ann Arbar, Mich: UMI Research Press.

Budhananda Swami, (1982), *Can One Be Scientific and Yet Spiritual,* Culcutta Advaita Ashrama.

Burn Lucilla, (1990), *Greek Myths,* Hyderabad: Orient Blackswan Private Limited.

Chandy, Amaryll Beatrice (1985) *Magical Realism and Fantastic,* New York and London: Garland Publishing, Inc.

Chatterjee, Partha, (1986), *Natinalist Thoughts and the Colonial World*: A Derivative Discouse?, London: Zed.

________, (1993), The National and Its Fragments, Princeton: Princeton University Press.

Chettiar, S.M.L. Lakshmanan, (2002) *Folk Lore of Tamil Nadu,* New Delhi: National Book Trust.

Chitre Dilip, (ed.) (1967), *An Anthology of Marathi Poetry,* Bombay Nirmala Sadanand Publishers.

Chitre Dilip, (trans), (1991), *Says Tuka*, New Delhi: Penguin Publication.

Chitre Dilip, (trans), (1996), *Shri Jnandev's Anubhavamrut: The Immortal Experience of Being,* New Delhi: Sahitya Academy.

Choudhari, Satya Dev, (2002), *Glimpses of Indian Poetics,* New Delhi: Sahitya Academy.

Clareson, Thomas D. (1971), *SF: The Other Side of Realism,* Bowing Green, Ohio: Bowing Green University Popular Press.

Colin N. Manlov, (1975), *Modern Fantasy: Five Studies*, New York: Cambridge University Press.

Cook, Michael, (2002), *The Koran: A Very Short Introduction,* New York: Oxford University Press Inc.

Culler, Jonathan, (2002), *Barthes: A Very Short Introduction,* New York: Oxford University Press Inc.

________ (1982), on Deconstruction: Theory and Criticism After *Structuralism*, Ithacol: Cornell University Press.

Dallapiccola A.L., (2003), *Hindu Myths,* Hyderabad: Orient Blackswan Private Limited.

Das, Manoj, (2010), *Sri Aurobindo,* New Delhi: Sahitya Academy.

Dasgupta R.K., (2008), *Philosophy and Philosophers,* Ramkrishna Mission Institute of Culture: Kolkata Gol Park.

Dasgupta, T. et.al. (eds), (2007), *Race and Racialization:* Essential Readings, Toronto: Canadian Scholars Press.

David - Neel, Alexandra, (2000), *Buddhism: Its Doctrines And Methods,* Kathamandu: Pilgrims Book House.

Deshmukh P.S., (1993), *The Origin and Development of Religion in Vedic Literature,* Bombay: Oxford University Press.

Deshpande, G.P. (2002), *Selected Writings of Jotirao Fule*, New Delhi: Leftword.

Deshpande, P.Y., *Sant Tukdoji Maharaj:* A Wonder-Man of India, Nagpur: Seva Prakashan.

Dev, Anjana Neira, Tiwari Bajrang Bihari, Khanna Sanam, *Indian Literature: An Introduction,* Delhi: Dorling Kinderslay (India) Pvt. Ltd.

Devi G.N. (ed.) (2007), *Indian Literary Criticism: Theory and Interpretation*. Hyderbad: Orient Longman.

Dhillon Harjinder Singh, (2000), *Shah Husain,* New Delhi: Sahitya Academy.

Easwaran Eknath, (2006), *The Sacred Literature of the World,* Mumbai: Jaico Publishing House.

Einstein, Albert, (1956) Department *Ideas and Opinions,* London: Alvin Redman Limited; 3rd Edition.

Eliade, Miracea, Editor in Chief (1987), *The Encyclopaedia of Religion,* 16 Vols, New York: Macmillan.

Fannon, Frantz (1952), *Black Skin and White Mask*, (Trans.), Charles Lam Markmann, London: Pluto, 1986.

Fannon, Frantz (1965), *The Wretched of the Earth,* New York: Grove Press (Original French, 1961).

Figueiria, Maria Ine's Oscar de Noronha, (2007), *Episodio Oriental: Readings in Indo-Portuguese Literature,* Panjim: Fundacao Orient & Third Millennium.

Ford Boris, (1998), *From Orwell to Naipaul*, Penguin London: Books.

Foucault, Michel, (1974), *The Order of Things: An Archaoelogy of the Human Sciences*, London and New York: Tavistock.

Frolov, Ivan, (1981), *Manscience-Humanism: A New Synthesis*, Moscow: Progress Publishers.

Frost, Mervyn, (2009), *Global ethics,* New York: Routledge.

Frye, Northrop, (1937), *Anatomy of Criticism*, Princeton, N.J: Princeton University Press.

Faucault, Michel, (1974), *The Order of Things: An Archaeology of the Human Sciences,* London and New York, Taxistock.

Gandhi M.K., (1960), *Village Industries,* Navjivan Publishing House, Ahmedabad.

Gandhi M.K., (1953) *Towards, New Education,* Ahmedabad, Navjivan Publishing House.

Gandhi, Leela, (1998), *Post-colonial Theory: A Critical Introduction*, New York: Columbia University Press.

Gandhi, M.K. (2001), *India of My Dreams*, Ahmedabad: Navjivan Publishing House, 2001.

Gardner, Jane F. (1993), *Roman Myths,* Hyderabad: Orient Blackswan Private Limited.

Gates, Henry Louis, Jr. (1989), *The Signifying Monkey: A Theory of African-American Criticism,* Oxford and New York: Oxfor University Press.

Genette, Gerald, (1980), *Narrative Discourse*, (trans.), Lewin, Jane E, Oxford: Basil Blackwell.

George K.M., (1989), *Kesari Balkrishna Pillai,* New Delhi: Sahitya Academy.

Gerber, Richard, (1973), *Utopian Fantasy*, New York: McGraw Hill, New York.

Ghalib, Mirza, (2008), Salil *Diwan-Ghalib,* Kuldip, (tr.), Delhi: Rajpal & Sons.

Gibran, Kahil, (1993), *The Prophet,* New Delhi: UBS Publishers and Distributors Ltd.

Gilory, Paul, (1993), *The Black Atlantic: Modernity and Double Consciousness*, Cambridge, MA: Harvard University Press.

Giri, Swami Avdheshanand (1992), *Journey to Self,* Ambala Cantt: Prabhu Prem Prakashan.

God News Bible, (2008), Mumbai: St. Pauls.

Golahit S.B., (2007), *Rural Development Programme: Theory and Practice,* New Delhi: Adhyayan Publishers and Distributors.

Greenblatt, Stephen, (2000), Practicing New Historicism, Chicago, IL and London: University of Chicago Press.

Guha, Ranajit and Gayatri Chakravorty Spivak, eds., (1988), *Selected Subaltern Studies,* New York: Oxford University Press.

Guha, Ranajit, (1999) *The Elementary Aspects of Peasant Insurgency in Colonial India*, Delhi: Oxford University.

Guha, Ranajit, ed. (1985), *Subaltern Studies IV: Writings on South Asian History and Society,* New Delhi: Oxford University Press.

Hainsworth, Peter & Robey, David, (2012), *Italian Literature: A Very Short Introduction,* New York: Oxford University Press.

Hariyanna M., (2008), *The Essentials of Indian Philosophy,* Delhi: Motilal Banarsidas Publishers Pvt. Ltd.

Hume, Kathlyn. (1984), *Fantasy and Mimesis: Responses to Reality in Western Literature,* New York: Methuon.

Hutcheon Linda, (2004), *A Poetics of Postmodernism: History Theory Fiction,* London: Routledge.

Illustrated Biography of Sri Aurobindo, (2007), Delhi: RBC International.

Iyer, Vijayalakshmi, (2007), *The World Great Speeches,* Delhi: GNOSIS.

Jain Hiralal, Upadhye A.N, (2000), *Mahavira: His Times and His Philosophy of Life,* New Delhi: Bhartiya Jnanpith.

Jameson, Fredric R. (1981), *The Political Unconscious: Narratives as Socially Symbolic Act*, London: Methuen.

Jameson, Fredric R. (1998), *The Cultural Turn: Selected Writing on the Post Modern,* 1983-1998, London and New York: Verso.

Jhaveri Mansukhlal, (1978), *History of Gujarati Literature,* New Delhi, Sahitya Academy.

Joseph, Siby K. Edited, (2012), *Contextulising Gandhian Thought,* Wardha: Institute of Gandhian Studies.

Kabir by Kunwar Anil Kumar, (2008), *Kabir Vani*, Delhi: Manoj Publications.

Kane, P.S. (2017), *The Rashtrasant: The Socio-Political Thought of Sant Tukadoji Maharaj*, Nagpur: Vijay Prakashan.

Kaul, J.N., Edited, (1975), *Higher Education, Social Change and National Development,* Shimla: Indian Institute of Advanced Study.

Kohli Mohinder Pal, (1992), *Guru Tegh Bahadur,* New Delhi: Sahitya Academy.

Kohli Surinder Singh, (1990), *Bulhe Shah*, New Delhi: Sahitya Academy.

Kosambi, D.D., (1962), *Myth and Reality in the Formation of India Culture,* Bombay: Popular *Prakashan.*

Kothiyal, G.N., (2006), *The History of World Religion*, Delhi: Adhyayan Publishers and Distributors.

Kumar, J. Keval, (2009), *Mass Communication in India*, Mumbai: Jaico Publishing House.

Lane, Richard J., (2006), *Fifty Key Literary Theorists*, New York: Routledge.

Lawson, Victoria, (2007), *Making Development Geography*, UK: Hodder Education.

Lokeswarananda, Swami, (2002), *Religion and Culture*, Kolkata: The Ramkrishna Mission Institute of Culture.

Lucas, George, (1980), *Essays on Realism*. (ed. and intro.), Ridney Lingstone and translated by David Fernabach, Cambridge: Mass, MIT Press.

Lyotard, Jean Francois, (1971), *Discourse/Figure*, Paris: Klincksieck.

Lyotard, Jean Francois, (1979), *The Postmodern Condition*, (Trans.) Geoffery Bennigton and Brian Massumi, Ninneapolis, MN: Minnesota University Press and Manchester: Manchester University Press, 1986.

Majeed Javed, (2009), *Muhammad Iqbal: Islam, Aesthetics and Postcolonialism*, New Delhi: Routledge.

Masih, Y. (2010), *Introduction to Religions*, Philosophy, New Delhi: Motilal Banarasidass.

Maududi Sayyid Abdul A'la (2007), *Towards Understanding Islam*, New Delhi: Morkazi Maktaba Islami Publishers.

Mehrotra Arvind Krishna, (ed.) (2008), *A Concise History of Indian Literature in English*, Ranikhet: Permanent Black.

Mehta, Uday, Puniyani, Ram, Editors, (2011), *Modern Gurus: Religion and Liberation Theology*, Thiruvanthapuram: Mythri Books.

Modak M.S., (1970), *Spinoza and The Upanishads: A Comparative Philosophy*. Nagpur University, Nagpur.

Moghni Abdul, (2004), *Islam and Terrorism*, New Delhi: Markazir Maktaba Islami Publishers.

Morris, Rosalind C. (ed.), (2010), *Can the Subaltern Speak?*, New York: Columbia University Press.

Mujeab, M., (2009), *Ghalib*, New Delhi: Sahitya Academy.

Mukherjee, Lal Gopal, Behari, Bankey (2007). *Songs from Bhartrihari*, Gorakhapur: Geeta Press.

Murti M. Srimannarayana, (1997), *Bhartrhari: Grammarian*, New Delhi: Sahitya Academy.

Paul de Man, (1986), *The Resistance to Theory*, Minneapis, MN: University of Minnesota Press.

Nagbhushan, Swami O.L. (ed.), (2007), *The Sign: Vachanas of 12th Century*, O.L. Nagabhushan Swami, Laxmi Chandrashekhar, Vijaya Guttal, (tr.), Hampi: Karnataka University.

Naik Zakir, (2007), *Concept of God in Major Religions*, New Delhi: Madhur Sandesh Sangam.

Naik Zakir, (2007), *The Quran: Modern Science, Compatible or Incompatible*, New Delhi: Madhur Sandesh Sangam.

Naik, M.K., (2007), *History of Indian English Literature*, New Delhi: Sahitya Academy.

Nandakumar, (2004), *Poems of Subramania Bharati*, New Delhi: Sahitya Academy.

Nayar, Pramod K., (2008), *Postcolonial Literature: An Introduction*. New Delhi: Dorling Kindersley (India) Pvt. Ltd.

Nayar, Pramod K., (2010), *Contemporary Literature and Cultural Theory*, New Delhi: Dorling Kindersley (India) Pvt. Ltd.

Nilsson, Usha, (2009), *Surdas*. New Delhi: Sahitya Academy.

Norris Christopher, (2003), *Deconstruction; Theory and Practice*. New York: Routledge.

Oldenberg, Herman (2017), 2nd Print, *Buddha: His Life, His Doctrine, His Order*, Delhi: Motilal Banarsidass Publishers Pvt. Ltd.

Panigrahi Ramesh Prasad, (2003), *Kalicharan Patnayak*, New Delhi: Sahitya Academy.

Paramananda Swami, *The Problem of Life and Death,* Madras Sri Ramkrishna Math, 1961.

Paranjape J.B., (2003), *Critical Investigations,* Nagpur: Datasons.

Powell Jim (2001), *Postmodernism for Beginners,* Chennai: Orient Longman Ltd.

Prabhananda Swami, (2001), *Max Muller and His Contemporaries.* Kolkata: The Ramkrishna Mission Institution of Culture.

Pradhan V.G., Pradhari, 1967, *Jnaneshwari,* Vol. I. London: Green Allen & Unwin Ltd.

Prasad K.B. Prabhu, (1993), *Sarvajna,* New Delhi: Sahitya Academy.

Prasoon Shrikant, (2009), *Indian Saints & Sages,* New Delhi: Hindoology Books.

Puniyani Ram, (ed.), (2005), *Religion, Power and Violence,* New Delhi: Sage Publication, New Delhi.

Puniyani, Ram, (2012), *God Politics,* New Delhi: Vitasta Publishing Pvt. Ltd.

Ramchandran T.N., (1999), *Sivagnaan Munivar,* New Delhi: Sahitya Academy.

Rabkin, Eric S., (1979), *Fantastic World: Myths, Tales and Stories,* New York: Oxford University Press.

Radhakrishan Sarvapalli, (2007), *The Dhammapada*, Varanasi: Pilgrims Publishing.

Rai Sunil K., (2004), *Jacques Derrida: An Introduction*, Delhi: Adhyayan Publishers and Distributors.

Ramachandran T.N., (1994), *Saint Sekkizhar,* New Delhi: Sahitya Academy.

Ramsukhadas Swami, *Srimad Bhagavadgita Sadhaka* - Sanjivini (with Appendix J. Vol. I Commentary. Gita Press: Gorakhpur, India.

Ramzan Shad, (1999), *Khazir Malik Safai,* New Delhi: Sahitya Academy, 1999.

Ranganathananda Swami, (1982), *Swami Vivekanand and His Humanism,* Culcutta: Advaita Ashrama.

Ranganathananda Swami, (2000), *Science and Religion,* Culcutta: Advaita Ashrama.

Rao B. Rajanikant, (1991), *Ramadasu*, New Delhi: Sahitya Academy.

Rao K.S. Ramkrishna, (2006), *Muhammad: The Prophet of Islam,* New Delhi: Madhur Sandesh Sangam.

Roy, Anjali Gera, (ed.) (2006), *Wole Soyinka: An Anthology of Recent Criticism*, New Delhi: Pencraft International.

Ruskin, John, (1996), *Unto This Last,* Ahmedabad: Navjivan Publishing House.

Russell Bertrand, (1980), *The Problems of Philosophy,* London: Oxford University Press.

Spivak Chakravorty Gayatri, (2003), *Death of Discipline,* New York: Columbia University Press.

Sadarangani Neeti M., (2004), *Bhakti Poetry in Medieval India: Its Inception, Cultural Encounter and Impact.* New Delhi: Sarup & Sons.

Said, Edward, (1994), *Culture and Imperialism,* New York: Vintage Books.

Said, Edward, (2001), *Orientalism,* New Delhi: Penguin Books India Ltd.

Sangave Vilas A. (1981), *The Sacred Shravan belagola: A Socio - Religious Study,* New Delhi: Bhartiya Jnanpith.

Sangave Vilas A., (2001), *Aspects of Jain Religion,* New Delhi: Bhartiya Jnanpith.

Sarvabhutananda, Swami, (2004), *Life, Mind and Consciousness,* Kolkata: Ramkrishna Mission Institute of Culture.

Sarvabhutananda, Swami, (2009), *The Perenial Values of Indian Culture,* Kolkata: Ramkrishna Mission Institute of Culture.

Sarvabhutananda, Swami, (2011), *Spirituality and Science of Consciousness,* Kolkata: Ramkrishna Mission Institute of Culture.

Satre, Jean-Paul, Hazel E. Barnes, (1943), (tr.), *Being and Nothingness,* Paris: Gallimard.

Satre, Jean-Paul, (2002), *Bernard Freechtman,* (tr.) *What is Literature?,* London: Routledge.

Schelling, Andrew (ed.), (2011), *The Oxford Anthology of Bhakti Literature,* New Delhi: Oxford University Press.

Sen, Amartya, (2004), *Social Exclusion: Concept, Application, Scrutinity,* New Delhi: Critical Quest.

Sharma, Arvind, (2007), *The Quest for Serenity In World Religions,* New Delhi: D.K. Printworld (P) Ltd.

Sharma, Deo Prakash, (2000), *Harappan Seals, Sealings and Copper Tablets,* New Delhi: National Museum.

Sharma, Prabhu Datta, (tr.) (2005), *Kabeer*, Jaipur: Research Publications.

Sharma, Rajendra, (2009), Mikhail Bakhtin's, *Theory of the Novel,* New Delhi: Dominant Publishers and Distributors.

Sharma, Satyendranath, (1985), *Madhavadeva,* New Delhi: Sahitya Academy.

Shekhar Chandra, M. Prasad Gangadhar, (2008), *Eternally Talented India*, Secunderabad: Vivekananda Life Skill Academy.

Shirwadkar Vasant, *The Wandering Saint: Life and Teaching of Gadge Baba,* Shree Gadge Maharaj Prakashan Samiti.

Singh, Ch. Manihar, (1996), *A History of Manipuri Literature,* New Delhi: Sahitya Academy.

Singh, Manihar, (2003), *History of Manipur: Literature,* New Delhi: Sahitya Academy.

Sinha, Sunita, (ed.) (2009), *Reconceiving Postcolonialism: Vision and Revisions*, New Delhi: Atlantic Publishers & Distributors (P) Ltd.

Spivak Chakravorty, Gayatri, (1987), *In Other Worlds: Essay in Cultural Politics*, London: Methuen.

Spivak Chakravorty, Gayatri (1988), *Selected Subaltern Studies,* (ed.), with Ranjit Guha, Oxford and New York: Oxford University Press.

Spivak Chakravorty Gayatri (1999), *A Critique of Postcolonial Reason: Toward a History of the Vanishing Present,* Cambridge, M.A.: Harvard University Press.

Spivak Chakraborty, Gayatri (2003), *Death of Discipline,* New York: Columbia University Press.

Stern, Willard, (1957), (tr.) *Erich Auerbach's Mimesis: The Reproduction of Reality in Western Literature,* New York: Double day, 1957.

Subramanyam, Ka Naa, (1987), *Tiruvalluvar and His Tirukkural,* New Delhi: Bharatiya Jnanpith.

Suddhatmaprana, Prayrajika, (2010), *Indian Saints and Mystics,* Kolkota: Ramkrishna Mission Institute of Culture.

The Text and the Context: A Euncounter with Jnanpith Laureates, (1994) New Delhi: Bhartiya Jnanpith.

Tagore G.V. 1993, *Eknath,* New Delhi: Sahitya Academy.

Talger Pramod and Verma S.B, (ed.) (1987), *Literature in Translation: From Cultural Transference to Metonymic Displacement*, Bombay: Popular Prakashan.

Talib Gurbachan Singh, (2001), *Guru Nanak,* New Delhi, Sahitya Academy.

Tathagatananda, Swami (2009). *Albert Einstein: His Human Side.* New York: The Vedanta Society of New York.

Taury Gideon, (1987), *Translation Across Culture.* New Delhi: Bahari Publication.

Thakar, Vimala, (1987), *Life To Be Related,* Blaricum: Bookfund Vimala Thakar.

Thakar, Vimala, (2002), *Totality In Essence.* Delhi: Motilal Banarasidass Publishers Pvt. Ltd.

Thakar, Vimala, (2004), *Blossoms of Friendship,* Delhi: Motilal Banarasidass Publishers Pvt. Ltd.

The Quran (Trans) (2008), New Delhi: Madhur Sandesh Sangam.

Tirumani M., (2007), *India of My Dream,* New Delhi: Sarup & Sons, 2007.

Tiwari, K.N. *(2009), Comparative Religion*, Delhi: Motilal Banarasidass Publisher Pvt. Ltd., Second Revised Edition.

Townend, Christine (2010), *The Teachings of Vimala Thakar,* Gontier, Jack, (ed. and tr.), Delhi: Motilal Banarasidass Publishers Pvt. Ltd.

Trivedi, Harish, Mukherjee, Meenaskshi, (2006), *Introgating Post-Colonialism: Theory, Text and Context.* Shimla: Indian Institute of Advanced Study.

Tukadoji, (2023), *Gramgeeta,* (Trans.), Ratnakar D. Bhelkar, New Delhi: Atlantic Publishers and Distributors (P) Ltd.

Usmani, B.D. (2008), (ed) *Encyclopaedia of Mass Communication,* Vol. I. Mumbai: Himalaya Books Pvt. Ltd.

Vanmikanathan G., (1980), *Ramalingar,* New Delhi: Sahitya Academy.

Vanmikanthan G., (1996), *Appar,* New Delhi: Sahitya Academy.

Victor P. George, Rao S.D.A. Joga, (2002), *Saints and Gurus: Perspectives on Spiritual and Social Renaissance in Contemporary India,* New Delhi: D.K. Printworld (P) Ltd.

Vijayasree C., Subbarayudu G.K., Siddiq Ali, Leela Lakshmi Narayen, (1998) Nobel *Laureates in Literature* (1986-1997), Delhi: Pencraft International.

Vivekanand, Swami, (2010), *Chicago Address,* Kolkata: Advaita Ashrama.

Vivekananda Swami, (2008), A *Concise Encyclopaedia of Hinduism* ,Vol. I, A-G, Vol. II, H-P, Vol. III, R-Z, Banglore: Ramkrishna Math.

Watson C.W., (2005), *Multiculturalism,* New Delhi: Viva Books Private Limited.

Wisker Gina, (2007), *Key Concepts in Postcolonial Literature,* New York: Palgrave Macmillan.

Yadav, Kumkum, (2003), *Tribals In Indian Narratives,* Shimla: Indian Institute of Advanced Study.

Yerankar Shriram, (2006), *Secularism in India*: Theory and Practice, New Delhi: Adhyayan Publishers & Distributors.

Zaidi Ali Jawad, (2006), *A History of Urdu Literature,* New Delhi: Sahitya Academy.

Zakariyya Fouad, (2005), *Myth and Reality in the Contemporary Islamist Movement*. London: Pluto Press.

मराठी

अडसाडे, अण्णासाहेब, (2001), महानुभव दर्शन, नांदगांव खंडेश्वर: महानुभव विश्व भारती।

अधारे, रमेश, (2010), मुद्रा महाराष्ट्राची, अमरावती: श्री शिवाजी शिक्षण संस्था।

अभ्यंकर, शंकर वासुदेव, (2008), अकराप्रधान उपनिषदे, पुणे: आदित्य प्रतिष्ठान।

अभ्यंकर, शंकर वासुदेव, (2008), हिन्दू धर्माची रचना, पुणे: आदित्य प्रतिष्ठान।

अभ्यंकर, शंकर वासुदेव, (2008), हिन्दू धर्माची वैशिष्टे, पुणे: आदित्य प्रतिष्ठान।

अभ्यंकर, शंकर वासुदेव, (2008), ब्राम्हणग्रंथे, पुणे: आदित्य प्रतिष्ठान।

अभ्यंकर, शंकर वासुदेव, (2008), मनुस्मृति, पुणे: आदित्य प्रतिष्ठान।

अभ्यंकर, शंकर वासुदेव, (2008), यज्ञसंस्था, पुणे: आदित्य प्रतिष्ठान।

अभ्यंकर, शंकर वासुदेव, (2008), सहा वेदाङ्ग्रे, पुणे: आदित्य प्रतिष्ठान।

अभ्यंकर, शंकर वासुदेव, (2008), श्री भगवद्गीता, पुणे: आदित्य प्रतिष्ठान,

अभ्यंकर, शंकर वासुदेव, (2008), चार वेद, पुणे: आदित्य प्रतिष्ठान।

अभ्यंकर, शंकर वासुदेव, (2008), स्मृतिग्रंथ, पुणे: आदित्य प्रतिष्ठान।

आंबेडकर, भीमरावजी, (2007), बुद्ध आणि कार्ल मार्क्स, वर्धा: मिलिद प्रकाशन, 2007।

आगलावे, सरोज, जोतीराव फुले: सामाजिक तत्वज्ञान, पुणे: सुगावा प्रकाशन।

ऑमव्हेट, गेल, (1995), वासाहतिक समाजातील सांस्कृतिक बंड, (भाषांतर), पुणे: सुगावा प्रकाशन।

ऑम्व्हेट, गेल, (2010), जोतीबा फुले आणि स्त्री-मुक्तीचा विचार, मुंबई: लोकवाङ्मय गृह।

ऑम्व्हेट, गेल, (2011), समतावादी साहित्य: एक चिंतन, कोल्हापुर: समतावादी सांस्कृतिक चव।

इर्लेकर, सुहासिनी, (1999), महदंबेचे धव, पुणे: स्नेहवर्धन पब्लिशिग हाऊस।

इनामदार, एस.डी., (संपा.), (2007), मर्मभेद, मे. पुं. रेगे यांचे टीकालेख, पुणे: प्रतिभा प्रकाशन।

इनामदार, हे.वि., जोशी वसंत स., (2005), एकनाथकालीन मराठी वाङ्मय, पुणे: स्नेहवर्धन प्रकाशन।

एकनाथ, एकनाथी भागवत, गीताप्रेस, सं. 2064।

एरंडे, अशोक, (संपा.) (2007), विठोबाची शिकवण, तरवडी: मुकूंदराव पाटील स्मारण समिती।

करन्दीकर, वि.रा., (2009) समर्थ रामदास, नवी दिल्ली: नॅशनल बुक ट्रस्ट, इंडिया।

कन्हाडे, सदा, (1995) समाज आणि साहित्य, मुंबई: लोक वाङ्मयगृह।

कसबे, रावसाहेब, (2007) मानव आणि धर्मचितन, पुणे: सुगावा प्रकाशन।

कडबे, रघुनाथ, (2001) राष्ट्रसंत तुकडोंजीचा जीवन प्रवास, भाग-1, नागपुर: अमोल प्रकाशन।

कडबे, रघुनाथ, (2003) राष्ट्रसंत तुकडोंजीचा जीवन प्रवास, भाग-2, नागपुर: अमोल प्रकाशन।

कडवे, रघुनाथ, (2008), राष्ट्रसंतांच्या ग्रामगीतेची वैज्ञानिक दष्टी, नागपुर: अमोल प्रकाशन।

कामत, अशोक, (2010), ग्रामगीता, सुबोध निरुपण, पुणे: गुरूकल प्रतिष्ठान।

काले, कल्याण, पुंडे दत्तात्रय, (2004) दामोदर पंडित कृत वछाहरण, पुणे: स्नेहवर्धन पब्लिशिग हाऊस।

कोलते, वि.भि., (1995), प्राचीन साहित्याच्या अंतरंगात, पुणे: स्नेहवर्धन पब्लिशिग हाऊस।

कोसंबी, धर्मानंद, (2003), जातक कथासंग्रह, भाग 1, 2, 3, वर्धा: सुधीर प्रकाशन।

कानडे, विश्वास, (2006), चितन, नागपुर: विजय प्रकाशन।

कानडे, विश्वास, (2004), प्रदेश साकल्याचा, नागपुर: सचिन साहित्य।

कानडे, मु.श्री., (2005), काही संत: काही शाहीर, पुणे: स्नेहवर्धन पब्लिशिग हाऊस।

कुलकर्णी, मदन, (2008), देशियता ते जागतिकीकरण, नागपुर: विजय प्रकाशन।

कुलकर्णी, द.भि. (1977), चार शोधनिबंध, नागपुर: नागपुर विद्यापीठ प्रकाशन।

खरात, शंकरराव, (2005) संताची सामाजिक दष्टी, पुणे: कॉन्टिनेन्टल प्रकाशन, 2005।

खांदवे, भाऊसाहेब, (2000), 'दीनबंधु', कृष्णराव भालेकर, अहमदनगर: गाज प्रकाशन।

खोरगडे, कुमुदिनी, (1984), राष्ट्रसंत तुकडोजी यांच्या समग्र वाङ्मयाचे चिकित्सक अध्ययन, अमरावती: रामचंद्र खोरगडे।

खेरडे, सुनन्दा, (2001), संत ज्ञानेश्वर ते राष्ट्रसंत तुकडोजी, पुणे: श्रीप्रज्ञा प्रकाशन।

गणेश देवी, (अनु.) म.सु. पाटील, (2008), स्मृतिभ्रंशानंतर; भारतीय साहित्य समीक्षेची परंपरा आणि तिच्यातील परिवर्तन, पुणे: पद्मगंधा प्रकाशन।

गोसावी, र.रा., गोसावी वीणा, (2008), श्री चोखामेका चरित्र, पुणे: सारथी प्रकाशन।

गोसावी, वीणा, (2008), संत रोहिदास चरित्र, पुणे: सारथी प्रकाशन।

घटाटे, कृष्ण माधव, भटकर विजय, (2010), मधुराद्वेताचार्य श्री गुलाबराव महाराजांची विज्ञानदष्टी, अमरावती: श्री ज्ञानेश्वर मधुराद्वैत सांप्रदायिक मंडल।

घुमरे, वि.भा., (2010), रमण महर्षि, नागपुर: श्री भारती प्रकाशन।

चित्रे दिलिप पुरुषोत्तम, (1990), पुन्हा तुकाराम, मुंबई: पॉप्युलर प्रकाशन।

चौघुले, (2006), संत, समाज आणि अध्यात्म, मीरा रोड (पू): मधुरा प्रकाशन।

चौधरी पां.दा., (1999), अस्तित्वादाची भूमिका, अमरावती: सोमकुंवर पब्लिकेशन्स।

चौधरी, कृष्णा, (2005), महात्मा जोतीराव फुले: पूर्वसूरी आणि प्रभाव, नागपुर: ऋचा प्रकाशन।

जाधव रा.ग., (1995), कविता आणि रसिकता, औरंगाबाद: परिमल प्रकाशन।

जाधव, रा.ग., (1986), कला, संस्कृती व साहित्य, पुणे: सुगंधा प्रकाशन।

जाफरी, अली सरदार, (2010), नव्या जगाला प्रणाम, श्रीपाद जोशी (अनु.), नवी दिल्ली: नॅशनल बुक ट्रस्ट ऑफ इंडिया।

जोशी, म.रा. (1981), वाङ्मयीन परंपरा आणि ज्ञानेश्वरकन्या, नागपुर: श्री गुलाबराव महाराज जन्मशताब्दी प्रकाशन।

जोग, वि. स. (1981), मार्क्सवाद आणि मराठी साहित्य, नागपुर: विजय प्रकाशन।

ठाकरे, के.सी. (2000), श्री गाडगेबाबा, मुंबई: श्री गाडगे महाराज प्रकाशन समिति।

ठाकूर, रवींद्र, (संपादक) (1999), क्रांतिजागर, पुणे: स्नेहवर्धन पब्लिशिग हाऊस।

ढसाल, नामदेव, सतीश कालसेकर, प्रज्ञा लोखंडे, (2009), मी भयंकराच्या दरवाज्यात उभा आहे!। मुबंई: शब्द प्रकाशन।

ढेरे, रा.चि., (2011), संत, लोक आणि अभिजन, पुणे: पद्मगंधा प्रकाशन।

ढेरे, रा.चि., (2008), मुसलमान मराठी संतकवी, पुणे: पद्मगंधा प्रकाशन, तृतीय आवृत्ती।

तावरे, स्नेहल, (1990), ज्ञानेश्वरी व विसावे शतक, पुणे: स्नेहवर्धन प्रकाशन।

तिप्पेरुद्रस्वामी एच. (2003), बसवेश्वर. रोहिणी तुकदेव (अनु.), नवी दिल्ली: साहित्य अकादमी।

तुलपुले, शं.गो., (2009), रमण महर्षि, कृ. स्वामिनाथम, (अनु.), दिल्ली: साहित्य अकादमी।

तुकारामदादा गीताचार्य, (2000), सार्वभौम ग्रामसभा, अड्याल-टेकडी: आत्मानुसंधान प्रकाशन मंडल।

द्वादशीवार, सुरेश, (2010) मन्वंतर: समूहाकडून स्वत:कडे, पुणे: साधना प्रकाशन।

देशमुख, उषा मा. (2010), मैत्र, नागपुर: माया प्रकाशन।

देशमुख, उषा मा. (2012), देवाचिया द्वारी, नागपुर: ज्ञानेश प्रकाशन।

देशमुख, उषा मा., (2004), संत साहित्य दर्शन, पुणे: स्नेहवर्धन पब्लिशिग हाऊस।

देशमुख, चितामणी, (1953), दामोदर धर्मानंद कोसंबी, मुंबई: ग्रंथाली।

देशपांडे, प्रकाश केजकर, (2006), संत कविता: एक दष्टिकोण, औरगांबाद: स्वरुप प्रकाशन।

देशपांडे, ग.त्र्यं. (1963), भारतीय साहित्यशास्त्र, मुंबई: पॉप्युलर प्रकाशन।

नगरकर, रा.शं. (संपा.), (2000), मुनि केशिराज-संकल्पित दष्टान्तपाठ, पुणे: स्नेहवर्धन पब्लिशिग हाऊस।

नारखेडे, लक्ष्मणदादा नारखेडे, (2001), नाणे एक बाजू दोन, गुरूकुंज मोझरी: आत्मानुसंधान प्रकाशन मंडल।

नेमाडे, भालचंद्र, (2004), तुकाराम गाथा (निवडक अभंग), नवी दिल्ली: साहित्य अकादमी।

पठाण, यु.म. (2014), संतसाहित्य: शोध आणि बोध, पुणे: दिलिपराज प्रकाशन प्रा.लि.।

पठाण, यु.म. (2011), संतसाहित्य नवचितन, पुणे: दिलिपराज प्रकाशन, प्रा.लि.।

परांजपे, जयंत, (1986), ग्रेस आणि दुर्बोधता, नागपुर: पा.ना. बनहट्टी।

पवार, गो.मा., (2007), विठ्ठल रामजी शिंदे, नवी दिल्ली: नॅशनल बुक ट्रस्ट ऑफ इंडिया।

पाटील, आनंद (2007), तरवा, नागपुर: आकांक्षा प्रकाशन।

पाटील, आनंद (2010), समीक्षा 'अपहरण', औरंगाबाद: रजत प्रकाशन।

पाटील, आनंद, (2007), तौलनिक साहित्य: नवे सिद्धांत आणि उपयोजन, औरंगाबाद: साकेत प्रकाशन।

पाटील, सुभाष, (2005), संत तुकाराम आणि रेव्ह, टिलक: एक भावानुबंध। पुणे: स्नेहवर्धन पब्लिशिग हाऊस।

पाटील, चंद्रकांत, (2001), आणि तोपर्यंत, औरंगाबाद: स्वरूप प्रकाशन।

पाटील, दीनमित्रकार मुकूंदराव, (2006), देवांची परिषद पहिली, तरवडी: दीनमित्रकार मुकूंदराव पाटील स्मारक समिति।

पदवाड, बाल, (1984), राष्ट्रसंत: वैचारिक क्रांती, नागपुर: विजया प्रकाशन।

पदवाड, बाल, (1987), कर्मयोगी तुकारामदादा गीताचार्य, अड्याल: श्रीगुरुदेव आत्मानुसंधान टेकडी।

पुंजे, सरिता बं., (2000) राष्ट्रसंत तुकडोजी महाराजांच्या वाङ्मयातील रसविमर्श, नागपुर: संस्कार प्रकाशन।

पंडित, बाबाजी महाराज, सं. 2064 श्री ज्ञानेश्वरी गूढार्थदीपिका, गोरखपुर: गीता प्रेस।

पंजाबी, विद्याधरदादा, (संपा), (2008), लीलाचरित्र: वस्तुस्थिति, नागपुर: महानुभव संदेश, आचार्य श्री ऋषिराजबाबा प्रतिष्ठान।

पंजाबी, विद्याधरदादा, (संपा), (2009), लीलाचरित्र, पिपला: महानुभव सेवा प्रकाशन।

फरकाडे, श्रावण, (संपा), (2007), बहुजनांचा मार्गदर्शक संत कबीर, आमला: राज प्रकाशन।

फुले, महात्मा ज्योतिबा, (1999), गुलामगिरी, नागपुर: आंबेडकर बुक ट्रस्ट।

फुले, महात्मा ज्योतिबा, (2007), सार्वजानिक सत्यधर्म, नागपुर: नेहा प्रकाशन।

फुले, महात्मा ज्योतिबा, वासुदेव मुलाटे (संपा), (1999), शेतकंयाचा असूड, औरंगाबाद: स्वरूप प्रकाशन।

बेलूरकर, रा.मो. (2007), खंजरी, श्रीक्षेत्र वरखेड: श्री माणिक प्रकाशन।

बेडेकर, शरद, (2005), ईश्वर चिकित्सा आणि निरीश्वरवाद, मुंबई: ग्रंथाली।

बोकरे, म.गो., (1973), विदर्भातील झोलकयांच्या आर्थिक व इतर समस्या, पुणे: सुगावा प्रकाशन।

भगत रा.तु., सहसंपादक-सावरकर सुभाष, (2009), राष्ट्रसंत तुकडोजी महाराज गौरव ग्रंथ, कोल्हापुर: चैतन्य प्रकाशन।

भिसेकर, गजानन आत्मारामजी, (2010), मायमाऊली विमला ठकार, पुणे: वत्स-विनायक प्रकाशन।

भोले, भास्कर, लक्ष्मण (1966), महात्मा जोतीराव फुले, नवी दिल्ली: साहित्य अकादमी।

मनोहर, यशवंत, (1999), परिवर्तनवादी जीवनमूल्ये आणि वाङ्मयीन मुल्ये, नागपुर: ठिय्या प्रकाशन।

मनोहर, यशवंत, (2001), नवे साहित्यशास्त्र, नागपुर: विजय प्रकाशन।

मर्ढेकर, बाल सीताराम (1977), मर्ढेकरांची कविता, मुंबई: मौज प्रकाशन।

मालशे, मिलिंद, जोशी अशोक, (2009), आधुनिक समीक्षा सिद्धांत, मुंबई: मराठी विद्यापीठ, मुंबई विद्यापीठ, मुंबई आणि मौज प्रकाशन।

माईणकर, म.गो., (1974), वैदर्भिय संस्कृत वाङ्मय आणि काव्यशास्त्रीय विचार, नागपुर: नागपुर विद्यापीठ।

माली, मा.गो., सावरकर सुभाष (संपा.) (1999), महात्मा फुले दुर्मिल वाङ्मय आणि समकालीन चरित्रे, अमरावती: मराठी जनसाहित्य परिषद।

माटे, श्री.म., (2006), संत पंत व तंत, पुणे: स्नेहवर्धन प्रकाशन।

मुकर्जी, दिलीपकुमार, (2009), श्री चैतन्य महाप्रभु, नवी दिल्ली: नॅशनल बुक ट्रस्ट।

मेंढे, निलकंठ, (2011), जनसाहित्यः चितन आणि चिकित्सा, अमरावतीः मराठी जनसाहित्य परिषद।

मोहिते, शिवाजीराव, (2007), ईश्वरनिष्ठांची मांदियाली, पुणेः कर्मवीर प्रकाशन।

मोहिते, शिवाजीराव, (संपा.), (2008), वरकरी संपद्राय आणि संत साहित्य, पुणेः कर्मवीर प्रकाशन।

मोहोड, बाबा (संपा.), (1998), राष्ट्रसंतांची पत्रे, गुरुकुंजः श्री गुरुदेव प्रकाशन।

युनूस, कार्ल वेबर, मोहमंद, गोविद गोडबोले, (अनु.), (2009), गरिबीमुक्त विश्वाची निर्मिती, औरंगाबादः साकेत प्रकाशन।

राघवन, ए.श्री. निवास (1986), नम्मालवार, नलिनी साधले, (अनु.), नवी दिल्लीः साहित्य अकादमी।

वडस्कर, या.बा. (1988), जनसाहित्याच्या दिशेने, पुणेः मेहता पब्लिशिग हाऊस।

वाडेकर, देविदास दत्तात्रेय, (1974) मराठी तत्वज्ञान महाकोश (तृतीय खंड), पुणेः मराठी तत्वज्ञान महाकोश मंडल।

विवेकानंद, स्वामी, (1999), धर्माचे स्वरुप आणि साधन, नागपुरः रामकृष्ण मठ।

विवेकानंद, स्वामी, (2003), राष्ट्राला आवाहन, नागपुरः रामकृष्ण मठ।

शास्त्री, मुरलीधर, कन्हैया कुंदप, (अनु.) (1979), चक्रपाणिः अेक विश्लेषण, भुसावलः आराध्य प्रकाशन, आशा खोत।

शेंदरे, नमिता (2000), संत तुकाराम-संत तुकडोजीः तौलनिक स्त्रीदर्शन, नागपुरः ॐ प्रकाशन।

सरवदे, भीमराव, (2004), पेरियार रामस्वामी यांची गाजलेली भाषणे, नागपुरः समता प्रकाशन।

सरदार, गं.बा., (2004), संत वाङ्मयाची सामाजिक फलश्रुती, मुंबईः लोकवाङ्मय गृह, पाचवी आवृत्ती।

सरदेसाई, एस.जी., (1992), दिलीप बोस, मार्क्सवाद आणि भगवद्गीता, मुंबईः लोकवाङ्मय गृह।

सरदेसाई, एस.जी., बोस, दिलिप (1992), मार्क्सवाद आणि भगवद्गीता, मुंबईः लोकवाङ्मय गृह।

सकपाल, बापूजी, (2009), श्री चक्रधर, नवी दिल्लीः नॅशनल बुक ट्रस्ट, इंडिया।

सारंग, विलास, (2000), अक्षरांचा श्रम केला, मुंबई: मराठी विभाग, मुंबई विद्यापीठ व मौज प्रकाशन।

सावरकर सुभाष, (1993), वैदर्भिय रीती, अमरावती: मराठी जनसाहित्य परिषद।

सावरकर, सुभाष, (1993), जनसाहित्य, अमरावती: मराठी जनसाहित्य परिषद।

सावरकर, सुभाष, (2004), ग्रामगीतारहस्य, स्पंद 1, अमरावती मराठी जनसाहित्य परिषद।

सावरकर, सुभाष, (2007), राष्ट्रसंत तुकडोजी: जीवन व कार्य, अमरावती: मराठी जनसाहित्य परिषद।

सावरकर, सुभाष, (2008), ग्रामगीतारहस्य, स्पंद 2, अमरावती: मराठी जनसाहित्य परिषद।

सावरकर, सुदाम, (1985), जीवनयोगी, खंड 4, अमरावती: साहित्यप्रभा प्रकाशन।

सावरकर, सुदाम, (1987), जीवनयोगी, खंड 6, अमरावती: साहित्यप्रभा प्रकाशन।

सावरकर, सुदाम, (1987), जीवनयोगी, खंड 7, अमरावती: साहित्यप्रभा प्रकाशन।

सावरकर, सुदाम, (1992), जीवनयोगी, खंड 9, अमरावती: जनसाहित्य साधना प्रकाशन।

सावरकर, सुदाम, (1993), जीवनयोगी, खंड 10, अमरावती: जनसाहित्य साधना प्रकाशन।

सावरकर, सुदाम, (1999), जीवनयोगी, खंड 1, अमरावती: साहित्य प्रभा प्रकाशन।

सावरकर, सुदाम, (2001), जनसंस्कृतीचे आधारस्तंभ, अमरावती: मराठी जनसाहित्य परिषद।

सावरकर, सुदाम, (2006), जीवनयोगी, खंड 3, अमरावती: मराठी जनसाहित्य, द्वितीयवृत्ती।

सावरकर, सुदाम, (2007), जीवनयोगी, खंड 2, अमरावती: मराठी जनसाहित्य परिषद।

सावरकर, सुदाम, (2010), जीवनयोगी, खंड 11, अमरावती: मराठी जनसाहित्य परिषद।

सावरकर, सुदाम, (2010), जीवनयोगी, खंड 8, अमरावती: मराठी जनसाहित्य परिषद।

साखरे सीमा (संपा.), (2008), शिदे ताराबाई, स्त्री-पुरुष तुलना, नागपुरः सीमा प्रकाशन।

सालूंखे, आ.ह., (2006), विद्रोही तुकारामः समीक्षेची समीक्षा, साताराः लोकायत प्रकाशन।

सालुंखे, आ.ह., (2008), मनुस्मृतीच्या समर्थकांची संस्कृती, लोकवाङ्मय गृह, मुंबई।

सालुंखे, आ.ह., (2008), चितनः बलीराजा ते रवींद्रनाथ, साताराः लोकायत प्रकाशन।

सालुंखे, आ.ह., (2011), महाभारतातील स्त्रिया भाग 2, साताराः लोकायत प्रकाशन।

सालुंखे, आ.ह., (2011), संवादः सहृदय श्रोत्यांशी, साताराः लोकायत प्रकाशन।

सालुंखे, आ.ह., (2011), परिवर्तनः शास्त्रही, कलाही, साताराः लोकायत प्रकाशन।

सुर्वे, नारायण, (1992), माझे विद्यापीठ, मुंबईः पाप्युलर प्रकाशन।

सुर्वे, नारायण, (1992), माणूस, कलावंत आणि समाज, मुंबईः पाप्युलर प्रकाशन।

सुर्वे, नारायण, (1995), जाहीरनामा, मुंबईः पाप्युलर प्रकाशन।

स्वामी, शिवतत्वानंद, (2000), धर्माचा गाभा अनुभव, नागपुरः रामकृष्ठ मठ।

सं. 2064 श्रीसकल संतवाणी (मराठी), खंड पहिला, गोरखपुर गीताप्रेस।

सं. 2065 श्री तुकाराम महाराजांची गाथा, गोरखपुरः गीताप्रेस।

हतकणंगलेकर, म.द., (2008), भाषणे आणि परीक्षणे, पुणेः श्री विद्या प्रकाशन।

हुसेन, एस. अबीद, प्रकाश देशपांडे केजकर, (अनु.), (2009), भारताची राष्ट्रीय संस्कृती, नवी दिल्लीः नॅशनल बुक ट्रस्ट ऑफ इंडिया।

श्रीसकल संतवाणी मराठी, खंड दुसरा, गोरखपुरः गीताप्रेस।

श्री नामदेवांची गाथा, गोरखपुरः गीताप्रेस।

ज्ञानेश्वर (2007), ज्ञानेश्वरी, श्रीक्षेत्र नेवासाः श्री ज्ञानेश्वर महाराज संस्थान।

हिन्दी

अज्ञेय, (2000), कितने नावों में कितने बार, नई दिल्लीः भारतीय ज्ञानपीठ।

अज्ञेय, (2008), आँगन के पार द्वार, नई दिल्लीः भारतीय ज्ञानपीठ।

गौतम, एस.एस., (2007), रविदास ने कहाः ऐसा चाहूँ राज मैं, दिल्लीः गौतम बुक सेंटर।

नारंग, गोपीचंद, (2004) संरचनावाद, उत्तर-संरचनावाद एवं प्राच्य काव्यशास्त्र, देवेश, (अनु.), नई दिल्लीः साहित्य अकादमी।

गौतम, एस.एस., (2006), चार्वाक दर्शन, दिल्लीः गौतम बुक सेंटर।

चतुर्वेदी, परशुराम (1981), संत काव्यधारा, इलाहाबादः किताब महल।

तिवारी, रामपूजन, (2002), सूफीमत, वाराणसीः ज्ञानमण्डल लिमिटेड।

नेमाडे, भालचंद्र, (2004), तुकाराम, चंद्रकांत पाटील, (अनु.), नई दिल्लीः साहित्य अकादमी।

द्विवेदी, हजारीप्रसाद, (2008), कबीर, नई दिल्लीः राजकमल प्रकाशन प्रा.लि.।

विवेकानंद, (2002), जाति, संस्कृति और समाजवाद, नागपुरः रामकृष्ण मठ।

विवेकानंद, (2002), भारत और उसकी समस्याएँ, नागपुरः रामकृष्ण मठ।

विनोबा, (2006), गीता प्रवचन, वाराणसीः सर्व सेवा संघ प्रकाशन।

येवलेकर, दिनकर, (2011), युगदष्टा राष्ट्रसंत तुकडोजी का राष्ट्रीय जीवन निर्माण में योगदान, कानपुरः विकास प्रकाशन।

विनोबा, (1993), विज्ञान-युग में धर्म, कान्ति शाह (संपा.), वाराणसीः सर्व सेवा संघ।

व्यास, श्याम सुन्दर (2012), रसखान, नई दिल्लीः साहित्य अकादमी।

स्नातक, विजयेंद्र (2012), रहीम, नई दिल्लीः साहित्य अकादमी।

शर्मा, ब्रम्हदेव, (2006), एक और भूमकाल, नई दिल्लीः सहयोग पुस्तक कुटीर (ट्रस्ट)।

रामबक्ष, (2011), दादू दयाल, नई दिल्लीः साहित्य अकादमी।

श्रीवास्तव, परमानंद, (2012), जायसी, नई दिल्लीः साहित्य अकादमी।

त्रिशरण, विजय कुमार (2008), महाकवि रविदासः समाज चेतना के अग्रदूत, दिल्लीः गौतम बुक सेंटर।

क्षमासागर, मुनि, (2005), अपना घर, नई दिल्लीः भारतीय ज्ञानपीठ।

Journals, Special Issues & Speeches

Journals

American Historical Review, Dec. 1994, Vol. 99, No. 5.

Critical Enquiry, Knowledge

Exploration, Indian Journal of Multi-discipline, Nagpur, Vol. I, II, 2011, Vol. I, II, 2012, Vol. I, II 2013.

Indian Literature, Sahitya Academy, New Delhi.

International Journal of Translation, New Delhi.

Journal of Indian Writing in English, Gulburga (Karnataka)

Economic and Political Weekly

Journal of South Asian Studies

Indian Journal of Human Relations, Jaunpur (UP)

The Translator, St. Jerome Publishing

The Translation Review, Center for Translation Studies (Electronic Journal) cosponsored by International Association of Translation and Intercultural Studies.

New Horizon, Agra

The *Indian Journal of English Studies*, Vol. XLV, 2008.

Voice of Saint Tukadoji, Adyal-Tekdi (Quaterly in English), From July 1998 to October 2022.

World Literature

मराठी

अक्षर वैदर्भी, अमरावती।

कविता-रती, धुले।

प्रसाद, पुणे।

पंचधारा, मराठी साहित्य परिषद, पुणे।

ललित, मुंबई।

लोकराज्य, मुंबई।

साहित्यसूची, पुणे।

सत्यशोधक विशेषांक: बहुजन संघर्ष, 1996।

श्री गुरूदेव, गुरूकुंज मोझरी, 1943-68।

शब्दसृष्टि, मुंबई।

हिन्दी

अलाव, दिल्ली।

भारतीय साहित्य, साहित्य अकादमी, नई दिल्ली।

वागार्थ, भाषा साहित्य परिषद, कलकत्ता।

हंस, भारतीय ज्ञानपीठ, नई दिल्ली।

सखी, वाराणसी।

Special Issues

मराठी

राष्ट्रसंत तुकडोजी महाराज विचार साहित्य सम्मेलन पाचवें, कोराडी, 8 फरवरी 2003।

लोकराज्य 1 ते 16 ऑक्टोबर 1984, राष्ट्रसंत तुकडोजी महाराज अमृत महोत्सव विशेषांक।

लोकराज्य, नवम्बर 2000, विशेषांक।

प्रचारभीष्म शामरावदादा मोकदम जन्मशताब्दी स्मरणिका, 2007-2008।

राष्ट्रसंताचा क्रांतिदूत, 2008।

राष्ट्रसंत प्रणित जनसाहित्य सम्मेलन स्मरणिका, 30 अप्रैल, 2009, जन्मशताब्दी विशेषांक।

स्मृतिग्रंथ, राष्ट्रसंत तुकडोजी महाराज विशेषांक 2001।

स्मरणिका, राष्ट्रसंत तुकडोजी महाराज विचार साहित्य सम्मेलन, नववे, जरूड 27 जनवरी 2008।

स्मरणिका, अखिल भारतीय सत्यशोधक समाज, 28वें अधिवेशन 1999, तरवडी (मुकुंदनगर)।

श्री गुरूदेव, नवम्बर 2004, राष्ट्रसंत स्मृति विशेषांक, नवम्बर 2004।

हिन्दी

कल्याण वेद-कथा, तिहत्तवें वर्ष का विशेषांक, गोरखपुर: गीताप्रेस, सं. 2061।

कल्याण संत-अडक, बारहवें वर्ष का विशेषांक, गोरखपुर: गीताप्रेस, सं. 2064।

संतवाणी, उनतीसवें वर्ष का विशेषांक, गोरखपुर: गीताप्रेस, सं. 2061।

Speeches

मराठी

जाधव, रा.ग., अध्यक्षीय भाषण, राष्ट्रसंत तुकडोजी महाराज साहित्य सम्मेलन, 2007।

पठाण, यु.म. अध्यक्षीय भाषण, राष्ट्रसंत तुकडोजी महाराज साहित्य सम्मेलन, 2002।

बेलुरकर, रामकृष्णदादा, अध्यक्षीय भाषण, राष्ट्रसंत तुकडोजी महाराज साहित्य सम्मेलन, 2006।

English

Narashimhaiah, C.D. 'An Inquiry Into the Indianness of Indian English Literature', New Delhi: Sahitya Academy, 2003.

Khan, M.Q., 'Interrogating 'Orientalism' and 'Going Native', Presidential Address, 52nd All India English Teachers Conference by Indian Association of English Studies, 2008.

Index